In the Service of Empire

Empire's Other Histories

Series Editors: Victoria Haskins (University of Newcastle, Australia), Emily Manktelow (Royal Holloway, University of London, UK), Jonathan Saha (University of Durham, UK) and Fae Dussart (University of Sussex, UK)

Editorial Board: Esme Cleall (University of Sheffield, UK), Swapna Banerjee (CUNY, USA), Lynette Russell (Monash, Australia), Tony Ballantyne (University of Otago, New Zealand), Samita Sen (Jadavpur University, India, and University of Cambridge, UK), Nurfadzilah Yahaya, (National University of Singapore, Singapore), Onni Gust (University of Nottingham, UK), Martina Nguyen (CUNY, USA) and Meleisa Ono-George, (University of Oxford, UK)

Empire's Other Histories is an innovative series devoted to the shared and diverse experiences of the marginalized, dispossessed and disenfranchised in modern imperial and colonial histories. It responds to an ever-growing academic and popular interest in the histories of those erased, dismissed or ignored in traditional historiographies of empire. It will elaborate on and analyse new questions of perspective, identity, agency, motilities, intersectionality and power relations.

Published:
Unhomely Empire: Whiteness and Belonging, c.1760–1830, Onni Gust, 2020
Extreme Violence and the 'British Way': Colonial Warfare in Perak, Sierra Leone and Sudan, Michelle Gordon, 2020
Unexpected Voices in Imperial Parliaments, edited by José María Portillo, Josep M. Fradera, Teresa Segura-Garcia, 2021

Forthcoming:
Spiritual Colonialism in a Globalizing World, Christina Petterson
Vagrant Lives in Colonial Australasia: Regulating Mobility and Movement 1840–1920, Catherine Coleborne
The Making and Remaking of 'Australasia': Texts, Mobility and Circulations in the Southern World, Tony Ballantyne
Gender, Violence and Criminal Justice in the Colonial Pacific, Kate Stevens
Across Colonial Lines: Commodities, Networks and Empire Building edited by Devyani Gupta and Purba Hossain
Arctic Circles and Imperial Knowledge: The Franklin Family, Indigenous Intermediaries, and the Politics of Truth, Annaliese Jacobs Claydon
Imperial Gallows: Murder, Violence and the Death Penalty in British Colonial Africa, c.1915-60, Stacey Hynd
Anti-Colonialism and the Crises of Interwar Fascism, Michael Oritz

In the Service of Empire

*Domestic Service and Mastery in
Metropole and Colony*

Fae Dussart

BLOOMSBURY ACADEMIC
LONDON • NEW YORK • OXFORD • NEW DELHI • SYDNEY

BLOOMSBURY ACADEMIC
Bloomsbury Publishing Plc
50 Bedford Square, London, WC1B 3DP, UK
1385 Broadway, New York, NY 10018, USA
29 Earlsfort Terrace, Dublin 2, Ireland

BLOOMSBURY, BLOOMSBURY ACADEMIC and the Diana logo are
trademarks of Bloomsbury Publishing Plc

First published in Great Britain 2022

Cover image: A British family celebrating Christmas in India by E. K. Johnson
(Photo by Rischgitz/Getty Images)

A catalogue record for this book is available from the British Library.

Library of Congress Cataloging-in-Publication Data
Names: Dussart, Fae, author.
Title: In the service of empire : domestic service and mastery in metropole
and colony / Fae Dussart.
Description: London ; New York : Bloomsbury Academic, 2022. | Series: Empire's other
histories | Includes bibliographical references and index. |
Identifiers: LCCN 2021039871 (print) | LCCN 2021039872 (ebook) | ISBN 9781350121164
(hardback) | ISBN 9781350121171 (pdf) | ISBN 9781350121188 (ebook)
Subjects: LCSH: Household employees–Great Britain–History–19th century. |
Household employees–India–History–19th century. | Imperialism–Social aspects–Great
Britain–History–19th century. | Imperialism–Social aspects–India–History–19th century. |
Great Britain–Social conditions–19th century. | India–Social conditions–19th century.
Classification: LCC HD8039.D52 G727 2022 (print) | LCC HD8039.D52 (ebook) |
DDC 640/.460941–dc23/eng/20211115
LC record available at https://lccn.loc.gov/2021039871
LC ebook record available at https://lccn.loc.gov/2021039872

ISBN: HB: 978-1-3501-2116-4
           ePDF: 978-1-3501-2117-1
           eBook: 978-1-3501-2118-8

Series: Empire's Other Histories

Typeset by Integra Software Services Pvt. Ltd.

To find out more about our authors and books visit www.bloomsbury.com
and sign up for our newsletters.

For Luka, Alia and Mischa

Contents

Acknowledgements

I would like to thank Catherine Hall for her guidance as the supervisor of the PhD this work grew out of, and for her staunch support of me ever since. Staff at Clwyd County Record Office, the Public Record Office, the Wren Library and the Asia Pacific and African Collections at the British Library helped me find useful material. Judy Lloyd generously shared Gertrude Lloyd's private papers with me. Rebecca Spang, Leonore Davidoff, Joanna De Groot, Victoria Haskins, Claire Lowrie, Swapna M. Banerjee, Carolyn Steedman, Laura Schwartz, Alison Light, Erin O'Connor, Nicola Foote, Mrinalini Sinha, Jane Hamlett, Laura Ishiguro, Onni Gust, Jonathan Saha, Daniel Grey, Divya Tolia-Kelly, Katie Walsh, Ceri Oeppen, JoAnn McGregor, Dave Ockwell, Brian Short, Ben Rogaly, Simon Rycroft and Zoe Laidlaw have been wonderful interlocutors and colleagues, who have supported me, listened and given invaluable feedback on work associated with this research at various points over the many years it has taken to develop it. Alan Lester, Victoria Haskins, Esme Cleall and Emily Manktelow have been great friends and great colleagues and my gratitude to them for closely reading sections of this book at various stages in its development is immense. Emily talked sense to me at various moments of overwhelming anxiety in the final stages of writing, for which I am hugely grateful. I am grateful for the encouragement and engagement of my dear friends Elizabeth Knight, Adam Knight, Rob Higham, Alpa Shah, Tejal Patel, Phil Makinson, Chris D'Oliveira, Nick Hartley, Charlie Courtenay, Nina Conti and Sara Berman. Esther Freud helped me develop confidence as a writer and taught me that writing a book is a matter of actually sitting down and writing the book – much like drawing an owl, it is harder than it sounds. Maddie Holder and Abigail Lane at Bloomsbury have been supportive and exceptionally patient through the whole process. I also owe thanks to my extended family: Molly and Georges Dussart, Mike Brearley, Mana Sarabhai, Lara Brearley and Jacobo Quintanilla have all provided me with the support (material and emotional) that has been essential to the completion of this work. I would not have been able to do the research that has resulted in this monograph, or indeed write it, without the labour of Taru Patel and Abigail Urayani. My children, Luka and Alia, have been amazing, keeping me busy and laughing in a tough year disrupted by Covid. Last but absolutely not least, Mischa, whose support from start to end, and beyond, means that this monograph finally exists. I'm hugely grateful.

This book is based upon research undertaken for my PhD thesis, which many years ago was funded by the Arts and Humanities Research Board. Parts of this monograph have been previously published in my chapters: 'Strictly Legal Means: Assault and Abuse and the Limits of Acceptable Behaviour in the Servant-Employer Relationship in Metropole and Colony 1850–1890' in Victoria Haskins and Claire Lowrie (eds.) *Colonization and Domestic Service. Historical and Contemporary Perspectives*, Routledge, © 2015 reprinted with permission from Taylor and Francis http://www.tandfonline.com and 'Family and Household: Domestic Service in Colonial India' in Jane Hamlett (ed.) *A Cultural History in the Age of Empire*, 2021, Bloomsbury Academic, an imprint of Bloomsbury Publishing PLC, and in my articles: '"To Glut a Menial's Grudge": Domestic Servants and the Ilbert Bill Controversy of 1883' © 2013 Fae Dussart and The Johns Hopkins University Press, first published in *Journal of Colonialism and Colonial History* 14.1 (2013) and reprinted with permission from Johns Hopkins University Press, and '"That Unit of Civilisation" and "the Talent Peculiar to Women": British Employers and their Servants in the Nineteenth-century Indian Empire'© 2015 Fae Dussart and Taylor and Francis, first published in *Identities*, 22, 6, (2015) and reprinted with permission from Taylor and Francis http://www.tandfonline.com.

Bringing the servant-master/mistress relationship in Britain and in India into the same analytic frame adds an important dimension to understanding the complex ways in which differences between categories of people were empowered during the nineteenth century.[2] Relations with servants were integral to shaping the sense of an English 'middle class' and the gender norms that so defined the men and women of that class. The servant-employer relationship was also important within the conceptualization and execution of the imperial project, which in the nineteenth century involved the acquisition and settlement of vast swathes of the globe by white Britons. The development of this project shaped the ways in which servant/master/mistress identities were constructed. An ambivalent rhetoric of immaturity was adapted to connect servants with putatively inferior 'Others', whether lower class or of colour. This process was heterogeneous, uneven and contradictory, and the identities of servant/master/ mistress became sites upon which notions of class, gender and racial difference were consolidated and contested.

Paid domestic labour was, and continues to be, the oil that greases the machinery of industrialized, capitalist societies. It is labour that is necessarily defined as low skill and low status, because it must always be *worth less* than the other work it releases members of households to do. The value of this transaction cannot always easily be measured. The association of domestic labour with pollution and tedium shapes its ostensible worth: its low social value allows it to be under-priced in economic terms despite its critical importance in the functioning of modern societies. This means that often the financial cost of outsourcing domestic work is outweighed by the earnings of family members who would otherwise be cooking, cleaning and caring. However, at times this is not the case – the work that family members are released to do by paid domestic workers might be unremunerated, voluntary and/or charitable. It may not be obviously work at all, but could look like lunching, or shopping. But being a person who 'lunches' when other people do the domestic work that could otherwise occupy that time is an existence with significant connotations of social and cultural power. What it means to be a person who lunches, often assumed to be 'a lady who lunches', is informed by and informs powerful, historically rooted ideas about gender, class and, as this book argues, race.

---

[2] Frederick Cooper and Ann Laura Stoler, *Tensions of Empire: Colonial Cultures in a Bourgeois World* (Berkeley: University of California Press, 1997), 4.

Class, gender, race and colonialism

In the second half of the twentieth century, in response to the political, economic and cultural changes wrought by the dismantling of the British Empire and the emergence of labour as a political force to be reckoned with, the objectives of History broadened. Historians began to recognize the complexity, depth and range of different processes of change and to analyse them in new ways. A new generation of academics developed novel theories and methodologies, interrogating the designation of certain lives – primarily those of people who were not white, male, heterosexual and/or upper class – as insignificant, or even invisible, within the frameworks of 'traditional' historical enquiry. Central to the approaches of much of this work were two principles; first, that the forms of human existence today are the outcome of historical processes. Thus, no human practice is static; all demand a historical perspective which uncovers the dynamics of change over time. Second, no aspect of human culture is essential or universal; all are historically and geographically specific.[3] These principles enable a sense of the layered and mobile intricacies of the past, of the intersections and interactions of all aspects of human life from thought, to language, to action. Furthermore, the notion that no aspect of human culture is essential entails a sense of the constructedness of that culture; assumptions about the permanence and naturalness of social identities associated with categories such as 'class' or 'race' are necessarily called into question. The ever-expanding cast of historical actors' identities no longer just *are*, but are *constructed relationally* within discourse, and are plural, diverse, in flux, and marked by conflict.[4] Feminist and post-colonial approaches to history writing have been crucial in applying this understanding to reconfigure 'traditional' interpretations of the past, and have been important for this study.

During the early 1970s women's history emerged as a strand of Women's Liberation and feminist historians sought to reconfigure histories of class, addressing women's absence in mainstream history writing.[5] Feminist historians

---

[3] John Tosh, *The Pursuit of History. Aims, Methods and New Directions in the Study of Modern History*, 3rd edn (Harlow: Longman, 2000), 9; Paul Rabinow, *The Foucault Reader* (London: Penguin 1991), 4.

[4] Discourse will be understood to mean a historically and culturally specific body of language practice which structures 'knowledge' and facilitates power, confining people within its regulatory scope as it situates them in a certain linguistic way. See Michel Foucault, *The Archaeology of Knowledge* (London: Routledge, 1972). See Paul Rabinow's *Foucault Reader* for a useful introduction to Foucault's main theoretical themes.

[5] See the introductory essay in Catherine Hall, *White, Male and Middle Class. Explorations in Feminism and History* (Cambridge: Polity, 1992) for an autobiographical account of the development of feminist history writing from the 1970s.

began to write about women workers and women activists, questioning their invisibility in existing history, devising the analytical category of gender to think through the relational formation of normative masculine and feminine identities, and the intersection of these with class.[6] Meanwhile, using discourse analysis to re-think the way in which identities are formed and given meaning, post-colonial scholars challenged the notion that race is a fixed objective category.[7] They posited racial identities as discursively constructed and constantly in the making, suggesting that both nineteenth-century contemporaries and traditional historians, to secure the unstable otherness of colonizer and colonized, continuously crafted a 'grammar of difference', to use Cooper and Stoler's elegant phrase.[8] Class, gender and race, rather than essential states that pre-exist human relationships, are matters of process, of feeling and of performance. They aren't fixed, but enacted, and in the moment of enactment, created.

Colonialism was not something that was transported from metropolitan Britain overseas, but metropole and colony and their attendant hierarchies of identity were mutually constitutive.[9] In recent years scholars in a range of

---

[6] For important examples of this work see Sheila Rowbotham, *Hidden from History. 300 Years of Women's Oppression and the Fight against It* (London: Pluto, 1973); Barbara Taylor, *Eve and the New Jerusalem. Socialism and Feminism in the Nineteenth Century* (London: Virago, 1983); Joan Scott, *Gender and the Politics of History* (New York: Columbia University Press, 1988).

[7] Catherine Hall 'Introduction: Thinking the Postcolonial. Thinking the Empire' in Catherine Hall (ed.), *Cultures of Empire. A Reader* (Manchester: Manchester University Press, 2000), 19. In the 1980s Black feminists were critical in developing this insight. See for example Evelyn Brooks Higginbotham, 'African-American Women's History and the Metalanguage of Race', *Signs*, 17 (1992): 251–374.

[8] Frederick Cooper and Ann Laura Stoler (eds.), *Tensions of Empire* (Berkeley and Los Angeles: University of California Press, 1997), 3–4. Other examples of early work that saw 'race' as socially constructed include Nancy Stepan, *The Idea of Race in Science. Great Britain 1800–1960* (London: Palgrave Macmillan, 1982); Douglas Lorimer, *Colour, Class and the Victorians: English Attitudes to the Negro in the Mid-Nineteenth Century* (Leicester: Leicester University Press, 1978); Michael Banton, *Racial Theories*, 2nd edn (Cambridge: Cambridge University Press, 1998); David Theo Goldberg (ed.), *Anatomy of Racism* (Minneapolis: University of Minnesota Press, 1990).

[9] See Frederick Cooper and Ann Laura Stoler, *Tensions of Empire*, 1–56 for their important discussion of the need to rethink a research agenda and consider how 'both colonies and metropoles shared in the dialectics of inclusion and exclusion, and in what ways the colonial domain was distinct from the metropolitan one'. This requires treating 'metropole and colony in a single analytic field, addressing the weight one gives to causal connections and the primacy of agency in its different parts' pp 3–4. Other key texts include Catherine Hall, *Civilising Subjects. Metropole and Colony in the English Imagination 1830–1867* (Cambridge: Polity, 2002); Partha Chatterjee, *The Nation and Its Fragments: Colonial and Post-Colonial Histories* (Princeton: Princeton University Press, 1993); Mrinalini Sinha, *Colonial Masculinity. The 'Manly Englishman' and the 'Effeminate Bengali' in the Late Nineteenth Century* (Manchester: Manchester University Press, 1995), which considers the relational construction of the identities of two elite groups – the Western-educated middle-class Indian and the English gentleman and shows how this happened 'in the context of an imperial social formation that included both Britain and India.' 2.

disciplines, and in places beyond the narrow corridors of the Western academy, have complicated this insight, turning their attention to the multiplicity of colonialisms and colonial identities, and to the creation of 'modern Western civilization' through the colonization of Latin America by European powers.[10] Recent interventions by historical geographers (and geographical historians) have questioned the utility of the metropole/colony binary altogether, suggesting that we might fruitfully decentre the metropole from our analyses of the imperial past and think instead of a multiplicity of places connected in webs or networks constituted by the mobility of things living and inanimate, material and abstract: 'a meeting-up of histories' as Doreen Massey has put it.[11] Here, while agreeing with the latter perspective, I suggest that the spatial imaginary of a metropole/colony binary did still matter to British colonizers, and that it was through locally grounded expressions of an over-arching ideology of domesticity that they refined their sense of what was 'metropolitan' and what was 'colonial', and thereby what it was to be imperial beings. White Britons throughout the Empire understood the home as a generative, transformative place, and a key resource for the making of a kind of 'Britishness' that was particularly English in character, something that reflected the dominance of England within the British Isles.[12] Although Britishness had a particular power throughout imperial space, it was variegated by its being articulated by spatially dispersed actors engaged in the process of making place. How people performed domesticity was critical in this process, through which ideas about what it meant to be metropolitan, and

---

[10] See for example the MCD project http://waltermignolo.com/the-collective-project-modernitycolon iality decoloniality/

[11] Doreen Massey, *For Space* (London: Sage Publications, 2005), 4. See also Alan Lester, *Imperial Networks. Creating Identities in Nineteenth-Century South Africa and Britain* (London: Routledge, 2001); Tony Ballantyne, *Webs of Empire: Locating New Zealand's Colonial Past* (Wellington: Bridget William Books, 2012).

[12] The slippage between 'Britishness' and 'Englishness' is problematic. I have used 'Britishness' as well as 'Englishness' throughout this monograph, perhaps at times incorrectly, to reflect the fact that the colonizers I am considering were not necessarily all English. Nonetheless, 'Englishness' had a particular power within the British Empire, which reflects the colonization by England of Wales, Ireland and Scotland. Of course, plenty of Scottish, Welsh and Irish people were enthusiastic colonizers of lands beyond the British Isles. It would be interesting to explore whether their household relations differed from those of the English, and from one another. See for example John M. Mackenzie with Nigel R. Dalziel, *The Scots in South Africa. Ethnicity, Identity, Gender and Race, 1772–1914* (Manchester: Manchester University Press, 2012); Lindsay Proudfoot and Dianne Hall, *Imperial Spaces. Placing the Irish and Scots in Colonial Australia* (Manchester: Manchester University Press, 2011); Barry Crosbie, *Irish Imperial Networks. Migration, Social Communication and Exchange in Nineteenth Century India* (Cambridge: Cambridge University Press, 2011); Andrew J. May, *Welsh Missionaries and British Imperialism. The Empire of Clouds in North-East India* (Manchester: Manchester University Press, 2012).

what it meant to be colonial (and what all the fine degrees of race, gender, class and ethnicity contained within those categories meant), were refined.

'Race' and 'civilization' are based upon gendered and gendering assumptions. The interaction of historically and culturally specific discourses produces tensely classed, gendered and raced identities that have access to different degrees and different kinds of power. As Joanna de Groot has argued, 'nineteenth-century representations and discourses of sexual identity and difference drew upon and contributed to comparable discourses and representations of ethnic, "racial", and cultural identity and difference' in terms of contemporary understandings of domination and subordination.[13] In the nineteenth century the construction of racial difference through the production of 'knowledge' about the non-European 'Other' intersected with the articulation of class and gender difference. This process worked both to construct relationally and to fracture the identities of colonizer and colonized, male and female, master and servant.[14] 'Others' did not necessarily have to be non-European, but could be constructed as 'aliens within', as people perceived as peripheral and implicitly threatening were defined as being beyond the bounds of the 'imagined community' of respectable Englishmen [*sic*]. In the nineteenth century certain groups – criminals, prostitutes, servants – were discussed in pejorative language that connected them through references to atavism, nature, barbarity, backwardness and bestiality with the people of so-called 'uncivilized' lands.[15]

---

[13] Joanna de Groot, '"Sex" and "Race": The Construction of Language and Image in the Nineteenth Century' in Susan Mendus and Jane Rendall (eds.), *Sexuality and Subordination* (London: Routledge, 1989), 89.

[14] There is now a lot of scholarship that examines the intersection of discourses of gender, race and class in identity construction in metropole and/or colony – too much to list here! Some key texts for this study are Antoinette Burton, *At the Heart of Empire: Indians and the Colonial Encounter in Late Victorian Britain* (Berkeley: University of California Press, 1998); Nupur Chaudhuri and Margaret Stroebel (eds.), *Western Women and Imperial Power: Complicity and Resistance* (Bloomington: Indiana University Press, 1992); Julia Clancy-Smith and Frances Gouda (eds.), *Domesticating the Empire: Race, Gender and Family Life in French and Dutch Colonialism* (Charlottesville: University Press of Virginia, 1998); E.M. Collingham, *Imperial Bodies: The Physical Experience of the Raj* (Cambridge: Polity, 2001); Catherine Hall, *Civilising Subjects*; Anne McClintock, *Imperial Leather: Race, Gender and Sexuality in the Colonial Context* (London: Routledge, 1995); Mary Procida, *Married to the Empire. Gender, Politics and Imperialism in India, 1883–1947* (Manchester: Manchester University Press, 2002); Mrinalini Sinha, *Colonial Masculinity*; Ann Laura Stoler, *Carnal Knowledge and Imperial Power. Race and the Intimate in Colonial Rule* (Berkeley: University of California Press, 2002); Elspeth Locher-Scholten, *Women and the Colonial State. Essays on Gender and Modernity in the Netherlands Indies 1900–1942* (Amsterdam: Amsterdam University Press, 2000); Esme Cleall, *Missionary Discourses of Difference. Negotiating Otherness in the British Empire, 1840–1900* (London: Palgrave, 2012); Emily Manktelow, *Missionary Families. Race, Gender and Generation on the Spiritual Frontier* (Manchester: Manchester University Press, 2013); Philippa Levine (ed.), *Gender and Empire* (Oxford: Oxford University Press, 2004).

[15] Leonore Davidoff, *Worlds Between. Historical Perspectives on Gender and Class* (Cambridge: Polity, 1995) 104–5.

Attention to how identities are relationally constructed through the operation and conflict of different discourses calls into question collective identities and the sets of characteristics seen as defining them, such as 'servants' or 'masters', 'Englishmen' or 'Indians'.[16] Discourse analysis allows us to uncover the conflicts in the construction of broad categories and reveals them as sites of constant contest and negotiation between competing influences. Historically and culturally specific discursive configurations produced unstable identities that were shaped by the intersection of mutable and contingent notions of difference. In the nineteenth-century British Empire, pre-existing notions of femininity and masculinity were elaborated and invested with new meaning. These femininities and masculinities were simultaneously fissured and shaped by the processes of definition and redefinition by which 'race' and 'class' difference was established and rendered meaningful. This process wasn't just about establishing the contours of categories of human difference. It also encompassed place-making, on a scale that ranged from the household to the nation and on to a spatialized conception of the Empire. Different forces operated and competed in this process, ranging from medical and legal practice to evangelical moral endeavour and ideological articulation within the literature, art, politics, religion and 'science' of the nineteenth century, through which people tried to make sense of the changing world in which they lived.

Domesticity

In Leonore Davidoff and Catherine Hall's pioneering text, *Family Fortunes*, the authors used the language of separate spheres to explore the gendering of public and private in eighteenth- and nineteenth-century England. Problematizing the English middle-class family, Davidoff and Hall revealed the linkages between processes of gendering, the structure of family relations and the construction of class difference. Using a wide range of source materials, they demonstrated that what goes on in the home has a resonance well beyond its walls. Davidoff and Hall showed how the development of a specifically middle-class culture in the nineteenth century involved the articulation of a domestic ideal, which necessitated the gendering of public and private space into masculine and

---

[16] John Tosh, *The Pursuit of History*, 188–9.

feminine 'spheres'.[17] According to this ideal, which manifested in a wide range of texts, the private sphere was defined as the site of the family, administered by a woman's gentle touch, while the public sphere was the world of 'work', where a man's strong hand was put to task. But, '[p]ublic was not really public and private not really private despite the potent imagery of "separate spheres". Both were ideological constructs with specific meaning which must be understood as products of a particular historical time'.[18] This 'particular historical time' was one when Britain's involvement in globalizing networks of trade, such as in opium and unfree labour, financed its industrialization, the extraction of resources from its empire and its development as a modern capitalist economy. Structures of domesticity and the intimate developed out of this context and were organized through reference to gender in nineteenth-century Britain.[19] At the same time, one's ability to conform (or at least to appear to conform) to a gendered domestic ideal was proscribed by wealth, and therefore, to an extent, linked to class and in an imperial context, race. Domesticity and different people's relation to it then were constitutive of class, race and gender difference in the nineteenth century.[20]

Domesticity is an ideology that governs practices of homemaking, defining the home itself. Historians of empire have investigated the functionality of domesticity and the politics of intimacy to the making of identities in metropole and colony. Through her work on intimate relations in the Dutch East Indies, Ann Laura Stoler has demonstrated that the regulation of affective bonds and sexual intimacies by the colonial powers was central to the making of colonial categories and to imperial ruling practices in both metropole and colony. As

---

[17] Leonore Davidoff and Catherine Hall, *Family Fortunes. Men and Women of the English Middle Class 1780–1850*, 2nd edn (London: Routledge, 2002). For a critique of 'separate spheres' as representing a new gender order defining the modern middle class see Amanda Vickery, 'Historiographical Review. Golden Age to Separate Spheres? A Review of the Categories and Chronology of English Women's History', *Historical Journal*, 36, 2 (1993): 383–414; See also Linda Kerber, 'Separate Spheres, Female Worlds, Woman's Place: The Rhetoric of Women's History', *Journal of American History*, 75, 1 (1988): 9–39; Judith Lewis, 'Separate Spheres: Threat or Promise?', *Journal of British Studies*, 30, 1 (1991): 105–15.

[18] Leonore Davidoff and Catherine Hall, *Family Fortunes*, 33.

[19] In this book domesticity will be understood to denote 'not just a pattern of residence or a web of obligations, but a profound attachment: a state of mind as well as a physical orientation. Its defining attributes are privacy and comfort, separation from the workplace, and the merging of domestic space and family members into a single commanding concept (in English, "home")' John Tosh, *A Man's Place. Masculinity and the Middle-Class Home in Victorian England* (New Haven and London: Yale University Press, 1999), 4.

[20] See Leonore Davidoff, *Worlds Between*, chapter 4 for a case study exploring linkages between class, gender and sexuality; See also Catherine Hall, *White, Male and Middle Class*, Part 2 for a collection of essays which consider gender, class and the relation of these axes of power to ideas about work, family and politics; See also Theodore Koditschek, 'The Gendering of the British Working Class', *Gender and History* 9, 2 (1997): 333–63; Sonya O. Rose, *Limited Livelihoods. Gender and Class in Nineteenth-Century England* (Berkeley: University of California Press, 1992).

Stoler argues 'domains of the intimate figured … prominently in the perceptions and policies of those who ruled'.[21] Conjugal relations, parenting practices, servant-employer relations in colonial homes were all crucial to the processes by which colonial identities were constituted:

> It was in the disarray of unwanted, sought after, and troubled intimacies of domestic space that colonial relations were refurbished and their distinctions made … Assessments of civility and the cultural distinctions on which racial membership relied were measured less by what people did in public than by how they conducted their private lives – with whom they cohabited, where they lived, what they ate, how they raised their children, what language they chose to speak to servants and family at home.[22]

So, structures of domesticity were crucial in defining the inclusions and exclusions of the communities that made up the Empire. Domesticity was, and is, a disciplinary regime. Cooking, cleaning and caring might encompass intimacy, love and pride, but they also can be practices that produce anxiety, uncertainty, fear and isolation. Managing the domestic world can also be a way of managing such destabilizing feelings. Not appearing appropriately domesticated can be seen as a mark of slovenliness, immorality or savagery. These factors framed the relationship between employers and servants in both colonial India and Britain in our period. Where Indian homes were represented as 'castles of ignorance and listlessness', the 'Englishman' was 'pre-eminent amongst the nations of the earth for his love of *home!*'[23] In the nineteenth century, domesticity as a set of practices created the imperial: perceptions of what 'home' stood for were expressed through ideas about civilization (always a relative concept) and its constituent practices and performances. These both united and differentiated Britishness across the globe, as they took root in and acculturated to dispersed cultural and physical environments, in ways that defined different kinds of people and place, but always within the broader coherence of Empire as a whole. Perhaps most importantly, gendered, raced and classed British domesticity, in which the home

---

[21] Ann Laura Stoler, *Carnal Knowledge and Imperial Power*, 7. There has been an explosion of work focussing on different aspects of colonialism and intimacy in the last two decades. On India see, for example, Antoinette Burton, *Dwelling in the Archive: Women Writing House, Home and History in Late Colonial India* (New York: Oxford University Press, 2003); Indrani Chatterjee (ed.), *Unfamiliar Relations: Family and History in South Asia* (New Delhi: Permanent Black, 2004); Durba Ghosh, *Sex and the Family in Colonial India: The Making of Empire* (New York: Cambridge University Press, 2006).

[22] Ann Laura Stoler, *Carnal Knowledge and Imperial Power*, 6.

[23] J. E. Dawson, 'Woman in India: Her Influence and Position', *The Calcutta Review*, CLXVI (1886): 347–9.

was ideally a unit of consumption and reproductive labour, only existed because
of the wealth and power afforded to Britain by the exploitations of empire. In
this way domesticity was part of the apparatus of coloniality.[24]

In nineteenth-century India, a specifically Anglo-Indian way of domestic
life emerged that was peculiar to its Indian context but was also connected
to wider ideas about 'Britishness' or 'Englishness'.[25] Anglo-Indians would
refer to themselves as Anglo-Indian, but also seemed to position themselves
interchangeably as English, British or European. Whatever community they
imagined themselves as a part of, Anglo-Indians' faith in their connection to
Home, to the Homeland, was an important part of their identities.[26] The use
of the word 'Home' to describe Britain was apposite; they imagined it in part
in terms of a certain kind of domesticity, which they would reference in their
Indian households. However, as Elizabeth Buettner has shown, on return to
Britain they frequently suffered disappointment that things were not as they
felt they should be. No longer part of a powerful white minority, many Anglo-
Indians found they could not afford the numbers of servants they were used
to or the domestic lifestyle they had envisaged themselves leading. Somewhat
estranged from metropolitan society, Anglo-Indian returnee communities
developed, with their own domestic cultures.[27] Beryl Irving remembered of the
Anglo-Indian community of Bedford, in which she grew up, that 'the houses were
crammed with Benares tables, strings of little carved elephants, placid buddhas
and malevolent Gods' while 'our mothers made good curries'.[28] The difference of

---

[24] The concept of coloniality was developed by Anibal Quijano as a way of conceptualizing the logic of
European/Western imperialisms and their legacies, particularly in terms of the making of the social
hierarchies and structures of knowledge that underpin 'modernity'. Quijano contended that Western
modernity depended for its existence on coloniality – on the systems of knowledge and the related
practices through which colonial structures of power were realized, and persist to the present day.
See Anibal Quijano, 'Coloniality and Modernity/Rationality', *Cultural Studies* 21, 2–3 (2007): 168–78

[25] I use Anglo-Indian throughout this book according to its contemporary usage to refer to white
Britons resident in India, who may or may not have also referred to themselves as British, English
or European depending apparently on context. I have seen few references to people as Welsh or
Scottish though there were many Scots and Welsh people in India at this time. Of course, who was
and was not included in the category of 'Anglo-Indian' was a vexed question and requires further
research.

[26] See Benedict Anderson, *Imagined Communities. Reflections on the Origin and Spread of Nationalism*
(New York: Verso, 1991) for an exploration of the idea of 'imagined communities'.

[27] For work on patterns of British family life in India and Britain in the late nineteenth and twentieth
centuries and a particularly interesting exploration of returnee communities see Elizabeth Buettner,
Empire Families. Britons and Late Imperial India (Oxford: Oxford University Press, 2004) especially
chapter 5; For a readable and comprehensive introduction to better-off British women's lives in India
see Margaret Macmillan, *Women of the Raj* (London: Thames and Hudson, 1988).

[28] Beryl Irving quoted in Elizabeth Buettner, *Empire Families*, 235.

those Britons who had permanently or temporarily made the outposts of empire their homes, signified by their development of an alternative version of British domesticity, strained simple links between whiteness and metropolitan national belonging. As an advice manual written for returnees from India suggested, Anglo-Indians were a different kind of English people, who understood 'each other's language' requiring 'no aid from a dictionary to understand the meaning of *"Durzee"* or *Ghorawallah*, and they do not want an explanation if you should happen to speak of a *pucka* house!'[29]

Categories of identity were never fixed, but were protean and malleable, their contents shifting as the movement of discourses across metropole and colony moulded them. What it meant to be a master or a servant varied according to the historically specific discursive context in which one was a master or a servant; in the nineteenth century this was a context that included both metropole and colony. Certainly, as this book demonstrates, Anglo-Indian women were active agents of empire, figuring themselves as doing the work of empire in the way they ran their homes.[30] Here, though, I suggest that imperialism was not something that only mattered in colonial places; 'imperial domesticity' was an ideology and associated set of practices that developed across imperial space. The work of 'civilization' went on in middle-class metropolitan homes where, just as in colonial households, domestic servants were supposedly educated by their involvement in and observation of the display of their employers' domesticity. Imperial domesticity was not unique to India; metropolitan domesticity was a part of it.

Domestic service

As Bridget Hill has written, 'Domestic service provides a point of entry into a host of interesting questions for the historian.'[31] Domestic service has commanded the attention of scholars in a range of disciplines, who have explored it to understand a key way that inequalities of power are naturalized

---

[29] Edward J. Waring, *The Tropical Resident at Home: Letters Addresses to Europeans Returning from India and the Colonies on Subjects Connected with Their Health and General Welfare* (London: John Churchill and Sons, 1866), 62–3.

[30] See Alison Blunt, 'Imperial Geographies of Home: British Domesticity in India, 1886–1925', *Transactions of the Institute of British Geographers*, 24, 4 (1999): 421–40 for an important exploration of 'imperial domesticity'. Also Mary Procida, *Married to the Empire*.

[31] Bridget Hill, *Servants. English Domestics in the Eighteenth Century* (Oxford: Clarendon, 1996), 7.

to sustain elite economic, political and cultural supremacy in the 'modern' world.[32] However, although some significant qualitative work has examined the articulation of power in the construction of nineteenth-century servant/ master/mistress class and gender identities in Britain, in most general studies of nineteenth-century society and culture written before the 1970s, and often since, domestic servants tend to have little more than a few paragraphs devoted to their lives, tending to feature as 'footnotes to larger dramas of class struggle'.[33] Work by Carolyn Steedman on eighteenth-century servants, and by Lucy Delap and Laura Schwartz on the twentieth century, has illuminated the critical importance of servants in the making of class categories and sensibilities, and has contested the hackneyed image of servants as always drooping under the weight of elite oppression.[34] Meanwhile, the critical importance of domestic service in the making of colonial societies has begun to receive the critical

---

[32] See Rafaella Sarti, 'Historians, Social Scientists, Servants, and Domestic Workers: Fifty Years of Research on Domestic and Care Work', *International Review of Social History*, 59, 2 (2014): 279–314, for a useful overview of this work. Key texts include Bridget Anderson, *Doing the Dirty Work? The Global Politics of Domestic Labour* (London: Zed Books, 2000); Shireen Ally, *From Servants to Workers: South African Domestic Workers and the Democratic State* (Ithaca: ILR, 2009); Mary Romero, *Maid in the USA* (London: Routledge, 1992); Dirk Hoerder, Elise van Nederveen Meerkerk and Silke Neunsinger (eds.), *Towards a Global History of Domestic and Caregiving Workers* (Leiden: Brill, 2015); Antoinette Fauve-Chamoux (ed.), *Domestic Service and the Formation of European Identity: Understanding the Globalization of Domestic Work, 16th–21st Centuries* (Bern: Peter Land, 2004); Rosie Cox, *The Servant Problem: Domestic Employment in a Global Economy* (London: I.B. Tauris, 2006); Grace Chang, *Disposable Domestics: Immigrant Women Workers in the Global Economy* (Cambridge: South End Press, 2000); Raka Ray and Seemin Qayum, *Cultures of Servitude: Modernity, Domesticity and Class in India* (Stanford: Stanford University Press, 2009); K. Adams and Sara Dickey (eds.), *Home and Hegemony: Domestic Service and Identity Politics in South and South East Asia* (Ann Arbor: University of Michigan Press, 2000); Samita Sen and Nilanjana Sengupta, *Domestic Days: Women, Work and Politics in Contemporary Kolkata* (New Delhi: Oxford University Press, 2016).

[33] Julia Wrigley, 'Feminists and Domestic Workers', *Feminist Studies*, 17, 2 (1991): 317.

[34] Carolyn Steedman, *Master and Servant: Love and Labour in the English Industrial Age* (Cambridge: Cambridge University Press, 2007); Carloyn Steedman, *Labours Lost. Domestic Service and the Making of Modern England* (Cambridge: Cambridge University Press, 2009); Lucy Delap, *Knowing Their Place. Domestic Service in Twentieth Century Britain* (Oxford: Oxford University Press, 2011); Laura Schwartz, *Feminism and the Servant Problem. Class and Domestic Labour in the Women's Suffrage Movement* (Cambridge: Cambridge University Press, 2019). Other important scholarship includes Pamela Horn, *Flunkeys and Scullions: Life below Stairs in Georgian England* (Stroud: Sutton, 2004), Pamela Horn, *The Rise and Fall of the Victorian Servant* (Stroud: Sutton, 1990); Alison Light, *Mrs Woolf and the Servants* (London: Penguin, 2008); Selina Todd, 'Domestic Service and Class Relations in Britain 1900–1950', *Past and Present*, 203 (2009): 259–65; Caroline Bressey, 'Black Women and Work in England, 1880–1920' in Mary Davis (ed.), *Class and Gender in British Labour History: Renewing the Debate (or Starting It?)* (Pontypool: Merlin, 2011): 117–32, Rozina Visram, *Ayahs, Lascars and Princes: Indians in Britain, 1700–1947* (London: Pluto, 1986); Kristina Straub, *Domestic Affairs: Intimacy, Eroticism and Violence between Servants and Masters in Eighteenth-Century Britain* (Baltimore: Johns Hopkins University Press, 2009); Bruce Robbins, *The Servant's Hand. English Fiction from Below* (London: Duke University Press, 1993); Higgs, Edward, 'Domestic Servants and Households in Victorian England', *Social History*, 8, 2 (1983): 201–10.

attention it demands.[35] Important work on domestic service in colonial India, which employed well over 2 million and was the fourth biggest occupation according to the 1881 Census, has in recent years not only attended to its significance for British imperial identities, but also sought to illuminate its wider cultural, economic and political importance and variability within the South Asia.[36] Having said this, despite notable exceptions – the work of Claire Lowrie, and also that by Julia Martinez, Claire Lowrie, Frances Steel and Victoria Haskins for example – there is still little scholarship that disrupts the national and local frames that structure much current scholarship on histories of domestic service.[37]

Inside/outside

As Davidoff has written, '[n]ineteenth century residential domestic service was a twilight world; domestic servants were not really part of the family (as many employers would have liked to believe), but neither were they legally or traditionally seen as unequivocally part of the paid workforce.'[38] Their work

---

[35] See 'Introduction' in Victoria Haskins and Claire Lowrie (eds.), *Colonization and Domestic Service. Historical and Contemporary Perspectives* (New York: Routledge, 2015) for an insightful overview of this scholarship. Key texts include Shirleene Robinson, *Something Like Slavery? Queensland's Aboriginal Child Workers, 1842–1945* (Melbourne: Australian Scholarly Publications, 2008); Barry Higman, *Domestic Service in Australia* (Melbourne: Melbourne University Press, 2002); Victoria Haskins, *One Bright Spot* (London: Palgrave, 2005); Victoria Haskins, 'Domesticating Colonizers: Domesticity, Indigenous Domestic Labor, and the Modern Settler Colonial Nation', *The American Historical Review*, 124, 4 (2019): 1290–3011.

[36] Elizabeth Buettner gives substantial attention to Indian servants and childcare in *Empire Families* (36–45), as does Cecilia-Leong Salobir in chapter 3 of *Food Culture in Colonial Asia: A Taste of Empire* (London: Routledge, 2001). E.M. Collingham discusses them in relation to the limits of anglicization in *Imperial Bodies* (103–13). Mary Procida devotes chapter 3 to servants in *Married to the Empire* arguing that servants freed Anglo-Indian women from 'the practical and ideological burdens of housework' so that they could 'turn their energy and attention to the work of empire both in the home and beyond' (105). Alison Blunt discusses domestic servants and the domestication of imperial power in 'Imperial Geographies of Home: British Domesticity in India, 1886–1925', *Transactions of the Institute of British Geographers*, 24, 4 (1999); See also Nupur Chaudhuri, 'Memsahibs and Their Servants in Nineteenth-Century India', *Women's History Review*, 3, 4 (1994): 549–62; Swapna M. Banerjee, *Men, Women, and Domestics*; Indrani Sen, 'Colonial Domesticities, Contentious Interactions: Ayahs, Wet-nurses and Memsahibs in Colonial India', *Indian Journal of Gender Studies*, 16, 3 (2009): 299–328; Nitin Varma, 'Servant Testimonies and Anglo-Indian Homes in Nineteenth-Century India' in James Williams and Felicitas Hentschke (eds.), *To Be at Home: House, Work, and Self in the Modern World* (Berlin: De Gruyter, 2018): 219–24. The essays in Nitin Sinha and Nitin Varma's volume *Servants' Pasts* are a ground-breaking intervention in the field: Nitin Sinha and Nitin Varma (eds.), *Servants' Pasts. Late-Eighteenth to Twentieth Century South Asia*, Vol. 2. (Hyderabad: Black Swan Pvt Ltd, 2019).

[37] Claire Lowrie, *Masters and Servants. Cultures of Empire in the Tropics* (Manchester: Manchester University Press, 2016); Julia Martinez, Claire Lowrie, Frances Steel and Victoria Haskins, *Colonialism and Male Domestic Service across the Asia Pacific* (London: Bloomsbury, 2018).

[38] Leonore Davidoff, *Worlds Between*, 3.

marked the difference between inside and out, private and public worlds; they
swept dirt out of the house, dealt with tradespeople, admitted visitors and cared
for their employer's possessions and their bodies, thereby releasing family
members from some, if not all, household labour.[39] As (mostly) women paid to
work in the home, domestic servants in Britain transgressed, even while they
were essential to, the boundaries of a powerful domestic ideal propounded in
verse, novels, paintings, pulpits and linked by contemporaries to morality and
the 'natural' difference between the sexes.[40] In British India domestic servants
were key interlocutors with, and representatives of, the 'native' environment
their employers sought to transform. However, despite efforts to remake India,
its climate and culture nevertheless shaped domestic life, with the employer-
servant relationship acting as a conduit through which India could flow into the
intimate and private recesses of Anglo-Indian life. Even while Anglo-Indians
attempted to constitute a version of the domestic ideal in the Indian context
for the sake of both their own sense of Englishness and their native servants'
edification, their dependence on those servants – on their local knowledge and
skill – revealed the fragility of the colonial 'project'.[41] Servants' labour was turned
towards making class, race and gender difference *feel* meaningful, while at the
same time the border crossing status of servants indicated the ephemerality of
such distinctions.

It is commonplace to imagine domestic servants as marginal figures,
probably because this is how they appear in archives, on the edges of their
employers' consciousness. But, as Delap has written, 'marginality is not the
most revealing of historical frameworks'.[42] The problem with marginality
is that it is a spatial concept that assumes the existence of a centre that gives
the margin its identity. Such a conceptualization is rooted in the epistemic
inequalities through which much 'Western' knowledge is organized. The centre
is British, it is white, it is middle class, it is the heteronormative family. We need
to reconfigure marginality, and consider the possibility a margin can also be
a centre, depending on perspective. The question really is whose perspective

---

[39] Leonore Davidoff, *Worlds Between*, 24; Leonore Davidoff, Megan Doolittle, Janet Fink and Katherine Holden, *The Family Story. Blood, Contract and Intimacy 1830–1960* (London: Pearson, 1999), 167.
[40] See Leonore Davidoff, *Worlds Between*, chapters 1 and 4 for further discussion of these ideas. See also Leonore Davidoff, Megan Doolittle, Janet Fink and Katherine Holden, *The Family Story*, 158–82 for a discussion of servants' ambiguous status and the tensions it produced in nineteenth century families.
[41] E.M. Collingham, *Imperial Bodies*, 8; chapter 3.
[42] Lucy Delap, *Knowing Their Place*, 4

has mattered, historically, and why?. When we talk about domestic servants as marginal, we are really thinking in terms of their access to power – their ability to determine the conditions of their existence. But perhaps it is more interesting to ask, in what ways domestic servants were *not* marginal, in order to understand how marginality can be problematic as a spatializing concept. In this book I have focussed more on domestic servants' liminality than their marginality to try and get at some of the complexities of the dynamics of power in their relationships with their employers.

Domestic servants within metropolitan British and colonial Indian households both kept and unsettled borders, creating a zone somewhere within them as they laboured. These borders manifested in a material sense as those between the house and the street, or between upstairs and down, or back and front, or verandah and interior, and so on. Much of the physical boundary-keeping done by domestic servants as they cleaned, cared, provisioned and policed visitors to the household also served to mark other kinds of differences, through which the distribution of social power was organized: differences of class, gender, race, and also ethnicity and age. In this sense, servants were liminal figures, agents of the creation of 'the place from which something begins its presencing'.[43] Who mastered and who served was the first distinction, but the flow of power could be ambivalent, something indicated by uncertainties around how much employers could trust their servants to care for, and about them, which was often expressed as anxiety about servants' resistance to the absolutism of their employers' authority. As Tanika Sarkar has suggested, asymmetries of intimacy may reflect servant resistance to oppression; servants' invisibility in archives may be *both* a mark of archivists' interest in elite lives *and* of servant agency: a choice to keep their selves for themselves.[44] And for servants, their seemingly small acts of empowerment, the lateral agency ('agency without intention') highlighted by Lucy Delap, perhaps illustrate an understanding of both the artificiality and the ineluctability of the systems of difference they were so important in making.[45] Domestic servants then had the potential to be dangerous figures, necessarily oppressed by the demands of domesticity, but simultaneously empowered by their intimate knowledge of their employers and their dependence. The ambiguous nature of the border zone created and occupied by servants was

---

[43] Martin Heidegger, quoted in Homi Bhabha, *The Location of Culture* (London: Routledge, 1994), 1.

[44] Tanika Sarkar, 'Caste-ing Servants in Colonial Calcutta' in Nitin Sinha and Nitin Varma (eds.), *Servants' Pasts*, 244.

[45] Lucy Delap, 'Agency and Domestic Workers' Calcutta' in Nitin Sinha and Nitin Varma (eds.), *Servants' Pasts*, 268–71.

reflected in other ambiguities. Were servants children or adults? They were often young and could be more physically immature than the children they might be charged to mind. Were they part of the family or not? They might be kin and certainly were ideally and legally dependent on the head of the household. Such uncertainties shaped the position of servants in nineteenth-century society and were reflected in their limited legal rights and denial of independent status.

Methodology and sources

Getting at the servant-employer relationship in the nineteenth century is problematic. The lack of historical interest in servants discussed earlier is reflected in their infrequent appearance in the categories of archives. Available sources relating to both Britain and India overwhelmingly document the perspective of employers and often afford only fleeting glimpses of servants working in the background.[46] Personal documents generated by nineteenth-century Indian servants in which they talk about their work are rare. The asymmetry of available source material is reflected by an asymmetry of focus in the book; there is more discussion of service in Britain than service in India.

There are exceptions to the tendency for personal sources to only rarely mention the servant-employer relationship. One oft-quoted source is the diary of Hannah Cullwick, the maid-of-all-work who, at the encouragement of her middle-class lover Arthur Munby, kept diaries throughout her working life.[47] To assume Hannah's attitudes were typical of servants generally would be rash, but nevertheless her accounts of work and relationships with employers and fellow servants make this an invaluable resource. Another exception is Jane Carlyle, whose relationship with her servants was a constant theme of her correspondence.[48] Similarly, for India the letters of the poverty-stricken soldier's wife Minnie Wood have been a useful counterpoint to the weight of elite

---

[46] Leonore Davidoff, *Worlds Between*, 19.

[47] Hannah Cullwick's diaries are in Box 98, Munby Collection, Wren Library, Trinity College, Cambridge University.

[48] There are various published collections of Jane Carlyle's correspondence. See J.A. Froude (ed.), *Letters and Memorials of Jane Welsh Carlyle*, 3 Vols (London: Longmans and Co, 1883); Townsend Scudder (ed.), *Letters of Jane Welsh Carlyle to Joseph Neuberg 1848–1862* (London: Oxford University Press, 1931); Leonard Huxley (ed.), *Jane Welsh Carlyle: Letters to Her Family, 1839–1863* (London: John Murray, 1924); Alexander Carlyle, *New Letters and Memorials of Jane Welsh Carlyle* (London: John Lane,1903); Alan and Mary McQueen Simpson (eds.), *I Too Am Here. Selections from the Letters of Jane Welsh Carlyle* (Cambridge: Cambridge University Press, 1977).

accounts, such as the letters of Lady Mary Hobhouse.[49] Though none of these sources can be seen as archetypal, they do afford important insights into the variable intimacies and tensions possible in the employer-servant relationship and often resonate with wider themes identified across more fragmentary source material. In order to identify these themes, manuscript and oral sources identified in record offices in London, Essex, Wales and the India Office Collection have been supplemented with other published autobiographies and diaries and cross-referenced with official records such as reports from social investigator Charles Booth, and letters between Members of the Government of India.[50] Analysis of census statistics for both India and England also gives some quantitative insight to an otherwise qualitative analysis.

Although as Edward Higgs has warned, '[r]elying on the use of domestic manuals' to write the history of domestic service is 'equivalent to reconstructing the average modern home from the pages of *Vogue*', domestic advice manuals have nevertheless been a fruitful resource for this book.[51] The genre of the domestic advice manual flourished in the nineteenth century. These books cannot tell us much about conditions of service or specific servant-employer relationships in India or in England *per se*; manuals and chapters on servants in more general books tended to describe ideal, rather than real, domestic set-ups. However, when placed in context, they reflect a 'structure of feeling' in terms of domestic service and the servant-employer relationship in the nineteenth century, and it is possible to trace the development of certain themes as the century progressed.[52] Moreover, in contributing to a discourse on service and servants they were a part of the process by which the identity of 'servants' (and by association 'mistresses/masters') as a sociocultural grouping was constructed and the terms of conduct for the servant-employer relationship were established, including the limits of acceptable behaviour. As a part of this discursive process, the writers of advice literature drew on normative notions of gender and class and racializing language, and in doing so contributed to the process by which those categorical distinctions were reified and invested with meaning.

---

[49] Letters of Maria Lydia Wood, MSS/Eur/B210, India Office Records Asia Pacific and African Collections, British Library; Mary Hobhouse, *Letters from India 1872–1877* (Edinburgh: printed for private circulation, 1906).

[50] I have used oral material from Paul and Thea Thompson's 'Family Life and Work Experience before 1918' (Essex University Oral Archive) and from the India Office Records Oral Archives.

[51] Edward Higgs, 'Domestic Service and Household Production' in Angela V. John (ed.), *Unequal Opportunities. Women's Employment in England 1800–1918* (Oxford: Blackwell, 1986), 127.

[52] Raymond Williams, *The Long Revolution* (London: Chatto and Windus, 1961), 48.

There is a heavy reliance on newspapers as a source for this book. I use them to access the elusive servant voice, examining a 'letters page' dialogue between servants and employers in *The Times* in which English servants asserted their selfhood and challenged a dominant employer discourse that constructed them as lazy and dishonest. I also employ them to investigate the desire of some servants to unionize at the end of the nineteenth century. Newspapers are used to examine the content and representation of court cases involving servants and employers in both metropole and colony.[53] It is important to note that newspapers are a problematic source due to the likelihood of editorial bias, their appeal to specific segments of the literate population and the possibility of letters printed in them being faked. However, as John Tosh has written, 'no text has ever been composed in isolation'.[54] My concern is with what the appearance of such texts at specific moments can represent in terms of the discursive construction of identities. Feeding back into the particular sociocultural contexts in and out of which they have been produced, textual representations can tap into and challenge, and/or reconstitute, ideas about and conflicts of opinion over behaviour and identity within the wider society to which they relate. In doing so they can suggest alternative possibilities and images for discursive and behavioural emulation, rejection or development. Thus representations of class, gender or race, or even just allusions to these axes of difference, can not only be read as constitutive within discursive constructions of identity, but can also reveal the play of wider ideological power over the meaning of differentiated identities. As Roger Chartier has written in relation to the early impact of print in sixteenth- and seventeenth-century France, 'representations of the social world themselves are the constituents of social reality'.[55] In this way, newspapers could serve as shapers of reality.[56] It is crucial, if the newspapers are to be of any use to us, to place the concerns and anxieties expressed within their pages in the wider sociocultural context out of, and into which, they emerged. Looking at the newspapers of the day may limit us to the opinions of the literate reading public, or even to the opinion of an editor, but with careful reading and attention

---

[53] In current parlance a 'character' would be a reference from an employer.

[54] John Tosh, *The Pursuit of History*, 124.

[55] Roger Chartier, 'Intellectual History or Sociocultural History? The French Trajectories' in Dominic LaCapra and Steven L. Kaplan (eds.), *Modern European Intellectual History: Re-appraisals and New Perspectives* (London: Cornell University Press, 1982), 30.

[56] Christopher A. Kent, 'Victorian Periodicals and the Constructing of Victorian Reality' in Don J. Vann and Rosemary T. VanArsdel (eds.), *Victorian Periodicals: A Guide to Research*, Vol. 2, 5 (New York: Modern Language Association of America, 1989), 5.

to detail we can trace conflicts and ambivalences within a paper's pages and in this way gain access to the making of nineteenth-century identities.

Chapter overview

Chapter 1 maps the structure of service in Britain, providing an analytical survey of the context to the master/mistress-servant relationship in the nineteenth-century metropole. It uses Census returns to assess numbers of servants and the gender division of labour. Advice manuals, articles, published autobiographies, novels and legislation are used to consider the myriad ways in which servant and employer rights, roles and responsibilities were variously defined by the employer class in the nineteenth century. This is to demonstrate the familiarity of the servant-employer relationship within British society and its long history as a conceptual tool.

In Chapter 2 the analytical focus moves to nineteenth-century India. As in the previous chapter, it uses Census data, amongst other sources, to build a picture of the structure of domestic service in colonial India. It argues that the servant-employer relationship in colonial India was essential to the development of colonial domesticity, through which management of the colonial home was constituted as critical to the imperial civilizing project. This had an impact on the way in which women conceived of their domestic role in India. White women attempted to manage their encounter with India in the nineteenth-century Anglo-Indian home through their relations with their Indian servants. However, these efforts were complicated by the conflict between metropolitan notions of domesticity and the circumstances of the Indian colonial context. These women positioned the home at the centre of the imperial civilizing project, using the language of imperial governance to describe domestic organization, translating metropolitan domestic ideology to develop a specifically Anglo-Indian domesticity. It was in the domestic sphere, however, that the limits of this process were most clearly revealed. As this chapter suggests, Indian domestic servants complicated efforts to recreate England within the private sphere. The domestic service relationship that was familiar to British imperial migrants was reconfigured through colonialism and fed into the making of colonial place in India. Anglo-Indians negotiated the Indian context through their explanation and definition of Indian servant roles and, despite themselves, represented an encounter that implicitly acknowledged Indian agency, even while they explicitly claimed triumph over it.

Chapter 3 explores the experience of middle- and upper-class employers in England, and particularly their perception, observance and transgression of the limits of acceptable behaviour in relation to ideas about who a master/mistress was and who a servant was. These limits were defined by private experience interacting with the public construction of roles and responsibilities and with wider discursive pressures. Through this ongoing process, the identities and rights of metropolitan servants and employers were ambivalently contested and shaped. Using autobiographies, letters and diaries, this chapter focusses on contests over employers' and servants' feelings about their respective responsibilities and rights. It argues that although the servant-employer relationship operated in variable ways 'behind closed doors', similar areas of tension emerge across households, as emotion was rationalized through the deployment of generic 'servant' characteristics by employers as a means to consolidate both their household and their class power.

In metropolitan Britain, domestic servants were in the process of making (and destabilizing) gendered class identities; in India they were key in the creation of 'Anglo-Indian' identities different both from Indian cultures and from metropolitan Britishness. This is the focus of Chapter 4. Anglo-Indian domestic practices, 'the transactions of the heart' that come with being fed, bathed, dressed, nursed, watched in moments of vulnerability or exuberance, by servants they understood as profoundly different from them, distanced Anglo-Indian people from friends, family and wider British society half a world away.[57] Theirs was an unstable, ambivalent identity that desired belonging in India but also was conscious and resentful of separation from Home. That ambivalence about where home was produced a tension amongst colonial settlers in India – a particular need to foster community and organize power – that resulted in a focus on what colonial place should be, how it should be ruled, what cultural work it should do. The insecurities that drove such debates crystallized in ideas about the appropriate management of domestic servants that had wider ramifications, as the next chapter will demonstrate.

Chapter 5 considers cases of assault and abuse involving domestic servants in Britain and in India to explore how the nature and legitimacy of violence were variously defined across different master-servant relationships, and how this intersected with broader practices of imperial governance and the power of the state to define the terms of 'civilization'. The chapter reflects upon the

---

[57] Thanks to Katie Walsh for the phrase 'transactions of the heart'.

tension between benevolent household pedagogy and regulatory control that often played out in discussions of the violence employers perpetrated on the bodies of servants. It sets these debates within the context of, on the one hand, eroded public sympathy for 'others' in colonial sites and on the other, increasing demands for rights by women and workers in the metropole in the second half of the nineteenth century, to demonstrate how race, class and gender might frame contests over the legitimacy of violence in ways that helped produce differentiations within categories of white Britishness.

Chapter 6 considers the way British servants contested and contributed to the construction of their characters in public dialogues with the employer class. Letters and articles published in *The Times* are used to assess how servants engaged in the public discourse on the servant-employer relationship, entering into a dialogue with employers over the extent of their authority. Second, this chapter concerns the efforts of some servants to unionize towards the end of the nineteenth century. The reasons why servants felt the need to unionize at this time are examined, as well as what their concerns as union members were and what the response of wider English society was to their unionization. This part of the chapter considers how efforts to unionize influenced and were influenced by ideas about the identities of servants and employers, by ideas about how the relationship between them should be conducted and by wider thinking about work and workers' rights in the late nineteenth century.

Conclusion

British imperialism did not simply affect the master/mistress-servant relationship in colonial places such as India. The experience of empire directly affected domestic service in England – imagine housemaids negotiating 'oriental' furnishings, their movement through a room proscribed by furniture and textiles from around the globe, or cooks being required to make uniquely colonial dishes, like curry, for their employers.[58] But more than this, English domesticity itself was an imperial ideology. In the context of the rapid industrialization of Britain, which was funded by the exploitations of Empire, 'domesticity' emerged

---

[58] See Margot Finn and Kate Smith, *The East India Company at Home 1757–1857* (London: UCL Press, 2018) and Jane Hamlett, *Material Relations. Domestic Interiors and Middle-class Families in England 1850–1910* (Manchester: Manchester University Press, 2010). There is also the fact that not all servants in Britain were white. See Caroline Bressey, 'Looking for Work: The Black Presence in Britain 1860–1920' *Immigrants and Minorities* 28, 2–3 (2010): 164–82.

as an effective method of organizing relations between people and place that underscored elite power throughout imperial space. This domesticity was an ideology that developed both as a result of empire and out of a dialogue with it, and domestic servants were both its objects and its agents. The notion that home was the cradle of empire was certainly as pertinent in Birmingham as in Bombay.

Servants' labour ensured the consumptive role of the domestic within the imperial economy, and was key in the middle classes establishing the cultural status and power that have remained a key feature of 'modern' societies. Servants' role was remade by the economic, political and social transformation that constituted industrialization and by the shifts in perceptions of human difference that that change engendered. This shift was financed by an imperial project which, in a context in which Britain was increasingly priding itself on its commitments to 'liberty' as a guiding principle, was itself legitimized by ideas about service and duty – the duty to serve the interests of 'civilization' by re-making relations of gender, race and class, eliding servitude with ideas about pedagogy and nature. These ideas were enacted on a domestic scale, largely by women who used servants to construct the domestic as an imperial project, in an attempt to claim a central role in the practice of imperialism. But this was not just a fantasy. This really was the work of imperialism. Through the master/mistress-servant relationship in the British Empire people were working out who they were, where they were positioned, in a new social framework – one that was global in scale and incorporated novel kinds of difference.

This study juxtaposes servant-employer relationships in England and in India, exploring aspects of both in an effort to understand how dynamics of gender, race and class variously shaped the relationship in metropole and colony and how the meaning and possibilities of 'service' were constructed across the two sites. Using close textual analysis of a range of qualitative and statistical source material to move between the general and the specific, it attempts to investigate in new ways the tension between intimacy and social distance that characterized the servant-employer relationship in both nineteenth-century Britain and its most important colony. It also tries to access the self-hood of servants who are too often portrayed as silent victims of omnipotent employers. The growth in representative institutions in nineteenth-century Britain afforded domestic servants the opportunity to assert themselves. It is instructive to consider the difference with India, where no such institutions existed, though as Durba Ghosh has demonstrated, domestic servants there did know and exercised what limited legal rights they had.[59] Consideration of domestic service and the relationships through which it was organized allows us to think productively about a range of interconnected issues including the nature of 'work', 'duty', the problematic distinction between categories of public and private, problems of intimacy and the ambivalent and contested processes through which intersecting hierarchies of power were and are constituted across space and time. Not only were domestic servants key components in the functioning of modern capitalist imperial economies, their 'otherness' played a material and imaginative role in place-making on different scales, from home, to colony, to nation, to empire, through which racial, class and gender identities were differentiated. As crucial interlocutors in colonial and metropolitan sites, servants played a key part in defining the relations that constituted those places as places.

---

[59] See chapter 5 in Durba Ghosh, *Sex and the Family in Colonial India. The Making of an Empire* (Cambridge: Cambridge University Press, 2006).

1

The structure of domestic service in nineteenth-century Britain

Though uniquely of their time and place, nineteenth-century domestic servants were preceded by a long history of service and servitude that framed their existence and shaped modern understandings of its purpose. For centuries ideas about service and duty had organized social relations in the British Isles. Put simply, everybody had a duty to serve someone, even the monarch, who served God. As we will see, the idea of service as something divinely ordained and owed up the social order was carried forward into the developing framework of class relations in nineteenth-century Britain, giving the lie to the idea of class as an open system of stratification. The first half of the nineteenth century saw a significant increase in the number of servant-employing households in Britain. The expansion in servant-employing households, and the increasing formalization of the employer-servant relationship, was part of a significant cultural shift, a seismic movement in the social fabric of British society as it shifted to become a society where households were units of consumption and reproductive labour, rather than production. This chapter will discuss the nineteenth-century culture of domesticity, its centrality to Victorian life and identity, and the numbers and roles of servants. It will then focus on a discussion of the decline of service and the so-called 'servant problem'.

Domesticity, class and gender in nineteenth-century Britain

In the nineteenth century British society experienced the turbulent effects of industrial capitalism. The establishment of a free market and the associated logic of individualism and competition were challenging and re-working received notions of hierarchy and patriarchy.[1] Social mobility was theoretically a

---

[1]   Leonore Davidoff, *Worlds Between* (Cambridge: Polity, 1995), 74.

possibility for many who a century earlier would have had little opportunity to alter their status. An old elite, whose wealth was based in landholding, was being challenged by a growing commercial and professional middle class. The transition from a joint to an individual wage, together with increasing employment of working-class women outside their homes, was also profoundly unsettling to patriarchal and hierarchical norms in the first part of the nineteenth century.[2] These developments were marked in the development of a status hierarchy that interacted with elaborated constructions of gender difference. Class definition did take place at the political and economic level: the developing proletariat and industrial bourgeoisie defined themselves through political organization in relation and opposition to each other, a shift stamped by the Reform Act of 1832 which gave middle-class men the vote, and by the repeal of the Corn Laws in 1846 around which political opposition to landed interests was articulated. However, status definition also took place at the cultural and ideological level, which interacted with political and economic expressions of both class and gender.[3]

The response of those who had obtained, or were aspirant to, upward mobility in the nineteenth century was one that manifested a tension between a profound anxiety about, and a supreme self-confidence in the rapidly changing social world. One way of relieving anxiety and boosting self-confidence is to differentiate, define, explain, educate and thereby control the world and secure one's place in it, and this is exactly what many nineteenth-century Britons attempted to do. Different agents operated in the processes of definition and classification ranging from political ideologues to medical and legal practitioners and evangelical moral crusaders. These forces intersected at that crucial site for modern identity, the family, which was invested with meaning as the basic unit of society as 'home' came to represent a stable refuge from an unstable and changing world. An image of a specifically bourgeois domestic ideal evolved, immortalized in the art and literature of the period. 'Home' took on a spiritual significance that elevated it above the mundanity of the quotidian. In John Ruskin's words, home was 'a sacred place, a vestal temple, a temple of the hearth watched over by Household Gods ...'.[4] It was the private sphere, ideally a unit of consumption sharply differentiated from the public world of work, politics,

---

[2] Wally Seccombe, 'Patriarchy Stabilised: The Construction of the Male Breadwinner Wage Norm in Nineteenth-Century Britain', *Social History*, 11 (1986): 67.

[3] See Leonore Davidoff and Catherine Hall, *Family Fortune. Men and Women of the English Middle Class 1780–1850*, 2nd edn (London: Routledge, 2002). s.

[4] John Ruskin, *Sesame and Lilies*, 1864 pocket edn (London: George Allen, 1906).

production and capital. The cut and thrust of the public sphere was almost universally represented as 'naturally' a masculine arena – the responsibility to financially maintain the family was ideally a man's alone. His role as provider for, protector of and, importantly, Master of his home and family was constitutive of his manliness, underpinning and re-working the traditional association of masculinity with authority, self-reliance, bravery, chivalry and reason:

> The Master: the Husband, the Father, the head of the House, the Bread-Winner is the responsible individual whose name and power upholds the household … he holds the place of highest honour; he is the supporter and sustainer of the establishment. He is also legally and politically responsible for all the other members of the family … such are the duties of a master, a husband and a father.[5]

This required that he have something to provide for, protect and rule over. In the nineteenth century the man's masculinity was associated with the existence of a private, domestic home, dependent on him, to which he could return at the end of the day as father, husband and master, to enjoy the fruits of other people's labour, purchased profitably by his own labour elsewhere. This home was also critical in a man's political identity – only independent men were eligible to vote. Independent men, to define their independence, required dependants: wife, children, servants. In the context of the British Empire, who would be dependent and who would not be, was determined by locally varied configurations of class, race and gender.

In relation to the developing ideal of masculinity, a lasting image of the ideal Victorian wife, daughter and sister evolved, an image that masked the exclusion of women from political and economic power by assigning them a domestic purpose and a distinct set of roles. Women were assigned a special position as the caretakers of religion and morality, ideally segregated within the private sphere of the home, free from the taint of market forces that would have undermined paternalistic authority.[6] As John Angell James wrote in his long-term bestseller *The Family Monitor*: 'What is gained by her in the shop is oftentimes lost in the house, for want of the judicious superintendence of a mother and mistress.'[7] The idea that market activity would undermine the purity and moral capabilities of women extended to any work involving manual labour, even within the home.[8]

---

[5] *Cassell's Book of the Household: A Work of Reference on Domestic Economy*, Vol. 1 (London: Cassell and Co, 1890), 27.

[6] Leonore Davidoff, *Worlds Between*, 74.

[7] John Angell James, *The Family Monitor, or a Help to Domestic Happiness* (1828) reprinted in T.S. James (ed.), *The Works of John Angell James*, 17 Vols. (Birmingham: Hamilton Adams, 1860–64), 56.

[8] Leonore Davidoff, *Worlds Between*, 74.

The attributes that fitted the ideal Victorian woman for her role in the private, domestic sphere were both overlaid with spiritual meaning and were seen to be the result of the mystical workings of nature. Innate 'biological' differences between men and women, supposedly identified by well-known 'experts' such as William Acton and Sir James Paget, scientifically 'proved' the idea that men and women should occupy different roles in different spheres of activity. This gave academic weight to the moral notion that 'separate spheres' benefited society at large.

The middle-class ideal of femininity was immortalized in Victorian poetry, literature, art and advice manuals. A symbol of social status in herself, the ideal Victorian lady manifested conspicuously the qualities of feminine gentility and appropriate morality. The construction of her gender identity, of ideal feminine identity (and relational masculine identity), was classed and classing, as its signifiers – the trappings of ideal domesticity – could only be fully achieved by those of a certain status. Those signifiers therefore worked to symbolize and construct broad conceptions of both class and gender difference, as well as nicer degrees of difference within the categories 'middle' and 'working' class and 'men' and 'women', as people tried to reconcile the tension between ideology and the material constraints on their lives.

Maintaining households in conformity with the domestic ideal of a non-working wife and children necessitated the employment of domestic servants. Seebohm Rowntree, in his study of York in the late nineteenth century, took the distinction between the working class and those above them in the social hierarchy to be marked by 'the keeping or not keeping of domestic servants'.[9] However, by definition, truly genteel women ensconced in a large and richly furnished private home could only be a small proportion of the population. Those who must work, therefore, should ideally only be engaged in domestic work that protected the purity of others – domestic service, charwomen, washerwomen or prostitutes – and thus conformed to the feminine ideal of women as the nurturers of the moral order of the private world.[10] Domestic service was seen as an appropriate preparation for young working-class girls for their future domestic roles. As W.R. Greg wrote, domestic servants 'do not follow an obligatorily independent, and therefore, for their sex an unnatural career: – on the contrary, they are attached to others and are connected with other existences

---

[9] Seebohm B. Rowntree, *Poverty: A Study of Town Life*, 2nd edn (London: Macmillan, 1901), 14.
[10] Leonore Davidoff, *Worlds Between*, 74.

which they embellish, facilitate and serve. In a word, they fulfil both essentials of a woman's being: *they are supported by and they administer to men.*'[11]

According to John Burnett: 'By their number, dress and function [servants] proclaimed in an outward and visible way the degree of success in life that their employer had attained and, by implication, conferred upon him membership of the [middle] class.'[12] Seeking to augment their social status, employers hired servants to maintain not only their lifestyles, but also as 'deference givers'.[13] The bourgeois domestic ideal had a power that stretched beyond the hazy borders of class categories. Even while tighter boundaries were drawn around the private sphere of home and family in the nineteenth century, more and more of those who aspired to middle-class status were bringing others into their homes to cook their food, nurse their children, clean their homes and deal with the most intimate aspects of their daily lives. Though servant-keeping was *de rigeur* for those who identified as middle-class, there was not necessarily a straightforward connection between servant-keeping and class status.[14] According to Eddie Higgs '[s]ervants were employed in the homes of retailers, farmers and members of all social classes'.[15] Throughout our period, farming, artisan and respectable working-class households hired paupers, local girls in need of work or took on kinfolk as servants. In houses lower down the socio-economic scale, servant labour released other members of the household to do other kinds of manual work, facilitating fine degrees of status within households.

As well as wife and children, domestic servants were defined within law as among the household head's dependants, rather than as employees. Although the mistress of a household would probably manage the servants, the head of the household, who was usually a man but could also be a single woman, was legally responsible for hiring and firing them, and for ensuring they were fed and clothed.[16] Domestic servants' dependence on the household head was necessary

[11] W.R. Greg, 'Why Are Women Redundant?' *National Review*, 15 (1862): 451.

[12] John Burnett, *Useful Toil: Autobiographies of Working People from the 1820s–the 1920s* (London: Allen Lane, 1974), 136.

[13] Quoted in Leonore Davidoff, *Worlds Between*, 24.

[14] See Edward Higgs, 'Women, Occupations and Work in the Nineteenth Century', *History Workshop Journal*, 23, 1 (1987): 59–80; Edward Higgs, 'Domestic Servants and Households in Victorian England', *Social History*, 8, 2 (1983): 201–10. Ebery and Preston's *Domestic service in late Victorian and Edwardian England, 1871–1914* (Reading: Reading Geographical Papers, University of Reading, 1976) is also essential reading for anyone interested in the Census and service.

[15] Edward Higgs, 'Domestic Service and Household Production' in Angela V. John (ed.), *Unequal Opportunities. Women's Employment in England 1800–1918* (Oxford: Basil Blackwell, 1986), 144.

[16] Edward Spike, *The Law of Master and Servant* (London: Shaw and Sons, 1839), 45; 'Bill for the better Protection of Young Persons under the Care and Control of Others as Apprentices or Servants', *Parliamentary Papers* (hereafter PP), 1851 (32) I.97.

within the ideology that gave meaning to and legitimized the definition of separate spheres and the attendant distinction of roles for men and women; defining servants as dependants within a family home obscured the fact that they were working women. Where the household head was a woman – as could be the case with widows and spinsters – the construction of the servant's childlike dependence bolstered the notion of the woman as motherly guide and domestic superintendent. Indeed, one domestic advice manual writer pseudonymously styled herself 'Mrs Motherly'. Nevertheless, the contrast between the notion that servants were family dependants and the reality of their difference to the families whose lifestyles they maintained emphasized their ambiguous status, implicitly blurring the class and gender boundaries that marked the edges of the middle-class domestic world.

Servants' failings had long been a source of complaint for their employers. However, as John Burnett has noted, the first half of the nineteenth century 'seems to have been unusually quiet on the subject'.[17] From around mid-century however, as domestic servant numbers began to increase rapidly, complaints about servants and advice as to how to deal with the problem of servants emerged with more frequency. Around the same time the genre of the domestic advice manual developed, creating a textual space in which women could publicly establish their domestic authority over both their homes and their 'subordinates'. Common themes encompassed issues of discipline and morality and the necessity for mistresses to ensure that their households' dependants observed behaviours appropriate to their lowly station. The servant problem, at this stage, focussed on the difficulties mistresses faced in enforcing deference, obedience, honesty and industry and the attendant risk that servant girls might fall into a life of vice and crime, possibly at the employers' expense.

From 1871, as the rate of domestic service slowed, commentators began to express increasing concern with the 'problem' of the scarcity of servants and its causes. Thus in the final decades of the nineteenth century the nature of the 'servant problem' shifted. Middle-class anxiety about the unwillingness of young girls of good character to enter service intensified, and with good reason. As a result of a range of material and ideological developments, such as the introduction of comprehensive elementary education in 1870, shifts in

---

[17] John Burnett, *Useful Toil*, 139.

ideas about citizenship and manliness, the possibility of alternative respectable occupations for women in factories, shops and offices and the arguments of feminists with regard to women, work and independence, fewer young men and women were choosing to become servants. The fact that they were making such a choice was extremely unsettling to their would-be employers as it challenged the principles upon which middle-class lifestyle and identity were predicated in the nineteenth century.[18]

The debate over the 'servant problem' in the final decades of the nineteenth century was a moment when the 'limits of ideological certainty' were exposed and tested. Such issues 'were the site of such intensive debates ... because they threatened to challenge *the* opposition upon which all other oppositions claimed to be based – the opposition between men and women'.[19] Servants were fundamental within the classed and gendered division of labour that sustained ideal middle-class domesticity. The ideology of domesticity legitimized and was legitimized by the meaningful definition of gender difference, through which women were excluded from openly wielding political and economic power:

> Locating the difference between men and women also set limits to the groups that actually had access to liberalism's promise of universal economic opportunities ... This process included generalizing the morality attributed to middle-class women to all women, translating the discrepancy between what one now has and what one could acquire into a psychological narrative of personal development, and subsuming the economic rewards capitalism seemed to promise into the emotional rewards that seemed available to every man in the castle of his home.[20]

Domestic servants were problematic within this process. Although ostensibly conforming to the gendered role of woman as caretaker of the domestic sphere, female servants did not perform domestic work because it was in their nature to do so, but because 'there was little that an unskilled girl who was under the unfortunate necessity of having to earn her own living could do except to clean,

---

[18] See Laura Schwartz, *Feminism and the Servant Problem. Class and Domestic Labour in the Women's Suffrage Movement* (Cambridge: Cambridge University Press, 2019) for a thoughtful study of 'the servant problem'.

[19] Mary Poovey, *Uneven Developments. The Ideological Work of Gender in Mid-Victorian England* (London: Virago, 1989), 10–11.

[20] Mary Poovey, *Uneven Developments*, 10–11.

cook and generally minister to others' wants'.[21] While conforming to the ideology that dictated 'a woman's place was in the home' in the sense that they performed domestic tasks in the private sphere as dependants of the master of the house, domestic servants, by virtue of their being working women earning their own living in a home that was for them a workplace, contradicted and even contested it in essence.

Various discourses worked to elide the challenge domestic servants posed to the theoretically sharp distinction between the classed and gendered 'separate spheres' of family and work, femininity and masculinity, which 'underwrote an entire system of institutional practices and conventions'.[22] Within advice literature service was frequently referred to as training for marriage. This made it possible to believe not only that the employer was doing the servant a service, rather than the other way round, but also that service was an appropriate education for a young working-class girl. Through service a working-class girl supposedly learned how to maintain the domestic sphere and to fulfil her role as a woman through her practice in the home of her benevolent employers. Religious arguments were marshalled to show that the relation between master and servant was a natural part of a divinely ordained hierarchy, and that the servant owed the master obedience as a result. Despite this, the ambivalence of the employer class towards their 'dependants', evidenced in contemporary writings on service and servants, is testament to a possibly unconscious and certainly unwilling recognition of the uncomfortable artificiality of such distinctions. It points towards the underlying and constant potential for changes in the ideological and material structure of gender and class relations, as articulated by feminists and socialists towards the end of the century.

The structure of service

Census returns must be treated with some caution with regard to domestic service. As Edward Higgs has pointed out, the occupational tables in the nineteenth-century census reports contain aggregates which disguise local variations and shifts over time, not to mention categorical changes between

---

[21] John Burnett, *Useful Toil*, 135.
[22] Mary Poovey, *Uneven Developments*, 8.

censuses as to the definition of a domestic servant.[23] Furthermore, a potentially large number of domestic servants were working in the households of kin, who may or may not have acknowledged the kin relationship in their census returns.[24] However, despite this the census material is useful in providing us with at least a rough idea of the scale of the occupation.

According to the Censuses, domestic servants were the largest occupational group of working women and indeed were the largest occupational group in the economy after agricultural labourers in the second half of the nineteenth century. In 1851, 751,641 women were categorized as servants.[25] Between 1851 and 1871, while the total of separate families increased by 36 per cent, the figure for female servants rose by over 56 per cent. In 1871, 12.8 per cent of the female population of England and Wales was engaged in domestic service or allied occupations.[26] In 1881 the number of resident female domestics in the census was 1,230,406 and by 1901 it was calculated as 1,285,072. The 1911 census gave the number of servants, including around 24,000 day servants, as 1,295,991. In 1891 the number of female servants had apparently peaked at 1,386,167 – over a third of all women employed. However, as Higgs has shown, this figure is likely to be inflated by the fact that the 1891 Census 'included with domestics all those female relatives returned in the census as employed in "helping at home", performing "housework" and so on', and thus it seems more accurate to regard the figures as indicating a gradual slowing down of the rate of expansion in the domestic service sector rather than an actual decline.[27] Nevertheless, servants were noticeably fewer in number, in relation to the number of families, in the final decades of the nineteenth century. In 1881 there were 218 female domestic servants per 1000 families in England and Wales; by 1911 this ratio had dropped to 170 domestics per 1000 families, hence the frequent expression of anxiety about servant 'shortages' in the late nineteenth and early twentieth centuries. Herbert. P. Miller expressed a common fear when he claimed that 'little foresight is required to see that unless a remedy is found for this state of things, the

[23] Edward Higgs, 'Domestic Servants and Households in Victorian England', 202; Mark Ebery and Brian Preston, *Domestic Service in late Victorian and Edwardian England, 1871-1914*, 11–15; see also Edward Higgs, 'Domestic Service and Household Production'.

[24] See Di Cooper and Moira Donald, 'Households and "Hidden" Kin in Early Nineteenth-Century England: Four Case Studies in Suburban Exeter, 1821–1861', *Continuity and Change*, 10, 2 (1995): 257–78. For a discussion of this in relation to mid-century Exeter.

[25] Census of 1851. Ages and Occupations, 1852–3, Vol. LXXXVII, parts 1 and 2.

[26] Pamela Horn, *The Rise and Fall of the Victorian Servant* (Stroud: Sutton, 1990), 26–7.

[27] Edward Higgs, 'Domestic Servants and Households in Victorian England', 202.

inevitable consequences will be that servants will dictate what terms they please, and employers will be obliged to accept them or become their own servants'.[28]

A large proportion of female domestic servants was under twenty (39 per cent of the total in 1860; 42 per cent in 1880; 31 per cent in 1911), though this proportion declined around the turn of the century as educational provisions improved after the passage of the 1870 Education Act, which introduced comprehensive primary education, and alternative occupations became available to young women.[29] Some commentators, such as Miller, blamed the decline on 'shortsighted parents, who attempt to artificially force [girls] beyond that station of life in which Providence has destined them to act'.[30] Nonetheless, the experience of service was still a common one for teenage girls; in 1881, 1 in 3.3 girls aged between fifteen and twenty was classified as a domestic servant.

The number of men in service had shown a decline since the 1850s. In 1851 there were 74,323 indoor male servants (not including coachmen, grooms or gardeners), a number which had fallen to 56,262 by 1881 and to 42,034 by 1911.[31] This may have been due to the fact that male servants tended to cost more than their female counterparts and were thought to be harder to control, but it is also likely that the increasingly exclusive association of domestic labour with 'women's' work and subordination, while the diversifying economy provided alternative 'manly' occupations for working-class men, did much to dissuade them from pursuing a career in indoor service as the nineteenth century progressed. The number of men in outdoor service – working as coachmen, grooms and gardeners – increased from 26,827 to 209,100 between 1851 and 1911. Gardeners saw the biggest increase – from 18,700 to 118,700 as compared with coachmen and grooms who increased in number from 37,400 to 90,400 between 1851 and 1911.[32] Ebery and Preston have argued that the huge increase in number of gardeners was due to the '[t]he rural myth [which] became embedded in English urban society through the thousands of little suburban estates and parks which were to be the urban equivalent of the Arcadian landscape. All these needed

---

[28] Herbert P. Miller, *The Scarcity of Domestic Servants: The Cause and the Remedy* (London: W. Lake and Son, 1876), 15.

[29] In 1880 attendance in school was made compulsory for children aged between five and ten and in 1891 fees in elementary schools largely disappeared.

[30] Herbert P. Miller, *The Scarcity of Domestic Servants*, 44.

[31] Census statistics taken from *General Reports of the Censuses of Population*: 1851: *PP*, 1853, LXXXVII; 1871: *PP*, 1873, LXXI; 1881: *PP*, 1883, LXXX; 1891: *PP*, 1893–94, CVI; 1901: *PP*, 1904, CVIII; 1911: *PP*, 1913, LXXVII.

[32] Mark Ebery and Brian Preston, *Domestic Service in Late Victorian and Edwardian England, 1871–1914*, 28–9, 112; Census of 1851.

full or part-time gardeners.'[33] Outdoor work did not carry the same stigma of unmanliness as indoor domestic service, it being manual labour outside the home, rather than cooking, cleaning and ministering to personal needs and wants inside the private sphere.

The demography of domestic service varied according to region. In mining and manufacturing areas, where servant employers constituted a smaller proportion of the total population and where there were other possible occupations for girls and women, the number of domestic servants was lowest. Servant employers in industrial areas had to recruit resident servants from further afield or go without. For example, Pamela Horn's research into the 1871 Census has shown that in the Lancashire cotton town of Colne only one in twenty three households had a resident servant (though more households may have employed day servants, or used kin as servants). Only a quarter of the Colne maids had been born in Lancashire, the majority being migrants from agricultural districts in Yorkshire, Cumberland, Westmorland and Wales. This pattern was common for industrial towns and London also relied on immigration to provide servants, though partly this was out of preference – city girls were thought to be less malleable, honest or hardworking than country girls.[34] Servants were more numerous in agricultural areas and towns such as Brighton, Bath and Cheltenham, 'the habitual resorts of the wealthier classes' according to the 1881 Census report, showed the greatest number of servants.[35] In London in 1881 the ratio of domestic servants was one in fifteen persons; in Brighton it was one in eleven and in Bath one in nine. In the agricultural counties of Norfolk, Suffolk and Essex the average was one to every twenty-one, but in industrial Lancashire it was one in thirty-one. In 1891 around one in five of all females over the age of ten living in Bath was a domestic servant, while in York, Reading and London the proportion was one in seven. However, in Halifax, Bury, Bolton, Rochdale, Blackburn and Burnley the ratio was only one in twenty.[36] By the time of the 1911 Census employers in the North of England had real difficulty in finding servants as the rate of growth in numbers of servants slowed. In Lancashire there were only 97 female indoor servants to every 1000 families and in the West Riding of Yorkshire 100 per 1000 families. In Bath, on the other hand, there were 307 servants per 1000, while

[33] Mark Ebery and Brian Preston, *Domestic Service in Late Victorian and Edwardian England, 1871–1914*, 29.
[34] Pamela Horn, *The Rise and Fall of the Victorian Servant*, 30–2.
[35] *General Report of the Census of Population*, 1881.
[36] Miss C.E.Collett, *Report on the Statistics of Employment of Women and Girls*, PP, 1894, LXXI, pt II, 22.

Class II families employing more than one servant was higher than 50 per cent in only one area – Easthampstead – in all but one area Class II families employed at least one servant.[45] Prochaska's argument that servants 'did not "necessarily" mark the division between the rich and the poor, between respectable middle and upper classes and their social inferiors' is valid; about 20 per cent of Class I households in mid-century York had no servants.[46] Nevertheless, over 50 per cent had more than one.[47] This suggests that a family was unlikely to consider and attempt to represent itself as middle or upper class and not employ one servant or more.

Many Victorian people saw conformity to the domestic ideal associated with middle classness, insofar as was possible, as an indicator of respectability, which was linked to the moral idea that one should constantly strive honestly to improve oneself and one's status. This idea – a key aspiration defining 'British' character – itself emerged in the wider discursive context of Empire, where from the early nineteenth century the domestic and family arrangements of 'natives' were understood to be backward, oppressive and even immoral. Thus, throughout our period farming, artisan and respectable working-class households employed poor girls cheaply from institutions such as workhouses and houses of mercy, in order to release the mistress from some of the dirtiest and most degrading chores.[48] These servants often did productive work in the household such as cheese-making or shop-minding. In Bradfield and Reading in 1871, 50 per cent of the servant keeping household heads in skilled manual occupations employed more than one servant.[49] Such girls would not be desirable employees for more established middle- or upper-class families, as Mrs Nassau Senior noted: 'The girls in service repeatedly tell me that they would have no chance of getting into a "good" family.'[50]

In 1896 Charles Booth divided servants into three basic categories, claiming that 'the roughest single-handed places' were run by the 'wife of an artisan or well-paid labourer who does the work of the household herself, with the assistance of a servant,' while a 'better class of servant' would work alone in the

---

[45] Mark Ebery and Brian Preston, *Domestic Service in late Victorian and Edwardian England, 1871–1914*, 64.

[46] F.K. Prochaska, 'Female Philanthropy and Domestic Service in Victorian England', *Bulletin of the Institute of Historical Research*, 54 (1981): 84.

[47] A. Armstrong quoted in F.K. Prochaska, 'Female Philanthropy and Domestic Service in Victorian England', 84.

[48] F.K. Prochaska, 'Female Philanthropy and Domestic Service in Victorian England', 82–3.

[49] Mark Ebery and Brian Preston, *Domestic Service in Late Victorian and Edwardian England, 1871–1914*, 64.

[50] Local Government Board, *Third Annual Report*, 344.

households of 'small clerks, where the mistress often takes a great pride in her house, doing a great deal of the work with her own hands, and superintending the whole of it'.[51] Booth's third category included 'those serving both in middle class households and in the large establishments of the wealthy, it being scarcely possible to make any practical division between these two classes of servants. Moreover, each of the three groups merges almost imperceptibly into the other, so that no hard or fast line can be drawn between them'.[52] Booth's difficulty in clearly marking off the boundaries of class within the hierarchy of servants reflects the lack of clarity at the borders of class categories in the nineteenth century. Furthermore, Booth's statement suggests that it wasn't necessarily the number, but the quality and status of the servant that helped define the social images of households in relation to each other at the end of the nineteenth century. In Bridget Hill's words: '[h]ouseholds varied in size and wealth, but their complement of servants did not necessarily reflect their income'.[53] Nevertheless, servants' existence allowed a merging of the difference between the employer and the employed with the difference between the master and the mastered. This dynamic did not necessarily work along the lines of the usual class boundaries to which we are accustomed, but operated to construct a status hierarchy *within* intersecting categories of class and gender that was nicely graduated both inside, and beyond the private home.

Many general servants were paupers, hired out from workhouses and charitable institutions at ages as young as six or seven, though more usually they were around twelve years old. The conditions of their working lives were frequently poor, particularly in the cities, where as sole servants and/or paupers and/or rural girls they were integrated into neither the household nor the local community.[54] These so-called 'slaveys' would often have to work from 5 am until midnight for a nominal wage, if anything at all. Note the connection with slavery, abolished in 1833, and made explicit in the name 'slavey', suggesting an affiliation between the servitude of the domestic drudge and that of enslaved peoples. 'These poor creatures', wrote J. Fenimore Cooper in 1837, 'have an air of dogged sullen misery that I have never seen equalled in any other class of human being'. He described one girl as entering his room at 'a sort of drilled

---

[51]   A single-handed establishment was one in which a servant worked alone as a maid-of-all-work or a general servant.

[52]   Charles Booth and Jesse Argyle, *Life and Labour of the People in London*, Vol. VIII, part II (London: Macmillan and Co, 1896), 213, 14.

[53]   Bridget Hill, *Servants*, 16–17.

[54]   Frank E. Huggett, *Life Below Stairs* (London: John Murray, 1977), 108.

trot, as if she had been taught a particular movement to denote assiduity and diligence, and she never presumed to raise her eyes to mine, but stood the whole time looking meekly down'.[55] The workload borne by such girls was enormous, and their tasks wide-ranging. For example, girls working as general servants in farming households would often have to help with the dairy and livestock, as well as be responsible for all the dirty and unpleasant household chores.

The servants rights and legal status

In a section on household law, the author of *Cassell's Household Guide* stated that 'of private relation subsisting between human beings, the first in importance is that of master and servant; the second, that of marriage, which, in the words of a great lawyer, includes the reciprocal rights and duties of husband and wife'.[56] Although 'the duties, privileges, and perquisites of servants' were 'details specially agreed upon between the contracting parties', there were certain features common to most residential service positions in the nineteenth century.[57] The position was located in a private home.[58] If married, the master was responsible for establishing a contract with a servant, as his wife had no independent status in law, although in practice the mistress would usually choose and engage the household staff. The master was responsible for all the servant's basic needs: food, housing and sometimes a small cash wage. If the master failed to 'find his servant in victuals' the servant could legally leave the position without notice. If the servant was 'of tender years' and unable to provide for and take care of him/herself:

> ... it is an indictable offence, in the nature of a misdemeanour, for the master, or mistress, to refuse, or neglect, to provide such servant with sufficient food or other necessaries, so as thereby to injure its health: and, it will be murder, or at least manslaughter, if death ensue; as likewise, if caused by pre-meditated negligence, or harsh usage.[59]

---

[55] J. Fenimore Cooper, *England*, Vol. III (London: Bentley, 1837), 123–4.
[56] *Cassell's Household Guide, New and Revised Edition*, Vol. I (London: Cassell and Co., n.d.), 130
[57] *Cassell's Book of the Household. A Work of Reference on Domestic Economy*, Vol. I (London: Cassell and Co, 1893), 31
[58] Leonore Davidoff, *Worlds Between*, 22. It has been noted that 'servants were not exclusively resident in the homes of paying employers', but 'may have been working as domestics in one or several other households during the day' (Edward Higgs, 'Domestic Servants and Households in Victorian England', 205). Servants might also be working in clubs or commercial properties. However, this book is concerned specifically with residential service in private homes.
[59] Edward Spike, *The Law of Master and Servant*, 45.

In 1851, after two highly publicized cases in which young servants were abused by their employers, legislative action was taken to improve the provisions of the law 'for the better protection of young persons under the care and control of others as apprentices and servants'. The Apprentices and Servants Act established that the master or mistress of any servant or apprentice under the age of eighteen was legally required to supply 'necessary Food, Clothing, or Lodging', and that failure to do so could result in up to three years' imprisonment. Furthermore, where any 'young person under the Age of Sixteen' was hired out as a servant from a workhouse, 'so long as such young person shall be under the Age of Sixteen' he or she was to be visited at least twice a year by the local relieving officer or other official appointed by the Poor Law Guardians.[60]

Servants did, therefore, have a legal right to freedom from neglect, though they only received specific legal protection from physical punishment by their employers in the provisions of the Offences against the Person Act of 1861.[61] Custom dictated that employer and servant had to give a month's notice before ending the contract, unless the servant did something 'flagrantly wrong – such as getting intoxicated, committing a theft, wilfully refusing to obey lawful orders, or staying out all night without being able to give a satisfactory reason for so doing', in which case instant dismissal was permitted.[62] If an employer did not want a servant to work the month he or she had to pay the servant a month's wages in lieu of notice.[63] The employer had the right to order the servant to wear a cap, provided it was not 'ridiculous and unusual', but was not allowed to search or detain a servant's box without permission.[64]

However, such rights could be ambiguous. The English legal system was notoriously ridden with prejudicial attitudes towards the different and the powerless. Domestic servants, as female workers of low-class status, were in a double bind. As Jill Barber has shown in her study of sexual harassment cases brought by servants in Wales in the nineteenth century, servants rarely took their employers to court and when they did, it was unlikely their actions would be successful.[65] More often than not servants stood in the dock rather than the

---

[60] Bill for the better Protection of Young Persons under the Care and Control of Others as Apprentices or Servants, *PP*, 1851 (32) I.97.

[61] Complaints had to be made to two JPs. See J.D.Caswell, *The Law of Domestic Service* (London: Grant Richards Ltd, 1913).

[62] *Cassell's Book of the Household. A Work of Reference on Domestic Economy*, 31

[63] A Barrister-at-Law, *The Home Lawyer. A Practical Handbook for the Household* (London: Cassell and Company, 1903), 25.

[64] A Barrister-at-Law, *The Home Lawyer*, 25–6.

[65] Jill Barber, 'Stolen Goods', 123–36.

witness box, having been prosecuted by employers for leaving their 'places' without due notice. There is a grim irony in the fact that it was not infrequent for a servant to state as her reason for her breach of the hiring agreement that she had suffered poor treatment at the hands of her employer. If the court disbelieved such claims the servant could be fined or even sentenced to three months hard labour.[66]

In return for food and lodging the servant was expected to be entirely available to the master and his family and guests, as this extract from a guide to the law of master and servant demonstrates[67]: 'A servant … has no right to call any portion of his time his own, but is bound to execute his master's commands at all reasonable times.'[68] The idea that servants were dependants rather than employees provided justification for their lack of a legal or customary right to freedom from the absolute power of their master. It is not insignificant that in the 1851 Act young servants are not described as being employed by their masters, but are under their 'care and control'. The law, confirmed in the case of *Turner v. Mason* in 1845, established that it was 'a master's province to regulate the conduct of his domestic servant' and that no duty to anyone else came before that owed to the master. In this case Ann Turner, a maid whose mother was thought to be dying, was refused permission to visit her. Ann went anyway and was immediately dismissed by her employer. Her employer's action was upheld in the subsequent court case, as it was considered doubtful 'whether any service to be rendered to any other person than the master would suffice as an excuse for defying a master's lawful command'.[69]

Though servants did often receive a cash wage '[t]he existence of a cash payment *in itself* does not mean escape from paternalistic control; it only creates possibilities for an alternative way of life' and wide variations in wages between households emphasized the informal nature of the cash payment.[70] As Leonore Davidoff has argued, it was not uncommon for female relatives to work as unpaid domestic servants and the intersection of domestic service and kinship duties meant that legally a servant had to clearly establish with an employer that service would be waged, otherwise the employer could assume that it was being

---

[66] Bridget Hill, *Servants*, 102.
[67] Leonore Davidoff, *Worlds Between*, 22.
[68] Edward Spike, *The Law of Master and Servant*, 45.
[69] Pamela, Horn, *The Rise and Fall of the Victorian Servant*, 130.
[70] Leonore Davidoff, *Worlds Between*, 20; 22–3. We must not underestimate the significance of the possibilities engendered by earning a cash wage. See also C.E. Collett, *Report on the Money Wages of Indoor Domestic Servants*, PP, 1899, XCII for details of actual wage rates.

given voluntarily[71]: 'In England the rule is that the mere fact of service does not itself ground a claim for remuneration, unless there be either an express bargain as to wages, or circumstances showing an understanding on both sides that there should be payment.'[72]

Residential servants were exempt from the Truck Act of 1831, which established that employers had to pay workers in the current coin of the realm and could not impose conditions on where the wages were spent. These Acts were an important step on the way to developing a cash nexus from which residential servants were excluded. The change in labour law of the 1870s, which transformed 'Master and Servant' to 'Employer and Workman', also did not apply to them. Servants' exclusion from this legislative shift enshrined their status as dependants in law, something that was reinforced by their being denied the vote in the franchise extensions of 1867 and 1884.

In theory the relationship between servant and employer operated as a familial one, though unfortunately for the majority of young girls and women, this was not the case. Ideally servants were invisible to the family whose lives they maintained, keeping to the back rooms and back stairs, sleeping in attics after working days as long as seventeen hours. As Edward Salmon wrote in 1888, '[b]eyond the paying of wages or the performance of duties the barrier between the drawing room and the servants' hall is never passed. Life above stairs is as entirely severed from life below stairs as is the life of one house from another.'[73] Such a clear physical distinction between family and servants as described by Salmon would only have been possible for middle- and upper-class families who could afford large houses and several servants. According to Charles Booth, in respectable working-class families the servant and mistress would 'go about the work together and eat the same meals, if not always at the same table' and it was 'when the kitchen ceases to be also the family dining room, that peculiar relations come into existence … whoever tries to ignore [the social barriers] finds before long how real and how inevitable they are … Domestic service provides no general bond – perhaps indeed, rather accentuates class difference.'[74] Booth noted that in working-class households the servant might not eat at the same table as the family. Even when the servant and employer were of similar

[71] Leonore Davidoff, *Worlds Between*, 23.
[72] Patrick Fraser, *Treatise on Master and Servant*, (Edinburgh: T & T Clark, 1882), 44.
[73] Edward Salmon, 'Domestic Service and Democracy', *Fortnightly Review* (March 1888), 411.
[74] Charles Booth and Jesse Argyle, *Life and Labour of the People in London*, 225–6.

class backgrounds markers of hierarchical difference were still relevant within the operation of the household.

In an expression of authority that showed a total disregard for a servant's individuality, employers would sometimes change a servant's name if the name was the same as a member of the family, or if they couldn't be bothered to remember the servant's real name. On hiring a new nursemaid called Emma, the sister of a nurse previously employed by her, Gertrude Lloyd resolved to call her new employee 'Mary for she is so ludicrously like her sister'.[75] Employers also had much control over their servants' futures. In order to get a place a servant had to provide her potential employer with a character reference from a previous employer. The issue of 'characters' was a problematic one. Although it was technically illegal for both employers and servants to supply false characters, there were consistent complaints throughout the period in letters, articles and manuals as to the pernicious incidence of the practice. However, the advantage was on the employers' side; employers were not legally obliged to provide references and could withhold a character to spite a servant whom they felt had wronged them in some way. A servant's livelihood depended on their 'character'. As one butler wrote to *The Times* in 1879: 'At the whim of the master, the servant starves or he lives'.[76] Within the wider context of the power masters or mistresses held over their servants the use of the word 'character' is significant – these references were rarely referred to as references. 'Character' is associated with the distinctiveness of personality and in this sense employers had control, not only over the likelihood of a servant's chances of future employment, but also over their personal reputation. The employer's control of the 'character' of a servant may thus be seen to symbolize their potential for exercising power over all aspects of the servant's existence from their livelihood right down to the definition of their personality.

The employers' complete authority over the servants' daily existence, combined with rituals of deference which will be discussed later in this chapter, contradicted the notion that the relationship between servant and master or mistress was anything other than the relation of subordinate to superior. For employers it was crucial to maintain a sharp distinction between the family and its servants, as the following survey of the representation of service in household advice manuals demonstrates.

---

[75] Gertrude Lloyd, eighteenth August 1891, '*Biography of Gerald Braithwite Lloyd*', manuscript privately owned by Mrs Judy Lloyd.

[76] Frederick Seward, letter, *The Times*, 21 August 1879 quoted in Pamela Horn, *The Rise and Fall of the Domestic Servant*, 54.

The representation of the servant-employer relationship in household manuals

Although not a nineteenth-century invention, it was during this period that the domestic advice manual was established as a genre. It was both a product and constitutive of the imperial imaginary of domesticity and of its gender, race, class and ethnic meanings. As Dena Attar has written: 'it is hard to overestimate the role of the household book in promoting the ideal pattern of middle-class domestic life. Women bought books in their millions.'[77] Hundreds of titles were published in the nineteenth century and the content was varied. Domestic manuals could take the form of receipt books, dictionaries, comprehensive general manuals, cautionary narratives illustrating moral precepts alongside practical advice or the miscellanies which emerged from the flourishing mid-century popular press, amongst other types. They could be specific, aimed at a defined market, such as servants, or could deal with a specific area of nineteenth-century domestic existence such as laundry, or etiquette. Alternatively, they could be general, produced for a wider market and imparting a broad range of moral advice and practical information. The genre also included books that offered advice about managing colonial households, and thereby constituted a literary space where the distinctiveness of metropole and colony might be articulated within a broader imperial framework in which 'civilization' and domesticity were conjoined.

The vast majority of these books were aimed at women and upheld the idea that women had certain domestic duties which were theirs by nature. However, in the second half of the nineteenth century, as alternative occupations to housewifery and service gradually became respectably available, 'the rhetoric authors used gradually changed, becoming more persuasive and less dictatorial, offering rational arguments for women to aim at nothing more than being good housekeepers or else painting enticing pictures of the happy homes it was women's lot to create'.[78] As well as reading them, women wrote many of these books. They wrote on the basis of their authority as mistresses of households, about the authority of mistresses of households, and in so doing, contributed to a discourse that situated women within the home as the custodians of all things

---

[77] Dena Attar, *A Bibliography of Household Books Published in Britain 1800–1914* (London: Prospect, 1987), 13.

[78] Dena Attar, '*A Bibliography of Household Books Published in Britain 1800–1914*', 34.

domestic, defined degrees of status and difference between them and laid claim to a special role for women in the making of a stable, 'civilized' society.

There were three kinds of advice manual written in relation to domestic service. These constituted books written by members of the servant employing class for servants, books written by the servant employing class for other servant employers and a few books written by servants which were recommended for mistresses but were primarily aimed at other servants.

From *Truslers' Domestic Management* (1819) through to Isabella Cowan's *The High Estate of Service* (1898) a ubiquitous theme of the books written for and about servants by servant employers throughout the century was the idea that servants should know their place as subordinates.[79] Biblical authority was invoked to justify this. In the books directed at servants the Bible was quoted to justify their subservience, while in the books written for mistresses, it was quoted to justify and regulate what was frequently called their 'rule'. As 'A Lady' wrote in 1852:

> We know that men and women are intended for various stations in life ... the rules they [the master and mistress] lay down must, therefore be obeyed with a willing spirit, and not considered as severe and harsh commands. St Paul says, "For rulers [and the master and mistress of a household may be so regarded (author's insert)] are not a terror to good works, but to the evil; do that which is good, and though shalt have praise of the same.[80]

Similarly, Adelaide Sophia Kilvert claimed that the 'Christian religion has placed the relation of master and servant on the right basis' and masters and mistresses owed to 'our Heavenly Master an account of those over whom we become rulers that in this station we should govern with justice and equity, in mercy and forbearance'.[81] Some of the texts aimed at mistresses stressed the responsibility of Christian employers to superintend their servants' moral and physical welfare:

> There is a sense in which we are all servants, for 'One is our Master, even Christ' ... We must get into our characters the same tenderness over the erring as He had, the same pity for the suffering, the same care for the faltering, if like Him we would do the work that is given us to do.[82]

---

[79] Dena Attar, '*A Bibliography of Household Books Published in Britain 1800–1914*', 38.

[80] 'A Lady' *Instructions in Household Matter or the Young Girl's Guide to Domestic Service*, 5th edn (London: John W. Parker and Son, 1852), 15–17.

[81] Adelaide Sophia Kilvert, *Home Discipline or Thoughts on the Origin and Exercise of Domestic Authority* (London: Joseph Masters, 1847), 32, 39.

[82] 'A Mistress and A Mother' *At Home* (London: Macintosh and Co, 1874), 8.

This responsibility was articulated as a responsibility towards society in general and other mistresses in particular, frequently with reference to women's nurturing proclivities within the domestic sphere. A popular theme of evangelical discourse, the notion of mothers' and mistresses' social responsibility became increasingly prevalent within household manuals as the genre flourished in the nineteenth century. As Lady Baker advised her reader, ' ... you and I ought to be a mother, not only to our own little ones, but also to the whole household':

> It seems to me that for every good and faithful servant that we come across in our lives (and I do not fear to say there are many) we are duty to our neighbours bound to put up with, and train some rough untaught one in our turn. Is it fair that we should, each one of us, expect to get the finished article and leave to our neighbours the task of making it?[83]

Mistresses were exhorted to recognize that 'the habits of the drawing room form the habits of the kitchen', and to 'raise the standards of a servant's morality to a point more nearly approximating their own' because 'immense good would result from it to society in general'.[84] While this concern suggests a recognition of the importance of servants to the maintenance of the domestic imaginary that structured middle-class gender, class and race relations, it is predicated on assumptions about servants' morality, or lack thereof. The author implied that servants were a source of immorality in wider society, and that it was the mistress's task to combat this tendency. In this way mistresses could not only establish a sense of moral superiority that infused their class position as 'betters' with value, but also drew on an imperial discourse in which the domestic was constructed as the heart of life and of public importance as the place where characters were made or broken. Women, as mistresses and mothers, thus participated in the development of an image of their feminine role as of public significance and social importance. As Catherine Buckton wrote at the end of the century 'domestic service is a trade of *national* and *vital* importance because it affects the health, comfort, and welfare of every household'.[85] As the statement by Lady Baker quoted earlier suggests, girls in service were the raw material of this trade; it was up to the mistresses to manufacture the finished product: good, obedient maids.

[83] Lady Baker, *Our Responsibilities and Difficulties as Mistresses of Young Servants* (London: Hatchard, 1886), 4, 5.

[84] *Home Difficulties*, 16, 8, 26.

[85] Catherine Buckton, *Comfort and Cleanliness. The Servant and Mistress Question* (London: Longmans, Green and Co, 1898), 46.

As the century progressed servants' subservience was still referred to as divinely ordained, particularly in tracts published by religious organizations. Such tracts usually consisted of a simple story with a moral conclusion in which the 'bad' servant ended up living in depravity and the 'good', obedient and religious servant achieved the reward of a good place. Although the idea that servants were at risk from the depredations of sin was a theme in books published for servants throughout the nineteenth century, it became a theme of books published for mistresses in the century's second half; as servants' dependence had become enshrined in law, their morality had become their mistresses' responsibility.

The association of servants with prostitution was particularly common from mid-century and was a real as well as rhetorical linkage, though discussions of the problem tended to focus on moral rather than material causes. Servants were thought to be particularly prey to policemen and soldiers who supposedly flattered the vanity that was assumed by many commentators to be a particular characteristic of servant girls and a major cause of their potential downfall. Although some observers were aware that if servants did slip into casual prostitution, which some did, it was as a result of poverty and/or unemployment, there was a willingness within Victorian society to view servants as having a natural predilection for vice. Henry Mayhew claimed that 'maid-servants live well, have no care or anxiety, no character worth speaking about to lose, for the origin of most of them is obscure, are fond of dress, and under these circumstances it cannot be wondered that they are as a body immoral and unchaste'.[86] In 1858 G. Oram wrote that 'it has ... been said, in the recent discussions which have taken place respecting the so-called social evil, "that domestic servants are to be found in large numbers among its victims." This, I fear, is too true.'[87] Lady Baker related to her readers 'one of the very saddest facts that ever came to my knowledge', and placed responsibility on mistresses' shoulders:

> The ranks of the great army of outcast women of England are largely recruited –
> it makes me shudder to think of it – from among our domestic servants. Oh, my
> friends, is it not a crying shame? Should it not be a bitter sorrow to us, mothers
> of England, mistresses of households, that this thing should be? Somehow, with
> all our boasted rules and regulations we must be making some awful mistake.[88]

---

[86] Henry Mayhew, *London Labour and the London Poor*, Vol. IV (London: Charles Griffin and Co, 1864), 258.

[87] G. Oram, *Masters and Servants: Their Relative Duties* (London: Hatchard, 1858), 44.

[88] Lady Baker, *Our Responsibilities and Difficulties as Mistresses of Young Servants*, 10.

Although presented as a concern for the welfare of servants, such discussions of mistresses' responsibilities contain ambivalent undercurrents that revolve around issues of authority and power. The styling of the mistress as a mentor to servants elided servants' status as employees and the emphasis on guidance often transmuted into one on management and control. In one book mistresses were advised that 'those under us must look up to us with reverence and fear mingling with their respect and love'.[89] There was also a sense, particularly in the second half of the nineteenth century, that servants presented some kind of threat. 'Internuncio' wrote that 'the mistress and her dependants have no friendly relations ... a sort of guerilla warfare is kept up between them ... Distrust and hostility are marked features of this domestic conflict'.[90] Similarly, in Amara Veritas's *The Servant Problem* (1899), servants were 'internal foes' and the home a battlefield.[91] In other books, the perception of servants as posing a threat was more tacit, inferred by continual reference to servants' dishonesty, or even their sexual vulnerability. As Lady Baker stated:

> How truly thankful we all are, from time to time, to light upon some steady, competent, middle aged servant, free from all the vanity of flirting ... who, equally helpful and hideous, will neither fall in love herself nor cause anyone else to do so. But how about the pretty little maid who answers the doorbell in spotless white cap and apron? Are we not in constant agonies over her, lest that same pretty face should prove her ruin?[92]

The perception of a need to manage servants, and the tone of mistrust that pervaded so many of the advice manuals, was predicated on a set of assumptions about servants that related to their gender and class status. As women their performance of domestic duties was the destiny of their sex, but paying for such work created knotty ideological and moral tensions. How does one place monetary value on something that is ideally beyond value? The act of selling what shouldn't be sold – ability to perform feminine duties in the domestic sphere – established a rhetorical linkage between servants and prostitutes. Also the presence of a working-class girl, associated by her class status with a potential for depravity, in the private home, may have posed a sexual threat, added to by the fact that it was she, rather than the mistress of the household, who had

---

[89] *Home Difficulties or Whose Fault Is It? A Few Words on the Servant Question* (London: Griffith and Farron, 1886), 23.

[90] 'Internuncio' *Mistresses and Servants* (London: John, F. Shaw, 1865), 7.

[91] Amara Veritas, *The Servant Problem* (London: Simpkin, Marshall and Co, 1899), 68.

[92] Lady Baker, *Our Responsibilities and Difficulties as Mistresses of Young Servants*, 8.

intimate knowledge of all its members, including the men. This threat was not necessarily a threat to the mistress's relationship with her master, but could be a threat to the respectability of the household, in relation to which familial and feminine status identity was defined. One writer expressed apprehensions about servants' inability to regulate their passions, and advised mistresses not to leave their servants alone in the house for any length of time:

> What can be more injurious, more fraught with temptation and danger – servants perhaps of both sexes left for weeks, even months, with … no check upon them … living together, day and night, without the intellectual pursuits or the conventional habits of society, which afford so much protection to the educated classes? What can happen but what does happen, – that year by year hundreds are tempted into sin of all kinds.[93]

The same author later talked about good servants 'becoming contaminated' by bad ones and exhorted mistresses to 'consider the souls of their kitchenmaid and underhousemaid at least as much as those of the visionary hordes around Timbuctoo'.[94] In this way the author used the wider imperial context both to establish a semantic and racializing link between the idea of such 'hordes' and servants and also to make a critique of telescopic philanthropy. Such an ambivalent attitude towards servants was a product of their peculiar position in the middle-class households in which they were defined as dependants, but which were dependent upon their labour. Moreover that labour was paid for, although the home was supposed ideally to be free from the taint of market activity. Finally, servants came to that home as avatars of a lower class that was in the nineteenth century, a real source of middle-class fear, mistrust and anxiety: 'But now, when "life below stairs" is totally distinct from life above, and the strong class feeling which I have described has had time to develop, the existence of dwellers within the household who are not yet of the family is felt – on one side at any rate, and that the side which is most concerned – to be intolerable.'[95] The encouragement and endorsement of mistresses' authority within manuals carried an implicit acknowledgement of servants' power to defy that authority and disrupt class and gender relations.

Despite continued references to divine authority, from the late 1850s authors of advice manuals placed stress on maintaining the symbols that signified status difference. Servants' dress was a major preoccupation. Servants were exhorted

---

[93] *Home Difficulties*, 9.
[94] *Home Difficulties*, 6, 19.
[95] A. Amy Bulley, 'Domestic Service. A Social Study', 183.

to dress in ways that suited their station for (it was argued) they could only look ridiculous if they attempted to dress like their superiors. As one mistress put it, 'A gaudily dressed servant looks, at best, like a coarse and vulgar lady; for with all the fine ribbons and gay colours that London can produce, a girl cannot whiten or soften the skin of her hands, or make her movements as graceful as those of a finished lady.'[96] Such statements contributed to the discursive construction of a hierarchy of status within the notion of 'femininity', bolstering the idea that all humans were not born equal. They also provide us with an insight into a certain anxiety on the part of 'ladies' to ensure the symbols of gentility were not debased by servants' use of them.

Another emphasis in advice manuals directed at servants was the necessity for them to be both silent and invisible. In some books this desire was framed within the definition of specific rituals of deference, such as not speaking unless spoken to, or keeping one's distance from one's superiors. One book, the *Servants' Behaviour Book*, was particularly concerned with such rituals, with only a nod to the oft-repeated values of honesty, sobriety, industry, etc., in its closing paragraph. The author, Mrs Motherly, emphasized a difference between servants and 'ladies', claiming that servants should not speak unless spoken to because

> ladies have been educated in a very different manner to you. They have read many books, have travelled and seen many sights, talked with educated people, and know a great number of things about which you know nothing. It is not likely that you can have anything to say that will amuse or interest a lady. When she talks to you, it is in kindness, and all the pleasure of the talk is on your side.[97]

Contrary to the idealized view of service, where servants, as dependants, are a part of the families they serve, Mrs Motherly encouraged girls to 'remember that, as long as you are in service, you are always in the house of another, and have strangers around you, and should not think, therefore, that because your mistress chooses to let her voice or step be heard, you are at liberty to do the same'.[98]

Mistrust of servants was most clear in writing concerned with their honesty and truthfulness. It was almost universally acknowledged that servants were dishonest and not to be trusted, and, as the century progressed, manual writers appear to have felt that they were getting worse. In 1859 'A Practical Mistress

[96] Mrs Motherly, *The Servants Behaviour Book* (London: Bell and Daldy, 1859), 87–8.
[97] Mrs Motherly, *The Servants Behaviour Book*, 20–1.
[98] Mrs Motherly, *The Servants Behaviour Book*, 40.

of a Household' wrote that 'about sixty per cent of the servants, in and out of place, would properly belong in the criminal class, if their antecedents as well as their present doings were known: this is no exaggeration. I believe I am understating the figures.'[99] The association of servants with the 'lower orders', and their presence in the houses of middle-class employers at this time may have sharpened the sense that there was an enemy within. 'Internuncio's' ambivalence is typical: 'It is an open question whether this greater independence which they are enabled to assume, and all the additional advantages of education which have fallen to their portion during the onward march, have really tended to elevate their moral character.'[100] Increasingly the concern in writings about servants was with the 'problem' of their desire for independence, and how this threatened both their own morality and the smooth running of households.

Servants' so-called 'love of change' became a prominent theme in the 1860s, around the time of the Reform Act. It was frequently stated that servants would not stay in their 'places' but were constantly on the move in search of better things. Such mobility was probably a result of the high demand and low supply of skilled servants in the later nineteenth century; however, the concern carried other connotations. Books aimed at servants encouraged them to stay with one employer for as long as possible:

> "A rolling stone gathers no moss," is an old and true saying; and by roaming from place to place your money is wasted, your time is wasted, your character is injured – for no one cares to engage a servant thus given to change; and, what is far worse than all these reasons – though they are bad enough – it fosters in you that restless spirit which, as I have before told you, is most pernicious.[101]

The same author claimed that '*Restlessness* ... is the characteristic of the present age' and devoted her whole book to the 'foolish reasons' why servants left their places. These include too much work (to which she retorted 'work never killed anyone'); temper ('there are but few cases where temper in any member of the household will justify a servant in leaving a situation'); particularity of mistresses ('the mistress against whom so heavy a charge was laid were really good ones ... Servants ... [cannot] imagine all the thought and care involved in the superintendence of daily life'); higher wages ('the wages given in the present day are acknowledged to be very high ... Is the result what one ought to expect?

[99] 'A Practical Mistress of a Household' in *Servants as They Are and as They Ought to Be* (London: W. Tweedie, 1859), 9.
[100] 'Internuncio', *Mistresses and Servants*, 11.
[101] 'A Friend', *A Word to Maidservants*, 8.

Is the work better done, and more of it? Alas! No. It is far otherwise.'); lack of freedom ('It is a plain fact, perhaps not a palatable one, that servitude in any capacity entails the loss of liberty ... Our Bible ... supplies a rule of conduct; in it we are told "women are to be the keepers at home"').[102]

Although this common theme – servants' 'love of change' – referred explicitly to geographical mobility, the advice against it made constant reference to social mobility. In many books servants were advised not to look for higher wages, not because of mistresses' pecuniary anxieties (though this may have been a reason) but because higher wages could facilitate the blurring of symbolic status boundaries:

> Whereas a really good servant, fifty, or even thirty years ago, had about half the sum that is now given to one in the same capacity, and upon that would always "appear respectable" as it is called – nay, would wear far better clothes, as well as lay by a good store for old age or sickness, or to set out with in life when she gets married: many now-a-days will fritter away their all, lay by nothing, and for what? 'To dress like a lady.'[103]

Thus the exhortation to servants to keep their 'places' can be seen to be not only about their place of employment, but also their place in a spectrum of classed femininity. Also, the distaste for servants' pursuit of higher wages suggests discomfort with them being paid at all. Immediately after discussing the 'evil' of seeking better pay, 'A Friend' invoked biblical authority to confirm that 'women are to be the keepers at home,' which suggests that she was uncomfortable with the idea of the relationship between servants and mistresses being a business one.[104]

There were a number of specific values that were repeatedly endorsed in manuals written for servants through the nineteenth century. These were honesty, truthfulness, sobriety, neatness and cleanliness. Authors appear to have perceived it necessary to drum these values into the minds of servants (particularly honesty). As we have seen, in texts written for mistresses about, rather than for, servants, the mistrust of the employing class is clear. To some extent this was a product of servants' association with the 'lower orders' from whom middle-class respectable people wished to distance themselves. According to Mrs Taylor, writing early in the nineteenth century, complaints about servants were 'strong indicators of the depravity of the lower orders, notwithstanding the

---

[102] 'A Friend', *A Word to Maidservants, passim.*
[103] 'A Friend', *A Word to Maidservants*, 15–16.
[104] 'A Friend', *A Word to Maidservants*, 25.

benevolent exertions of the last thirty years to banish ignorance, and vice as its offspring'.[105] Later in the century, the elaborate deference rituals endorsed by Mrs Motherly, combined with the desire neither to see nor hear her servants, served to elide any individuality a girl might have with a work persona that was predicated on the assumption of servants' collective lack of value in anything other than a service role. Underlying the recommendation of such rituals, also, was a sense that servants must be controlled. This resonated with other defensively toned writings of the later period which were concerned with highlighting servants' dishonesty and depravity as a social problem of wide significance. Servants were often associated with children, and seen as ignorant and irrational. As one writer claimed 'servants – as well as children – require to be managed with *kindness* and *firmness*. The greatest kindness we can exercise towards them is to endeavour, by a mild rein, to keep them in the path of duty'.[106] By reducing servants to a childlike status, mistresses tried to neutralize their fear of the threat, which was possibly sexual, that servants posed to domestic order. As we will see in Chapter 4, these were also traits attributed to servants by employers in India, where they were racialized into general 'native' characteristics in ways that legitimized white Britons' sense of entitlement to rule India and its people.

By the mid-nineteenth century, as racial theories gained credence, some writers made use of racializing language. In 1847 Adelaide Sophia Kilvert asked: 'Born and bred in ... squalid nothingness, how can we hope to find men or women derived from such a race fitted for the proper duties of a well-conducted family? ... Nurtured in poverty, the consequence of their vices, they are the slaves of their own passions, and surrounded by ignorance'.[107] As the century progressed, and particularly from the mid-century, authors of advice manuals began to refer to servants both as a class and as a race. Writing in 1865, 'Internuncio' asked ' ... is it really the truth that during the past half-century the nature of servants has undergone a rapid change, from good to bad, and that as a class, they are indeed come to be worthless?' He or she answers the question 'undoubtedly', and makes reference to the 'idleness of the race who serve', whose 'instincts are less under control and less governable' than those of their mistresses.[108] Though writers rarely made such explicit references in literature relating to English households, characteristics associated with the so-called

---

[105] Mrs Taylor, *Practical Hints, Practical Hints to Young Females on the Duties of a Wife, a Mother and a Mistress of a Family* (London: Taylor and Hessey, 1815), 36.

[106] 'A Practical Mistress of a Household' *Servants as They Are and as They Ought to Be*, 16.

[107] Adelaide Sophia Kilvert, *Home Discipline*, 28.

[108] 'Internuncio', *Mistresses and Servants*, 8–9, 10, 24.

'savage' indigenous people of colonized lands – such as inherent dishonesty or the inability to regulate passion – were often pejoratively associated with the generality of servants, as well as with the class from which they came. Through such slippages racializing constructs underwrote ideas about class inferiority/ superiority, and in the late nineteenth century, with the increased popularity of the idea of hereditary degeneracy, class degeneration. The emphasis on the necessity to maintain symbols of difference, chiefly articulated in discussions of servants' dress or their 'love of change', also related to this. It did not just imply that servants should be kept in their place, but that it was somehow unnatural for them to imagine themselves as anything other than servants, destined for nothing more than to serve their 'betters'.

The late nineteenth-century 'servant problem'

As numbers of servants dwindled in the later nineteenth century, middle-class writers gradually realized how much they depended on them. This may also have contributed to the sense of discomfort and distaste that characterized so much of the writing about servants in the second half of the nineteenth century. As 'A Mistress and A Mother' put it: 'the comfort and well-being of our whole domestic life, which in England lies so much within doors, depend very much upon our servants.'[109] Much of this anxiety was a result of the perceived 'shortage' of servants which was understood by many commentators to be the result of new ideas about independence, freedom, individuality and workers' rights. In an article in the *Westminster Review* A. Amy Bulley argued that the evidence of labour unrest, 'trades' union manifestoes, strikes, resulting in wholesale stoppage of business or pleasure among the well-to-do classes,' meant that 'the veriest recluse in the land' could not ignore 'the great upheaval' which was 'stirring the labouring class to its very depths'. However, Bulley's main concern was with 'silent forces,' which alongside the 'strongly pronounced demonstrations' were 'slowly but steadily undermining no small portion of the structure of our social life'. 'I refer to the rebellion in the ranks of domestic service' wrote Bulley, 'Rebellion is the only word; no other adequately expresses the facts.'[110]

As Bulley's words suggest, a new kind of 'servant problem' emerged in the final decade of the nineteenth century when many trade unions were increasingly

---

[109] 'A Mistress and a Mother', *At Home*, 3.
[110] A. Amy Bulley, 'Domestic Service. A Social Study', 177.

vociferous. Some servants themselves set up unions in the 1870s and 1890s which, though not entirely successful, caused significant sensation in the press. The threat of servants attempting to combine was enough to agitate employers. W.L.M of Surbiton Hill censured the *Surrey Comet* in 1872 for publishing letters by servants in which they talked about striking, complaining that 'what possible good can the publication of such stuff do, I am at a loss to conceive; while the harm that may be done is very great in unsettling the minds of really good servants'.[111] In 1890 Ellen Darwin argued that 'domestic service is a problem as momentous as that of Capital and Labour ... Social theorists and philanthropists ... are silent on this – a most important and significant side of human life, where the individuals of the two great classes, commonly known as Capital and Labour, come into the closest and most direct personal relationships'.[112] In 1893 Mrs Lewis described mistresses as being 'directly menaced with an invasion of the eight hours movement' in an article in *Nineteenth Century*.[113]

At this time a new generation of feminists was developing arguments for women's right to independence and self-reliance. It is possible that their ideas, alongside the opening up of new occupations for women and the expanded provision of elementary education, influenced girls' decision whether or not to go into service. Commentators on the servant problem certainly noted a new desire for independence as driving girls away from service. The feminist Clementina Black argued that the 'conditions of domestic service' were outdated and did not 'harmonize with sentiments of today'. She compared domestic service with other employments in which 'the person employed sells a certain number of hours of labour, and, when those hours are over, all relation ceases between employed and employer'. According to Black in other jobs the worker had 'a life of her own, absolutely apart from her industrial life. The servant has no such life of her own ... The domestic servant, in short, still lives under a system of total personal subservience.' Black identified that gradual growth of a feeling amongst women that 'total personal subservience' was 'intolerable and degrading' and linked it to young women's increasing reluctance to become servants. According to Black:

> it is this feeling which causes domestic service to be held in low social esteem by women who are often harder worked and less materially prosperous than most servants. The servant is despised not because she cooks, or scrubs, or nurses

---

[111] Letter, *The Surrey Comet*, 20 July 1872.
[112] Ellen W. Darwin, 'Domestic Service', *The Nineteenth Century*, 28, 39 (August 1890), 288.
[113] Mrs Lewis, 'A Reformation of Domestic Service', *The Nineteenth Century*, 191, 33 (January 1893), 138.

a baby, still less because she has to yield obedience to orders – every factory worker has to do that in working hours – but because she consents to put herself at some other person's beck and call.[114]

Unlike Black, who sought the reform of service and championed the cause of servants, most middle-class writers of articles generally agreed that 'this mischievous craving for independence' in working-class girls, as Lady Aberdeen put it, was not only a serious problem for servant employers, but also for the girls themselves. M.E. Benson wrote ominously that 'the foul talk that is forced into the ears of young girls who go to business, the black stories they hear, the evil words, the bad novelettes, the fierce temptations, are difficult to realise'.[115] In Benson's view domestic service constituted an opportunity for working-class girls to be educated in the ways of respectability through association with their 'betters', rather than those of their own class. Benson acknowledged the interest employers had in their servants' development, pointing out that since 'the lives of a large number of the future wives and mothers of the working classes' were 'so closely bound to ours ... it becomes our right and duty to see that the physical, mental and moral conditions of their lives are favourable to their development and happiness'.[116]

The various commentators on domestic service developed a range of solutions to the 'problem' in the last decade of the nineteenth century. There seems to have been general agreement that changes needed to be made by employers 'before we are driven to it by the rapidly increasing growth of independent employment for women, or before we reach that stage through which America is passing at present, where, we are told by American ladies, servants have it *all* their own way'.[117] However, what these changes should constitute was a contentious issue. Ellen Darwin thought that 'every servant should have, at least, every day, two hours definite leisure, during which she is her own mistress', that servants should be treated with greater trust by their employers, that every servant should be 'kept as much as possible in connection with her family' and friends, that servants should have a right to a fair character and that they should be better paid.[118] Lady Aberdeen saw the solution to the problem as in the establishment of

---

[114] Clementina Black, 'The Dislike to Domestic Service', *The Nineteenth Century*, 193, 33 (March 1893), 454–5.

[115] M.E.Benson,'In Defence of Domestic Service: A Reply', *The Nineteenth Century*, 164, 28 (October 1890), 623.

[116] M.E. Benson,'In Defence of Domestic Service: A Reply', 626.

[117] Ellen W. Darwin, 'Domestic Service', 295.

[118] Ellen W. Darwin, 'Domestic Service', 293–4.

'household clubs', daily meetings at which all members of the households could pursue artistic and educational interest, the object being 'to bring the general progress of our times towards education, self-culture, self-government, and co-operation, to bear upon those employed in domestic service'.[119] Lady Hamilton thought that such clubs 'to the heads of small households can afford but little help'. She argued for a rather more old-fashioned solution: '[i]f in our complex society, we are to retain the advantages of the households of earlier days, we must certainly re-adjust our relations with our servants ... But the essence of service is and must remain the same – Rule: and, until the prejudice against rule is eradicated, servants cannot be very numerous and will often be unsatisfied and unsatisfactory.'[120]

The 'servant problem' began to be taken up by other writers with feminist leanings in the late nineteenth century, though potential resolutions to the 'problem' proved hard to reconcile with embedded ideas about class hierarchies. For example, 'A Mistress and a Mother' claimed optimistically that 'the common bond of womanhood is a stronger tie between a mistress and a maid, than any difference of station can nullify or destroy' and drew attention to servants' vulnerability as women: 'they share alike the defencelessness of sex'.[121] Nevertheless, despite these claims to sisterhood, she still exhibited the sense of antagonism that characterized so much late century writing on servants recommending that

> whenever it is necessary to have a 'talk' with a domestic it must be in one's own sitting-room. As the king on his throne, the cleric in his pulpit, and the pedagogue in his seat *seem* to possess greater authority than elsewhere, so the mistress in her parlour chair. The chances of an impertinent reply are much less than if the maiden were encountered anywhere in her own domain.[122]

Putative sisterhood was thus fractured by a sense of antagonism that had much to do with the idea of the home as a place where the mistress's authority had to be paramount, in order to secure the stability of class relations in the imperial metropole. Amara Veritas and other writers approached the problem differently. After many chapters on the exasperating deficiencies of servants in her book *The Servant Problem*, Veritas argued that the problem of the relationship between

[119] Isobel Aberdeen, 'Household Clubs: An Experiment', *Nineteenth Century*, 181, 31 (March 1892), 396.
[120] Margaret Hamilton, 'Household Clubs: How Will They Affect Small Household', *Nineteenth Century*, 183, 31 (May 1892), 807; 809.
[121] 'A Mistress and a Mother', *At Home*, 3.
[122] 'A Mistress and a Mother' *At Home*, 7.

servants and mistresses was due to the fact that service was unregulated and unrespected work, which would be better placed on a formal business footing. This had not happened, she argued, because women did not have the right to vote and so their problems, such as with servants, were overlooked by men. 'Yes, we must have our lives placed upon an equal footing with our husbands …,' she proclaims, ' … our men at the head of affairs should long ere this have passed measures to defend their helpless mothers, sisters, and wives from internal foes':

> All good men reverence women, and it is to them we look for assistance and help. Some men will oppose – do oppose- the passing of 'The Franchise Bill for Women', but they are only men of a certain stamp, who look upon women as beings who have been created for their sole use, pleasure and amusement. Men such as these should be met on their own ground. Say to them: 'You depend on us for your pleasure and amusement. Well, then, make life easier and smoother to us, and until you do so we refuse our favours to you.' My sisters, if you said this and adhered to it, there would soon be a pretty general stampede to St Stephen's, and your Bill would not be long delayed in passing.[123]

While Amara Veritas appealed to a sisterhood of women, it was limited to women who employed servants. She wanted rights in order to gain some protection against the 'internal foe' that servants represented to her. Even though she claimed that putting service on a business footing would benefit servants by enabling service to be recognized as a skilled profession, so that servants could claim dignity in their labour, she was primarily concerned with the needs of servant employers for a steady supply of reliable servants. Other writers took a similar stance. '[T]he time has surely come', claimed Mrs Lewis, writing in *The Nineteenth Century* in 1893:

> for English housekeepers to consider the well-being of their homes and hearths, and to be beforehand with a practical scheme for the preservation of domestic privacy and comfort. It is not for them to remain so enslaved and disenfranchised as to accept unhesitatingly such conditions as may be prescribed to them. They have as much right as any other class of British subjects to choose for themselves the conditions under which they prefer to live.[124]

In this extract Mrs Lewis used the status of 'English housekeepers' as managers of 'workers' to make a claim for political rights for mistresses of servants, who she implied were denied those rights, unlike other members of the dispersed

---

[123] Amara Veritas, *The Servant Problem*, 13, 68, 179–80.
[124] Mrs Lewis, 'A Reformation of Domestic Service', 138.

community of 'British subjects'. By insisting that domestic labour was work, exemplified by a comparison with 'trade or houses of business', she suggested that a transformation of the meaning of separate spheres was necessary to preserve the distinction between public and private that sustained 'domestic privacy and comfort'.

Articles in the *Englishwoman's Review* in 1890 on the education of servants exhibited similar attitudes. These articles concerned a training college at Newnham on Severn, set up to teach 'the rudiments of housework' to 'little women'.[125] These lessons would make them 'helpful little daughters, and will be invaluable when they come to have homes of their own to work in, or to manage, or if they become domestic servants'.[126] According to one article the institution would encourage respect for domestic labour: 'the domestic work of women will not attain to its true dignity amongst us until it has its recognized place amongst the skilled trades, with its regular curriculum and certificated teachers. This conviction, which has been in the air, so to say, would now seem about to become embodied in a tangible and well organised plan'.[127] However, although the institution was set up for the education of both working- and middle-class girls, it did nothing to break down those class distinctions. Rather, its curriculum was specifically designed to reinvest them with meaning, training young women in the relational roles of mistress or servant established 'in the good old days'.[128] The school had three departments 'one for students of housewifery, one for upper- and middle-class girls, with a housewifery department attached to the ordinary branches of teaching, and one for the training of girls for service'.[129] As part of the education the girls training for service would wait on the upper- and middle-class girls, so that they could all learn how to properly acquit themselves in their respective roles:

> The idea of various grades of inmates has already been started there, and this is essential, for in order to learn how to wait on people there must be people to wait on. Large Industrial and Union schools do not turn out good servants, though they turn out good sweepers and scrubbers, because all are at one level ... and there is no one to serve.[130]

---

[125] 'The National Housewifery Association', *The Englishwomen's Review* (Jan 15 1890), 10.
[126] 'The National Housewifery Association', 10.
[127] 'A Domestic College', *The Englishwoman's Review* (July 15 1890), 293.
[128] 'A Few Thoughts About the Technical College at Newnham-on-Severn', *The Englishwoman's Review* (July 15 1890), 297.
[129] 'The National Housewifery Association', 11.
[130] 'A Few Thoughts About the Technical College at Newnham-on-Severn', 297.

As this quotation suggests, there was more to being a servant than being able to clean. Being a servant was also about creating and expressing status difference through the performance of deference rituals. The various writers' approval of this institution in the *Englishwoman's Review* was motivated by the fact it aimed at preserving, rather than transforming, the hierarchical structure of the servant-employer relationship, even within the context of providing training, and attempting to redefine domestic work as skilled labour.

But what about the servants themselves? Unfortunately their views were rarely published. In those books by servants that were published, such as *Servants Defended* (1847), servants were quick to point out that their masters and mistresses were not faultless, that domestic service was a trade requiring a certain degree of skill and knowledge and that servants, though much maligned, were usually hard-working and respectable. In their self-writings servants demonstrated a clear awareness of their importance to the maintenance of a middle-class lifestyle and asserted their belief in the dignity of their work. For example, the authors of *The Complete Servant* stated that: 'Subordination, indeed, attaches to your rank in life, but not *disgrace* ... Perhaps, there is not a more indispensably necessary description of persons in society than those who are denominated *Servants*.'[131] Similarly, Thomas Cosnett, in the popular *Footman's Directory*, which ran to several editions through the nineteenth century, stated scathingly that 'some persons speak of servants as if they were so much beneath them as to be unworthy of notice; but this adds nothing to their own respectability, and only betrays their ignorance and pride'.[132] Cosnett advocated servants knowing their place, but interpreted this 'place' through Christian principle in a way that claimed dignity for servants. Cosnett filled 'service' with honourable meaning, seeing the difference associated with class and status not in terms of a hierarchy of human value, but in terms of the distribution of different roles to be played in a grand scheme of God's devising. He showed that servants must act out a part that belied real skill, knowledge and ability:

> Were I to pourtray [*sic*] a good domestic servant, I should say, he must have *eyes* like a *hawk* but be as *blind* as a *bat*; ears like a *cat*, but be as *deaf* as a *post*; must have more *sensibility* than the *sensitive plant*, but yet be as *hard* as *stone*; must be as *wise* as a *counsellor*, yet as *ignorant* as an *ass*; his *movement swift* as that of an *eagle*, but *smooth* as that of a *swallow*; in *manners* and *politeness* a *Frenchman*, in *probity* and *virtue* an *Englishman*; in dress a *gentleman*; in *disposition* a *saint*;

---

[131] Samuel and Sarah Adams, *The Complete Servant* (London: Knight and Lacey, 1825), 17.
[132] Thomas Cosnett, *The Footman's Directory and Butler's Remembrancer* (London: T. Cosnett, 1825), 3.

in *activity* a *harlequin*; in *gravity* a *judge*: he must have a *lady's hand*, a *maiden speech*, and a *light foot*; in *protection* and *defence* he must be a *lion*; in confidence and trust like the law of *Medes* and *Persians*, 'which altereth not', in domestic management a *Moses*; in *chastity* a *Joseph*; in *pious resolution* a *Joshua*; in *wisdom* a *serpent*; in *innocence* a *dove*.[133]

Thomas Cosnett was a manservant, writing for menservants, who generally enjoyed higher status and better wages than their female counterparts. Cosnett's attitude was echoed by the butler John Robinson at the end of the nineteenth century when he wrote: 'Intrinsically there is nothing in service of which a man need be ashamed. There is nothing derogatory to a man's dignity or self-respect in the discharge of its humblest duties.' Nevertheless, Robinson was concerned with his loss of manly independence, claiming that 'the thorn lies in the fact that a man, for peace's sake, is reduced to a kind of degrading sycophancy; or to use a phrase common among servants, "he cannot call his soul his own"'.[134]

The advice manuals relating to service in the nineteenth century overwhelmingly document the views of the servant employing class, but at the same time, reflect wider concerns about gender and class difference and the putative difference between different human groups. Nevertheless servants did publish their own writings. In writing books for themselves they were claiming agency in the construction of their individual and work identities that was denied them in dominant discourses. As the century progressed there are subtle changes in representations of the servant-employer relationship. The necessity of servants to middle-class domestic comfort was increasingly acknowledged in manuals and articles, and their recommendations that servants be disciplined gave way to exhortations to kindness and better regulation of their work. At the same time however, the constructed 'difference' of servants began to draw on notions of inferiority and depravity that characterized the way in which 'Others' of non-English origin were also represented within a range of discourses.

Conclusion

The presence of domestic servants in bourgeois households helped their employers mark, and make sense of, differences of class, gender, race and ethnicity. Legally sited outside relations of labour that put a financial price on

---

[133] Thomas Cosnett, *The Footman's Directory and Butler's Remembrancer*, 175–6.
[134] John Robinson, 'A Butler's View of Men-service', *Nineteenth Century*, 184, 31 (June 1892), 932.

work, servants enacted performances of deference that were imagined to be embedded in the pre-modern past. The houses of the nobility for centuries had long employed grand domestic retinues and '[s]ervice to a master or mistress, to King and country, and to God all figured in accepted world views'.[135] In this way, nineteenth-century domestic servants provided their middle-class employers with a sense of continuity with the past, of a fundamental entitlement – the right of some people to command the service of other people – at a time when assumptions about what determined a person's place in the society were being challenged by the shift in relations of power that came with the growing and unbalanced connectedness of the modern human world. Domestic servants in the imperial metropole provided routine and comfort; they looked after emotional bodies that felt the insecurity of recently acquired power. Being able to command service was an important signifier of authority, which spoke to pre-modern notions of duty and fealty. In this sense Victorian domestic servants were in households, in part at least, to remind their employers of their success, success that, as much Victorian literature reminds us, might be snatched away by ill-luck and bad decision-making. Servants' labour released household members to do other kinds of work, and to lead other kinds of life away from the tedium and sweat of cleaning, cooking and caring. In the process, domestic servants mid-wifed the inequalities that are fundamental to the functioning of modern capitalist societies. Metropolitan domesticity was an expression of imperial power. Servants fulfilled economic and cultural functions that were critical to the development of the modern industrialized world that we live in today, and in the performance of their role embodied the connection between its organizing hierarchies and the character of its places and the societies that made them.

---

[135] Leonore Davidoff, Megan Doolittle, Janet Fink and Katherine Holden, *The Family Story*, 161.

2

Domestic service and the colonial home in India

India emerged as an independent nation state from the declining British Empire in 1947, the story of its coming-to-be enmeshed with that of modern Britain itself. Indeed, the economic, political and cultural importance of the subcontinent for Britain's modernity and status as a world power can hardly be underestimated. The extraction of resources from India and its position as a captive colonial market helped fuel Britain's industrial and economic development, driving the emergence of the consumer culture that underpinned the meaningful differentiation of metropolitan space into public and (ostensibly) private. The extent to which India, or indeed any colonial site, was a recognized part of metropolitan Britons' lives is contested, but there is no doubt that the subcontinental colony played a critical role in the emergence of a putatively 'British' sensibility that spanned imperial space.[1] This sensibility – this 'Britishness'– was articulated to a significant degree through the definition and practices of gendered and gendering, classed and classing, and raced and racializing 'domesticity'.

As we saw in the previous chapter, in Britain people thought of the home as a generative place, where the rules and categories of difference that were thought by contemporaries to underpin social stability were made and learned. This understanding did not simply travel to India and other places with colonial settlers and sojourners, where it was then applied to bolster imperial authority. Rather, it developed in a dialogue with and between those places, an imperial discourse of domesticity that encompassed, and was important in the making of both metropole and colony as connected and distinct. The fact that the idea of a

---

[1] See Bernard Porter, *The Absent-Minded Imperialists: Empire, Society, and Culture in Britain*, 1st edn (Oxford: Oxford University Press, 2004); Catherine Hall and Sonya O. Rose (eds), *At Home with the Empire. Metropolitan Culture and the Imperial World* (Cambridge: Cambridge University Press, 2006); John M. MacKenzie, '"Comfort" and "Conviction": A Response to Bernard Porter', *The Journal of Imperial and Commonwealth History*, 36, 4 (2008): 659–68.

purposeful domesticity was articulated in a vast range of texts and images; that a whole genre of advice literature emerged that served an international English-speaking readership; that domestic servants became emblematic of lower-class subservience in Britain and also in India, is evidence of this. The authority of metropolitan mistresses over their servants, the gender and class work that was done when they gave one another instruction as to how their households should be managed, or when they requested certain labours and behaviours from the servants themselves – this was the authority of mistresses who were located in the metropole of an Empire, whose position was informed by other, geographically distant 'British' places, other houses, other sites of command. At the same time, the consciousness of mistresses and masters of Anglo-Indian households in British India of the coloniality of their homes was expressed through anxiety about the security of their rule. This was a coloniality that was defined not only by their precarity within their geographical location and its local environment and culture, but also by their necessary difference from, and therefore contribution to the making of, metropolitan Home. Via an interpretation of a normative idea of what the home and its relations should be, each place could find its identity within an imperial formation, and be simultaneously connected to, and other to, another. The degree to which families and individuals could conform to normative domesticity played a part in constituting their class, gender and race identities across imperial space. Domestic servants were often the agents of these processes, occupying the border zones of encounter between regimes of difference.

The colonization of India in the long nineteenth century

Until 1858 colonial India was ruled by the joint-stock East India Company (EIC), which, from the late eighteenth century had, through conquest and treaty, undermined and displaced the existing Mughal rulers. This was the world's first experiment in corporate government, as the EIC seized territory and assumed the responsibilities of rule for the purpose of enriching its shareholders. The Company's rule was enforced by a huge private army of locally recruited Indian soldiers, and administered by its own civil service. From the 1770s the Company operated within the constraints of British government oversight, which was progressively enhanced in the first half of the nineteenth century as the Company's finances foundered on the rocks of costly territorial governance. After Company management of the colony failed catastrophically, resulting in the Uprising of 1857–8, the government assumed direct control of India, making it a Crown colony. India remained under direct British governmental control until its independence in 1947.

Under Company rule, until the early nineteenth century, most Britons who travelled to India did so primarily to make their fortunes, rather than engage in any explicit project of cultural transformation there. Francis G. Hutchins has suggested that, unlike those that followed them in the nineteenth century, 'India's conquerors were men ... unexcited by questions of morality'.[2] In the eighteenth century significant Enlightenment thinkers, such as Burke, Robertson, Jones and Maurice, while critical of certain aspects of Hindu culture, such as its perceived sensuality, produced 'largely appreciative works' on India, seeing it as a different, but also ancient and highly complex civilization that had fallen into decay due to Mughal mismanagement.[3] Ancient Hindu laws represented 'the jurisprudence of an enlightened and commercial people' according to Robertson while Warren Hastings claimed that Indian learning had achieved a 'higher degree of perfection many ages even before the existence of the earliest writers in the European world'.[4]

Following the defeat of Britain's imperial rival, Napoleonic France, in 1815, the idea that India should be ruled in an 'Indian idiom' was revived in official and academic circles, having fallen into disfavour under Cornwallis's administration from 1786.[5] Of course, so-called Indian traditions of rule were shaped by their identification and classification by late eighteenth-century colonial scholars and administrators, whose codification (and even construction) of 'indigenous' laws and customs helped facilitate a specifically colonial perception of what constituted an 'indigenous tradition'.[6] Furthermore, prior to the establishment

---

[2]   Francis G. Hutchins, *The Illusion of Permanence* (Princeton: Princeton University Press, 1967), 3.

[3]   Brian Young, '"The Lust of Empire and Religious Hate": Christianity, History and India, 1790–1820' in Stefan Collini, Richard Whatmore and Brian Young (eds.), *History, Religion and Culture: Essays in British Intellectual History, 1750–1850* (Cambridge: Cambridge University Press, 2000), 110. Of course, as the EIC integrated territorial government and commerce, there was a business incentive to denigrating existing Mughal supremacy.

[4]   William Robertson, *A Historical Disquisition Concerning the Knowledge Which the Ancients Had of India* (1791), 275, quoted in Brian Young, 'The Lust of Empire and Religious Hate', 94; Hastings quoted in Margaret Macmillan, *Women of the Raj* (London: Thames and Hudson, 1988), 9.

[5]   D.A.Washbrook, 'India, 1818–1860: The Two Faces of Colonialism' in Andrew Porter (ed.), *The Oxford History of the British Empire. The Nineteenth Century* (Oxford: Oxford University Press, 1999), 399; 404; the phrase 'Indian idiom' is from Javeed Majeed, *Ungoverned Imaginings. James Mill's 'The History of British India' and Orientalism* (Oxford: Oxford University Press, 1992), 22.

[6]   Mrinalini Sinha, *Colonial Masculinity. The 'Manly Englishman' and the 'Effeminate Bengali' in the Late Nineteenth Century* (Manchester: Manchester University Press, 1995), 4; See also J.D.M Derrett, 'The Administration of Hindu Law by the British', *Comparative Studies in Society and History*, 4 (1961): 10–52; Rosanne Rocher, 'British Orientalism in the Eighteenth Century: The Dialectics of Knowledge and Government' in C.A.Breckenridge and P. van der Veer (eds.), *Orientalism and the Postcolonial Predicament: Perspectives on South Asia* (Philadelphia: University of Pennsylvania Press, 1993), 215–59.

of Crown control of India in 1858, the motivation for the employment of 'traditional' methods of rule was the extension and consolidation of Company rule, rather than a respect for indigenous cultures.[7] Valorization of the ancient past did not mean that contemporary Indian cultures were held in high esteem: quite the opposite. As Jon E Wilson has shown, the EIC's conquest of India was bloody and chaotic rather than scholarly and genteel.[8] Nevertheless, until the late eighteenth century conscious efforts by colonizers to instigate radical social reform in India were limited.

The early nineteenth century saw a flurry of reformist activity. In Britain, as well as feeding into campaigns for changes to prisons and working conditions in factories, Evangelical and Utilitarian ideas shaped debates about the best way to do colonialism.[9] Colonial rule in India was argued to be sorely in need of 'the benefit of men capable of applying the best ideas of their age to the arrangement of its important affairs'.[10] Drawing on the scholarship of classical philologists, who had established Sanskrit as belonging to a common Indo-European family of languages, some early nineteenth-century scholars suggested Europeans and Indians shared common origins, thus providing justification for the idea that with guidance Indian people could become 'civilized' according to a definitive European standard.[11] Central to the early nineteenth-century perception of India's need for reform was a representation of Indian society as in a state of barbarous immaturity, lacking in the 'civilization' that supposedly defined the culture of the metropole.

An important part of the British ideal of 'civilization' was a particular manifestation of domesticity that was realized through the household. As we saw in Chapter 1, in Britain, industrialization had entailed the expansion of a middle class whose distinctive culture articulated the home as ideally a private, sanctified and feminized place of consumption, dependent on the reproductive labour of domestic servants. Through the application of this hegemonic discourse of domesticity the sensibilities that underpinned notions of class and gender difference gained substance, shaping the material realities of people's lives. This

---

[7] D.A.Washbrook, 'India, 1818–1860: The Two Faces of Colonialism', 385–420.

[8] See William Dalrymple, *The Anarchy: The Relentless Rise of the East India Company* (London: Bloomsbury, 2019) and Jon E. Wilson, *India Conquered: Britain's Raj and the Chaos of Empire* (London: Simon and Schuster, 2016) for thoughtful and provocative accounts of the chaotic, ad hoc nature of the establishment of the modern British empire in India.

[9] See Alan Lester and Fae Dussart, *The Origins of Humanitarian Governance. Protecting Aborigines across the British Empire* (Cambridge: Cambridge University Press, 2014).

[10] James Mill, *History of British India*, Vol. VI (London: Baldwin, Cradock and Joy, 1820), 402.

[11] Mrinalini Sinha, *Colonial Masculinity*, 20.

though was not a territorially bounded phenomenon, but was articulated in an imperial thought-world that not only included both metropole and colony, but where the metropole's distinctive modernity depended on colonial exploitation. In colonial India domesticity was equivalently important as in Britain, as a way of displaying British prestige and establishing the home as the heart of imperial civilization.[12] It was also as a way of regulating the behaviour of the home's inhabitants. Domesticity established the coloniality of the home, and the classed, gendered and raced identities of those who lived in relation to it.

The practices of rule employed by Company administrators had incorporated aspects of 'traditional' Indian ruling practice, such as the use of grand ceremonial display, in an effort to consolidate and legitimize their dominion. Under Company rule the Anglo-Indian's self-perception and projection as 'a new Indian nobility' drew on aspects of both British and Mughal rituals to produce a 'composite mode of communication, shaped by Indian ideas of appropriate forms of display, as well as their own notions of ceremony in medieval England and the splendour of oriental magnificence'.[13] This concern with displaying the prestige of putative nobility was not restricted to official life, but impacted on the domestic existence of both official and non-official Britons in India, many of whom lived in homes not dissimilar to those of the nobility in England. Eliza Fay described the banks of the river in Calcutta as 'absolutely studded with elegant mansions', while J.H. Stocqueler described Anglo-Indian residences in Calcutta as 'surrounded by extensive grounds, laid out in miniature representations of the beautiful parks of England'.[14] There were plenty of British people in India who did not live in quite such luxury, residing in colour-washed mud-brick bungalows or, if they lived in the cities, in boarding houses or flats. The spouses of ordinary British soldiers certainly enjoyed little luxury; for many, throughout the nineteenth century, their living arrangements constituted a 'screened-off corner in the barracks'.[15] Nevertheless, for all the British in India, regardless of its level of luxury, the interior of the Anglo-Indian home was from the early nineteenth century an important site for the display of British prestige. It was

---

[12] See Alison Blunt, 'Imperial Geographies of Home: British Domesticity in India, 1886–1925', *Transactions of the Institute of British Geographers*, 24, 4 (1999): 421–40 for an important exploration of 'imperial domesticity'.

[13] E.M. Collingham, *Imperial Bodies. The Physical Experience of the Raj c.1800–1947* (Cambridge: Polity, 2001), 15; 17.

[14] Mrs Eliza Fay, *Original Letters from India (1779–1815)* (London: Hogarth, 1925), 171; J.H.Stocqueler, *The Hand-book of India, a Guide to the Stranger and the Traveller, and a Companion to the Resident*, 3rd edn (London: W. H. Allen and Co., 1854), 132.

[15] Margaret Macmillan, *Women of the Raj*, 75–6.

also the place where gendered and classed ideas about whiteness were refined. Crucial to these processes were servants, preferably a large retinue of them. The relation between Indian servants and their Anglo-Indian employers was central to the colonial and imperial project, even while their presence revealed the precarity of domesticity as a disciplinary ideology.

As Indira Ghose has written: 'the later generation of East India Company rulers was anything but enamoured of Indian arts and culture'.[16] As the nineteenth century progressed Indian society was discussed in ways that stressed sociocultural decline, signified by the putative effeminacy, sensuality and feebleness of Indian people. Where in the eighteenth century high-ranking Company men married elite Indian women, or kept them as concubines (*bibis*), and lower-class British men might co-habit with lower status Indian women, by the early nineteenth century unions between British men and Indian women, and their children, began to be frowned upon.[17] As time went on, and the reform enthusiasm of the 1840s waned, the development of 'scientific' theories of racial difference allowed many mid-century British observers to perceive Indians as a totally different, and inferior, race from the British: 'In point of race the Hindoos have been regarded by naturalists as belonging to what they call the Caucasian, and even to the same family of that race as the white man of Europe! But this is a fantastical notion, for which there is hardly even so much as the shadow of a foundation.'[18]

The discursive construction of Indian character as inherently debased was 'proved' by the so-called 'Sepoy Mutiny' of 1857. This rebellion was sparked in May in Meerut, when rumours spread amongst Indian Army soldiers – *sepoys*– that pig and cow fat had been used to grease cartridges for new Lee Enfield rifles. The use of such animal products was offensive to both Hindu and Muslim soldiers, who were already disaffected by the negative effects of Company rule on their own and their communities' lives. The soldiers' rebellion spread rapidly across North India, encompassing civilian populations, with atrocities committed on all sides. After the rebellion had been brutally repressed by the British, control of India was removed from the hands of the East India Company and taken over by the Crown in 1858. The shift to Crown control saw the establishment of a

---

[16] Indira Ghose, *Memsahibs Abroad: Writings by Women Travellers in Nineteenth Century India* (Oxford: Oxford University Press, 1998), 4.

[17] See Durba Ghosh, *Sex and the Family in Colonial India* (Cambridge: Cambridge University Press, 2006) for an exploration of relationships between Indian women and British men, and what this meant for early colonial governance. See also William Dalrymple, *White Mughals: Love and Betrayal in Eighteenth-Century India* (New York: Penguin, 2002).

[18] McCullock and Others, *India: Geographical, Statistical, and Historical, Compiled from the London Times Correspondence* (London: G. Watts, 1858), 81

Government in India that was directly responsible, via the Viceroy in India and a Secretary of State for India in the India Office in London, to Parliament. Though nationalist movements emerged towards the end of the nineteenth century, India was to remain a Crown colony until its independence in 1947.

Anglo-Indian society in India

After the establishment of Crown control and the beginning of the Raj in 1858 the numbers of Europeans in India expanded, particularly as more women were encouraged to travel to the subcontinental colony. Nonetheless, by the time the first comprehensive Census of India was taken in 1881 the British population in India was still a tiny, if supremely powerful minority, scattered across rural areas and concentrated in towns in the North and North East of the region.[19] It has been estimated that about half the Europeans in India resided in the larger towns and cities, where they could find European shops, restaurants and clubs, unlike in the remoter towns, villages, army outposts and most hill stations.[20] Even as late as the 1880s, the British-born population was overwhelmingly male, young, and even if not single, it would appear that around half the married men had travelled to India without their wives[21]. Unless a husband had achieved a certain status in his official or army career, 'there was no place for wives in the Raj'.[22] For the unmarried man, as Alice Perrin wrote, 'India could be a very Paradise; to a married man it might easily become the reverse, what with anxieties about health and money and children, and the everlasting self-sacrifice that a family must needs entail'.[23] Many single men in India saved expense by living in the regimental mess, a boarding house or a club; a married man had to keep an independent establishment with its own servants. Even those men who had lived in their own houses as bachelors found their expenses significantly increased by the accoutrements of matrimonial bliss.[24] The testimony of Anglo-Indians, who

[19] *Census of British India taken on the 17 February 1881*, Vol. 1 (London: HMSO, 1883).

[20] Margaret Macmillan, *Women of the Raj*, 43.

[21] *Statistics of the British-Born Subjects recorded at the Census of India, 17th February 1881* (Calcutta, 1883): 1–2.

[22] Mary Procida, *Married to the Empire. Gender Politics and Imperialism in India, 1883–1947* (Manchester: Manchester University Press, 2002), 31.

[23] Alice Perrin, *The Anglo-Indians* (London: Methuen, 1912), 164.

[24] Mary Procida, *Married to the Empire*, 33; Swati Chattopadhay, '"Goods, Chattels and Sundry Items". Constructing nineteenth Century Anglo-Indian Domestic Life', *Journal of Material Culture*, 7, 2 (2002): 251.

recorded their experiences of colonial life in letters, journals, memoirs, advice books and interviews, also confirms the lack of a place in India for children or the elderly. In the 1870s Mrs Murray Mitchell noted '[t]wo points of difference between Indian and home society [which] strike the eye at once; here there are hardly any old people, and very few boys and girls'.[25]

Anglo-Indian society was highly stratified. The class categories that operated in the metropole were transformed in the Indian colonial context to a certain extent; social status was largely defined by a man's occupation and if he was married, his wife shared his status. Members of the Indian Civil Service were the elite. The Indian Political Service also ranked highly, as did the Indian Medical Service and the upper reaches of the Public Works Department. Clergymen and non-officials tended to form inferior social categories, though money could buy respect as some of the wealthier businessmen and planters discovered.[26] Indian Army Officers could rank highly, though they were often looked down on by civilians, and looked down on civilians in their turn. As Edith Dixon remembered:

> The army looked down at each regiment, the cavalry looked down on the infantry, the infantry all the soldiers, looked down on the civil department who on the other hand considered themselves to be the lords anointed, and then there were the government departments railways, PWD, salt revenue, all these things, which again were accepted into that society and they were expected to know their place.[27]

Knowing one's place was of prime importance in India. An etiquette developed that determined social behaviour from the order one went in to dinner, to whom one requested leave from (the *Burra* Memsahib – wife of the most senior official present rather than the hostess), and to the order one left in.[28] *The Warrant of Precedence in India* was an official guide to the order of precedence published

---

[25]	Mrs Murray Mitchell, *In India: Sketches of Indian Life and Travel from Letters and Journals* (London: T. Nelson and Sons, 1876), 71.

[26]	Margaret Macmillan, *Women of the Raj*, 47–8. Although it is important to note that those who worked for the civil service or became army officers would most likely be drawn from the middle class. Collingham has suggested that 'they came from a circumscribed section of the traditional middle class' and 'among both civilians and army officers the aristocracy, small-scale businessmen, artisans and men of the new entrepreneurial middle class, were under-represented'. E. M. Collingham, *Imperial Bodies*, 20.

[27]	Edith Dixon, MSS.Eur.T26, India Office Records, Asia Pacific and African Collections, British Library (hereafter IOR).

[28]	Margaret Macmillan, *Women of the Raj*, 47–8; Mary Procida, *Married to the Empire*. 43–4; Swati Chattopadhay, 'Goods, Chattels and Sundry Items', 265.

by the government from mid-century and as Macmillan has written, it became 'the bible of every hostess'.[29] Mary Procida and Swati Chattopadhyay have argued convincingly that the use of an administrative hierarchy to structure social relations in India resulted in the blurring of the distinction between public and private because the household 'was merely an extension of the public world of administration where all the rules and ceremonies of the latter applied'.[30] This had an impact on the way in which elite white women conceived of their domestic role in India. In advice manuals, literature and articles they positioned the home at the centre of the imperial civilizing project, using the language of imperial governance to describe domestic organization. As Steel and Gardiner wrote: 'an Indian household can no more be governed peacefully, without dignity and prestige, than an Indian Empire.'[31]

Satoshi Mizutani has elegantly explored the way that class animated the category of whiteness in India after 1858.[32] As in Britain, the proficiency with which employers managed their households was a marker of their sophistication, which contributed to the degree of their claim to the privileges of whiteness. Poor whites, of course, were at the bottom of the Anglo-Indian social order. David Arnold has argued that nearly half the European population living in India by the end of the nineteenth century could be classed as 'poor whites'.[33] Often recruited from the ranks of soldiers and sailors, they worked as semi-skilled workers and low-grade intermediaries between white officers and their Indian subordinates in government departments and private enterprises. Poor whites could also be found working as 'domestic servants, nurses, midwives, clerks, teachers and shop assistants for European employers'.[34] As in settler colonies, in the early days

---

[29] Margaret Macmillan, *Women of the Raj*, 48.

[30] Swati Chattopadhay, 'Goods, Chattels and Sundry Items', 265; Mary Procida, *Married to the Empire*, chapter 2.

[31] F.A. Steel and G. Gardiner, *The Complete Indian Housekeeper and Cook* (London: W. Heinemann, 1898), 9; Swati Chattopadhyay discusses this process at length in 'Goods, Chattels and Sundry Items'.

[32] See Satoshi Mizutani, *The Meaning of White. Race, Class and the Domiciled Community in British India, 1858–1930* (Oxford: Oxford University Press, 2012).

[33] David Arnold, 'European Orphans and Vagrants in India in the Nineteenth Century', *Journal of Imperial and Commonwealth History*, 7, 2 (1979): 104.

[34] David Arnold, 'European Orphans and Vagrants in India in the Nineteenth Century', 105. Work on white domestic servants in India might prove a fruitful area of future research, as Jana Tschurenev's research on orphanages and schools in Presidency towns indicates. Such schools promised to 'unruly paupers' into 'an industrious class of useful servants, obedient to the higher ranks of colonial society', Jana Tschurenev, 'Training a Servant Class. Gender, Poverty and Domestic Labour in Early Nineteenth-Century Educational Sources' in Nitin Sinha and Nitin Varma (eds.), *Servants' Pasts. Late-Eighteenth to Twentieth Century South Asia*, Vol. 2. (Hyderabad: Black Swan Pvt Ltd, 2019), 109, 137.

of Company rule, white European men often took Indian women as de facto wives.[35] However, as racist thinking increasingly shaped the politics of colonial authority in the nineteenth century, and the inclusions of whiteness were more rigorously policed, the Indian spouses of low-ranking white men were designated in their wills and testaments as servants; the master-servant relationship being seen by white society as a more appropriate form of relation between colonizer and colonized than that of husband and wife.[36] Generally despised by their social superiors, there were few opportunities for social advancement for poor white peoples and they would often live cheek-by-jowl with Indian people in the larger cities.[37] For example, the probate of Elizabeth Tilyard, a midwife who died in 1859, indicates that her small house in Calcutta was part of a neighbourhood inhabited by Indians as well as Anglo-Indians. Nevertheless, Elizabeth, like many other poor whites, employed three servants.[38] Minnie Wood, whose officer husband's profligacy resulted in the family's poverty, thanked her mother for sending money in a letter in 1857, claiming that 'I have to have two ayahs, dearest Mama … I enclose a list of the servants we keep, perhaps large to you, but essential out here'.[39] Though apparently teetering on the brink of destitution, Minnie needed her servants in order to constitute her racial and social status. Keeping servants was not only a necessary part of distinguishing oneself as a member of the ruling race. Servants were also crucial to the maintenance of social status within the Anglo-Indian community.

In fact, social distinctions within the white community became less relevant when the possibility of socializing with Indian people arose. In relation to Indian people, whiteness identified all Anglo-Indians as rulers. One returnee to England, on visiting his Grandfather's house, described it being 'strange that … the servants were white. I had never seen white ladies in that role before'.[40] Mary Hobhouse noted in a letter to England:

---

[35] See Adele Perry, *Colonial Relations. The Douglas-Connolly Family and the Nineteenth-Century Imperial World* (Cambridge: Cambridge University Press, 2015) for an exploration of marital and family relations in the making of British Columbia within an imperial context.

[36] Satyasikha Chakraborty, 'From *Bibis* to *Ayahs*. Sexual Labour, Domestic Labour and the Moral Politics of Empire' in Nitin Sinha and Nitin Varma (eds.), *Servants' Pasts. Late-Eighteenth to Twentieth Century South Asia*, Vol. 2 (Hyderabad: Black Swan Pvt Ltd, 2019), 70–1.

[37] David Arnold, 'European Orphans and Vagrants in India in the Nineteenth Century', 105.

[38] 'Estate of Elizabeth Tilyard', Inventories of Deceased Estates, L/AG/34/27/163, IOR, Asia Pacific and African Collections, British Library, cited in Swati Chattopadhay, 'Goods, Chattels and Sundry Items', 246.

[39] 16 September 1857, Letters of Maria Lydia Wood, MSS/Eur/B210, IOR.

[40] George Roche quoted in Elizabeth Buettner, 'From Somebodies to Nobodies: Britons Returning Home from India' in Martin Daunton and Bernhard Rieger (eds.), *Meanings of Modernity. Britain from the Late-Victorian Era to World War II* (Oxford: Berg, 2001), 225.

'Tis amusing to see all the subdivisions here; all, however, pretty well unite in keeping out the Hindu element. Mr Campbell gave a large soiree on Tuesday and invited numbers, but was afraid of what his European guests would think, and accordingly they separated like oil and water; and I was especially invited to the verandah, by some lady friends, to be out of the way of the natives.[41]

The 'Hindu element' also included those Europeans in whose veins some Indian blood was seen to pump. 'Eurasians' occupied a peculiar and difficult position in nineteenth-century India.[42] In one of her letters Anne Wilson termed them as 'one of the unfortunate classes of the community'.[43] Though they mostly styled themselves as European, they found themselves excluded both from Anglo-Indian and indigenous Indian society as the Anglo-Indian community drew ever more racially restrictive boundaries around its membership and the gulf between Indian and British society widened.

Exclusion worked two ways though. As other scholars have pointed out 'in the eyes of Hindus they [the British] were outcasts with the power to pollute'.[44] This offended and irritated many Anglo-Indians, as did the fact that many Indian women stayed hidden behind the walls of the *zenana*. They blamed such Indian cultural practices for the growth of a gulf between Indian and Anglo-Indian people, as Anne Wilson's words attest:

You must understand that some Europeans of the old school would not allow a lady to accept an Indian gentleman's proffered hospitality. They would not permit her to drive through an Indian town, be a spectator of tent-pegging, or receive an Indian as visitor, far less dine with him. They, in short, prefer her to be as wholly absent from every kind of Indian society as are the inmates of zenanas. Their argument is that until an Indian gentleman will allow them to meet his wife, they will not allow him to meet an English lady.[45]

Making a home from Home

You would be astounded if you could see the makeshift way people live in this land. It is difficult to realize that English people with their great love for comfort

---

[41] Mary Hobhouse, *Letters from India 1872–1877* (Edinburgh: printed for private circulation, 1906), 114.

[42] 'Eurasian' was the nineteenth-century term used to categorize people of mixed Indian and European descent.

[43] Lady Wilson (Anne C. Macleod), *Letters from India* (Edinburgh: William Blackwood, 1911), 181.

[44] E.M. Collingham, *Imperial Bodies*, 55. See also Margaret Macmillan, *Women of the Raj*, 8; 58–9.

[45] Lady Wilson (Anne C. Macleod), *Letters from India*, 33–4.

are willing to put up with such things. As long as they have plenty of horses, dogs and servants they are perfectly happy.[46]

Anglo-Indian life was remarkably transient. First of all, many Anglo-Indians were in India on a temporary basis. Many may have stayed for years and years, but it was always England that was 'Home'. Second, Anglo-Indians moved frequently within India, both because of work duties and as part of the annual pilgrimages between the plains and the mountains as the seasons changed. It was difficult for Anglo-Indians to identify with any one place. Rumer Godden's description of Anglo-Indians as 'cut flowers; that is why most of them wither and grow sterile, they cannot live without their roots, and so few of them take root' seems an appropriate one.[47] The transience of Anglo-Indian life, along with 'the impression of *aliens*'[48] that resulted from being part of a self-conscious white minority, was an incentive to Anglo-Indians to bond in ways they may not have done in the metropole. As Herbert John Maynard wrote in a letter to his mother in England: 'I expect you do not grasp the transience of things out here ... I meet all manner of people with whom I have had casual conversations in hotels and railway carriages, and this constitutes a bond between us which it is perhaps rather difficult to appreciate until one is away from one's own country.'[49]

In the effort to not take root, to not 'go native', the Anglo-Indian community idealized 'Home' and attempted to recreate its Englishness in microcosm inasmuch as their circumstances would allow. As Mizutani has shown, temporary residence was a critical factor in claims to whiteness, so metropolitan Home had a particular power that shaped the often unmoored domesticity of Anglo-Indian households.[50] The necessities of climate and frequent moves meant that Anglo-Indian houses in India could never exactly replicate those in the metropole. The open-plan bungalows favoured in India bore little resemblance to the storied townhouses of England. Nevertheless, efforts were made by Anglo-Indian women to gentrify the domestic environment. The author of *Indian Outfits and Establishment* suggested that 'By dint of hanging up photographs, pictures, brackets for odds and ends of china, Japanese scrolls, having books and papers

---

[46] Letter from Freda Maynard, 7 March 1897, in Katherine Lethbridge (ed.), *Letters from East and West* (Devon: Merlin, 1990), 134.
[47] Rumer Godden quoted in Margaret Macmillan, *Women of the Raj*, 44.
[48] Mary Hobhouse, *Letters from India*, 75.
[49] Katherine Lethbridge (ed.), *Letters from East and West*, 33.
[50] Satoshi Mizutani, *The Meaning of White*, 2.

about, and a piano ... a room can be made fairly pretty'.[51] Anglo-Indians even made such efforts when travelling and living in tents:

> A bowlful of Gloire de Dijon roses on the table next to me is a delight to my eyes; beyond is a little bookcase filled with our favourite books, and on the top of it is the guitar, the poor ill-used guitar! We have pictures on our walls, comfortable chairs, tables and rugs, and in short, are as snug as snug can be.[52]

But as we have seen, Anglo-Indian society was a product of a specifically colonial encounter and experience. Anglo-Indians could never eradicate the traces of that ongoing encounter, as it made them who they were. Nevertheless, this didn't stop them from trying. After all, 'the end and object is not merely personal comfort, but the formation of a home'.[53] Home was the cradle of empire and 'home' carried a double meaning in India (particularly after 1857 when more women joined their husbands in India) relating to both the metropole and the domestic sphere – 'that unit of civilization where father and children, master and servant, employer and employed, can learn their several duties' as Steel and Gardiner put it towards the end of the nineteenth century, in a formulation that echoed metropolitan advice literature, which also saw the home as critical to the production of a 'civilized' bourgeois society.[54] In this way the organization of the domestic sphere was posited as intrinsic to the wider project of civilization that encompassed both metropole and colony, and legitimized the exploitation and dispossession that underpinned their existence.[55] For women in both metropole and colony, the domestic sphere became the place where they worked in the service of empire, displaying the values of British civilization to servants and visitors, insisting on cleanliness, order and respect for the ruling race and/or class.

Maintaining households in an appropriately imperial fashion necessitated the work of many servants. Anglo-Indians required servants to sweep verandahs and clean floors and furniture, keeping the constant barrage of dust at bay during the hot months, and later in the year removing the stains caused by the monsoon damp. Servants were needed to cook elaborate meals on basic stoves, fetch water and wait at tables at both family and social events (Anglo-Indians often took their own servants to serve them when they dined at other people's houses).

---

[51] An Anglo-Indian, *Indian Outfits and Establishments: A Practical Guide for Persons about to Reside in India* (London: L. Upcott Gill, 1882), 63.

[52] Lady Wilson (Anne C. Macleod), *Letters from India*, 13.

[53] F.A. Steel and G. Gardiner, *The Complete Indian Housekeeper and Cook*, 7.

[54] F.A. Steel and G. Gardiner, *The Complete Indian Housekeeper and Cook*, 7.

[55] Mary Procida has discussed this at length in her book *Married to the Empire*.

Servants were needed to do laundry, beating their employers' calico dresses and cotton undergarments against heavy river stones to get them clean. Servants were required to admit callers and deliver cards, assisting their white employers' articulation of the rituals of 'Society' in the colonial setting. Liveried servants were needed to carry the heavy *jhampannies* in which wealthier Anglo-Indians reclined while travelling. Servants were required to sit on the verandah and pull the great fans that cooled houses in hot weather. Servants performed intimate personal services for their employers; they washed their employers' skin and dressed their hair. Servants were required to care for and even breastfeed children. The work of servants facilitated the domestic civilizing project, and as the 'natives' with whom Anglo-Indians had the most quotidian and close contact, they were ostensibly its primary recipients.

In the domestic sphere in India, however, 'the limits of anglicization' were clearly revealed.[56] As Elizabeth Collingham has pointed out, 'anglicization was neither a uniform nor an uncontested process'.[57] Far more than the climate and the transience, Indian domestic servants complicated efforts to ignore Indian society and culture and recreate England within the private sphere. They brought that society and culture right into the Anglo-Indian home and constantly reminded their employers of their dependence on it, both practically and in terms of their self-image as avatars of an imperial power.

The structure of service in Anglo-Indian households

Despite the resonance between metropolitan and colonial discourses of domesticity, the organization of domestic service in nineteenth-century India was different from in nineteenth-century England. Distribution of wealth, difference in customs, climate and domestic habits were all factors in the different structure of service in India. According to the author of a report on Madras in the 1881 Census, because houses were more open and more sparsely furnished due to the effects of the climate and the frequent moves, 'the work of the housemaid, of the charwoman, of the general houseservant is absent; and so, the housemaids, charwomen, and female general servants, who number close on one million in England and Wales, are wholly wanting in Madras – a not uninteresting fact,

---

[56] The phrase 'limits of anglicization' is E.M. Collingham's. See E.M. Collingham, *Imperial Bodies*, chapter 3.
[57] E.M. Collingham, *Imperial Bodies*, 93.

which may perhaps be seriously accepted among the mitigations of Indian life'.[58] Within the category 'servant' there were many variations, as the following extract from Dr Riddell's book *Indian Domestic Economy* indicates:

> The races of servants are very different at the three Presidencies; at Bombay there is a large proportion of Native Portuguese, Parsees, Mussulmans, and Hindoos, besides Eurasians; at Madras Native Christians take the place of Parsees at Bombay; and at Calcutta there is a mixture of every caste and grade in India. There are some among these who speak English, and who generally bear but very indifferent characters.[59]

There were also geographical variations in the way domestic service occupations were defined, as Flora Annie Steel claimed in *The Complete Indian Housekeeper and Cook*: 'In Bombay, Madras, Ceylon, and Burmah the manner of life is so different, that residents in these Presidencies will find it necessary to piece the duties of the various servants together into a new classification.' She also suggested that, despite the variations, there was one similarity between all Indian servants, which was that 'the majority of servants, from Himalaya to Cape Comorin, are absolutely ignorant of the first principles of their various duties'.[60] While many employers expressed similar frustration with their servants – the view expressed by Anne Wilson, that 'if one wants a thing done one must do it one's self, or at least superintend its being done,' was a common one in letters and manuals – such attitudes were not necessarily universal.[61] After all, the truth was that Indian servants' knowledge was key to Anglo-Indian survival in India. As Cecilia Leong Salobir has argued 'domestic chores, in food purchasing, preparation and serving, were relegated to the local people ... it was the servants' local knowledge that procured food'.[62] Mrs Eliot James was able to claim that 'we have been singularly fortunate in our dependents'[63] and employers, including those who decried some of their servants' characteristics, often expressed satisfaction with their servants' loyalty, patience and ability to negotiate problems faced by their employers due to their unfamiliarity with Indian customs, climate and circumstances. Even while 'Lady Resident' condemned servants' 'want of truth and the impossibility of placing any dependence on them', she also claimed

---

[58] *Report on the Census of British India taken on the 17 February 1881*, Vol. 1, 391.

[59] Dr R. Riddell, *Indian Domestic Economy and Receipt Book*, 7th edn (London: Thacker and Spink, 1871), 3.

[60] F.A. Steel and G. Gardiner, *The Complete Indian Housekeeper and Cook*, 54.

[61] Lady Wilson (Anne C. Macleod), *Letters from India*, 9.

[62] Cecilia Leong Salobir, *Food Culture in Colonial Asia* (Abingdon: Routledge, 2011), 60–1.

[63] Mrs Eliot James, *Indian Household Management* (London: Ward, Lock and Co., 1879), 43.

that there was 'a bright side', highlighting the emotional labour done by Indian servants in the creation of the colonial household:

> The unwearying patience and gentleness of all domestics with children, the kindness of horsekeepers to their horses, the way in which cooks accommodate themselves to having meals ready at all kinds of irregular hours, and the manner in which all servants submit to the querulousness produced by the climate in Europeans,– these and many other points are greatly to be praised.[64]

Newly arrived British women might have had little or no experience of employing servants, or indeed household management, before their migration to India and even if they had, that experience might be of little use to them in the Indian context. The proliferation of household manuals across the nineteenth century catered to a market uncertain about, rather than confident in, the expression of imperial authority in the home.

According to the Census of 1881, there were 2,149,629 male domestic servants in all India. This number must have vastly underestimated the actual number of servants, as women's occupations were not counted and every respectable Englishwoman had at least one ayah. Domestic servants were the fourth largest occupational group, after agriculturalists (though many agriculturalists also had a second occupation which was sometimes service), 'indefinite labour' and cotton manufacture. However, the report also states that 'the figures under this sub-order are largely understated'. The highest concentration of domestic servants was in Bengal, where almost half the entire number worked.[65] Of the total number of servants, the vast majority (1,707,454) worked in British Provinces and the majority of these (1,589,563) were defined as general servants.[66] There were far more male servants in India than in England. In a report on Madras it was observed that there were 'only 445 females to 555 males' in domestic service, while in England there were 894 female domestic servants to 106 male domestic servants per 1000.[67] Indian servants were often married with families of their own, with whom they lived in huts on the compound. Finding an unmarried servant could be difficult, as Minnie Wood discovered: 'My under-ayah took herself off on the day of the mutiny and has never come back. I find it most difficult to get another like her, for she was one who did not possess what is

---

[64] 'A Lady Resident', *The Englishwoman in India* (London: Smith, Elder and Co., 1864), 61.

[65] *Report on the Census of British India Taken on the 17 February 1881*, Vol. I, 349–52.

[66] *Report on the Census of British India Taken on the 17 February 1881*, Vol. I, 358. The Census doesn't say what proportion of this number worked in Anglo-Indian households and what proportion in Indian or other households.

[67] *Report on the Census of British India Taken on the 17 February 1881*, Vol. I, 391.

the greatest nuisance to us in this country, namely husband and children, and consequently she slept in the house at night.'[68] With the demands of their own families competing with the employing family's needs, Indian servants were not subject to their employers in the same way as English servants. As a result, the politics of dependence worked in different ways in India, as Minnie Wood's experience suggests.

In India, although individuals of any creed could perform most service roles, these roles were specialized and for many Hindus, could only be performed by individuals of certain caste. For example, a Hindu bearer, who would usually be of high caste, would not have anything to do with foodstuffs. Lower caste or non-Hindu table servants would be required for serving food, while a Muslim or Christian bearer could be persuaded to wait at table. Similarly, while a Catholic ayah of Portuguese descent might wash laces and stockings, a higher caste Hindu ayah might refuse to; a lower caste or non-Hindu under-ayah would therefore often be required to undertake personal cleaning duties for the mistress of the house. According to the Census of 1881, the majority of domestic servants were Hindus (74.74 per cent). A total of 23.73 per cent were Muslim and 1.52 per cent were tabulated as 'other', which may explain why caste restrictions on servants' roles were so often noted by Anglo-Indian employers.[69]

In their explanations of servant hierarchy, Anglo-Indians employers mapped the familiar structures of British households onto domestic organization in India. The indoor servants were generally regarded as 'upper' servants and the bearer was the head of the Indian servant hierarchy in Anglo-Indian households. His role was an important one, more or less equivalent to that of the housekeeper in English households. It was important to engage the right man, as the author of *Indian Household Management* advised: 'On your head servant or bearer depends much of your comfort; be, therefore, very particular in your choice, and do not engage too young a man.'[70] As well as discharging 'all the functions of a valet for the sahib' the bearer was, according to most accounts, also responsible for dusting furniture and looking after the lamps. He would receive guests or their cards and as a measure of his responsibility, was usually 'entrusted articles of value – money, jewels, clothes, &c' and was responsible for 'the general good behaviour of the staff'.[71] The bearer could act

---

[68] 16 September 1857 Letters of Maria Lydia Wood, MSS/Eur/B210, IOR.
[69] *Report on the Census of British India Taken on the 17 February 1881*, Vol. I, 376.
[70] Mrs Eliot James, *Indian Household Management*, 44.
[71] An Anglo-Indian, *Indian Outfits and Establishments*, 50.

as an intermediary between employer and staff. As Elizabeth Garrett wrote of the bearer, 'his master and mistress should be able to look to him in case of any dispute in the compound'.[72] Bearers were valued for their loyalty and trustworthiness and their employers often felt emotionally attached to them. For example, the Hobhouses intended to bring their bearer to England with them when they left India. In a fantasy of servant devotion, figured as the kind of love an ideal parent has for its child (though unlike most Anglo-Indians, he acknowledged its paid-for nature), Bertie Maynard wrote of his bearer, Khuda Buksh, that he

> was one of those Indians who for thirty rupees a month or thereabouts– shall we say eighteen pence a day – and a little "cherishing" … will serve with whole-hearted devotion a strange being of another complexion, of different religion and different thoughts; put up with his tantrums; bring meals into existence for him in the wilderness, wait for him for months, even for years, when he withdraws himself to that distant and mysterious "home" of his; love and guard his children; risk disease and death for his sake and under his protection, and most effectively thwart the machinations of others like himself to get other employers served first and served best; putting affection before justice and before self.[73]

Another key servant role, and apparently the only household role occupied by a woman, was the ayah's. According to Sinha and Varma, the ayah's role 'points to the emergence of a particular service category linked to a new kind of household and domesticity' that was 'neither unprecedented nor a clear break from the past' in the nineteenth century.[74] As an important symbol of colonial domesticity in India, the ayah evidences how imperialism might result in a synthesis of metropolitan, colonial and pre-colonial domestic roles across space, time and culture: usually an 'older' Indian woman, she would be employed to act as a lady's maid for the mistress of the household and as nanny to any children. In the early nineteenth century, most ayahs were of Muslim or Portuguese origin and might travel to find wage-work out of necessity. They would also often travel with the families that employed them, even sometimes to England. By the second half the nineteenth century, lower caste Hindu women began to find employment as ayahs. Whatever their background, ayahs were

---

[72] Elizabeth Garrett, *Morning Hours in India* (London: Trubner and Co., 1887), 20.
[73] Katherine Lethbridge (ed.), *Letters from East and West*, 158.
[74] Nitin Sinha and Nitin Varma, 'Introduction' in Nitin Sinha and Nitin Varma (eds.), *Servants' Pasts*, 30; Nitin Varma, 'The Many Lives of Ayah. Life Trajectories of Female Servants in Early Nineteenth-Century India' in Nitin Sinha and Nitin Varma (eds.), *Servants' Pasts*, 105.

key servants for 'the ideological project of producing a moral empire'.[75] As Satyasikha Chakraborty has suggested, the desexualized, maternal figure of the 'faithful Indian ayah ... morally distinguished elite Anglo-Indian households in the presidency towns from slave-holding polygamous "native" households, lower-class "mixed" households, and Catholic French and Portuguese imperial households'.[76] Many more wealthy households employed more than one ayah, particularly when there were children to be catered for. Memsahibs could become close to their ayahs and a good ayah was highly valued, as the author of *Indian Outfits* attested: 'a better maid I never wish to have; gentle, quiet, attentive, careful and trustworthy – in fact, a domestic treasure'.[77] Ayahs' work tended to involve providing personal services. She would often take care of her mistress's jewellery, wardrobe and hair, and would help to bathe and dress her mistress. She would tend to her employers when they were sick and would carry and care for children. As such the ayah and her employers experienced a physical intimacy that highlighted the racial and social differences between them, even when they were bridged by affection.

Wet nurses – *Dhayes* or *amahs*– were often hired to feed unweaned babies. They seem usually to have been engaged from the poorest echelons and were a source of great anxiety for many Anglo-Indian parents. Their necessary intimacy with the children they suckled and the dependency of those children on their milk transgressed the racial and class boundaries Anglo-Indians were so keen to maintain. *Amahs* were frequently accused of blackmailing their employers. Dr Riddell claimed that wet nurses 'make the most exorbitant demands, which from necessity you are often compelled to comply with' while Julia Maitland wrote that her *amah's* 'whims are the plague of my life'.[78] Florence Marryat even suggested *amahs* used special skills to inconvenience their employers:

> An amah also, or native wet nurse, offended by some word or action of her mistress, will revenge herself by causing her milk to dry up or 'backen', as it is technically termed, in a few hours, and what is more extraordinary still, will,

---

[75] Nitin Sinha and Nitin Varma, 'Introduction' in Nitin Sinha and Nitin Varma (eds.), *Servants' Pasts*, f/n56, 30; 31. Nitin Varma explores ambiguities of status in the ayah's role in, 'The Many Lives of Ayah. Life Trajectories of Female Servants in Early Nineteenth-Century India' in Nitin Sinha and Nitin Varma (eds.), *Servants' Pasts*, 73–107.

[76] Nitin Sinha and Nitin Varma, 'Introduction' in Nitin Sinha and Nitin Varma (eds.), *Servants' Pasts*, 30; Satyasikha Chakraborty, 'From *Bibis* to *Ayahs*. Sexual Labour, Domestic Labour and the Moral Politics of Empire' in Nitin Sinha and Nitin Varma (eds.), *Servants' Pasts*, 43.

[77] An Anglo-Indian, *Indian Outfits and Establishments*, 47.

[78] Dr R. Riddell, *Indian Domestic Economy*, 6; [Julia Maitland], 'A Lady' *Letters from Madras during the Years 1836–1839* (London: Author, 1846), 106.

when perhaps in possession of the dismissal she coveted, bring the draught back again almost as quickly.[79]

Anglo-Indian writers expressed fear of contamination by wet nurses. This was usually articulated in terms of a fear that the wet nurse would infect the child with sickness, but the subtext was one of a fear that supposed Indian degeneracy, particularly that of the low-status Indian, might be communicated to the suckling child. The cross-racial, cross-class physical closeness between wet nurse and child was crucial in the development of this fear. Advice manuals invariably recommended that the wet nurse be closely watched, her habits inspected and that her diet be carefully supervised.[80] Some families, such as the Lyalls, refused to engage such a servant. '[W]e are determined to eschew black foster mothers, and our triumph over other households who maintain negresses is great and deserved', wrote Alfred Lyall with pride to his sister in 1866.[81]

Cooks were also important within the Anglo-Indian household and Steel and Gardiner advised Memsahibs who had found a good one to 'do anything to keep him – short of letting him know that you are anxious to do so'.[82] Memsahibs were advised to avoid the kitchen, or at least give notice before they went into it because, according to Elizabeth Garrett, '[a]n Indian cook-room is so painfully unlike a kitchen at home that a visit to it affords little pleasure to the English matron'.[83] Steel and Gardiner did not mince their words, in their estimation the Indian kitchen 'is a black hole, the pantry a sink'.[84] Nevertheless, good cooks could work apparent miracles with limited equipment, as Anne Wilson discovered: 'As for the cook, all that he seems to need is two bricks or a hole in the ground. He takes the pots out of the panier ... lights his fire of wood or charcoal, and gives us dinner as good as he ever prepared in his kitchen at home'.[85] A cook's boy, or *masalchee*, who would do the washing up, assisted the cook. The *khansamah* was also a servant of significant responsibility. He oversaw 'the concerns of the table

---

[79] Florence Marryat, *'Gup' Sketches of Anglo-Indian Life and Character* (London: Reprinted from Temple Bar, 1868), 165.

[80] See for example 'A Medical Practitioner', *Domestic Guide to Mothers in India* (Bombay: American Mission Press, 1848), 70–5; 'A Lady Resident', *The Englishwoman in India*, 97; Dr R. Riddell, *Indian Domestic Economy*, 6. Indrani Sen has given close attention to the anxiety that shaped memsahibs' relationships with wet-nurses and ayahs in colonial households. See Indrani Sen, 'Colonial Domesticities, Contentious Interactions: Ayahs, Wet-nurses and Memsahibs in Colonial India', *Indian Journal of Gender Studies*, 16, 3 (2009): 299–328.

[81] Letter from Alfred Lyall, 15 July 1866, Lyall Collection, MSS Eur F132/4, IOR.

[82] F.A. Steel and G. Gardiner, *The Complete Indian Housekeeper and Cook*, 72.

[83] Elizabeth Garrett, *Morning Hours in India*, 19.

[84] F.A. Steel and G. Gardiner, *The Complete Indian Housekeeper and Cook*, ix.

[85] Lady Wilson (Anne C. Macleod), *Letters from India*, 15.

and of the servants attached to it', who were called *kitmutgars*, and would also go to the bazaar and do the marketing for the household.[86]

Servants in India did not live in the house as their counterparts in England did, but usually occupied huts on the compound where they lived with their families. The kitchen was also usually sited apart from the main house. Employers preferred that the external servants of the household did not enter the house beyond coming to the verandah to receive instructions or wages. Even indoor servants would ideally wait on the verandah until summoned by their employers with a call of '*Qui hye?*', though such restrictions were hard to place on servants who worked indoors. Bathrooms had doors opening onto the compound so that the servants who cleaned them would not have to walk through the house.[87] External servants included punkah pullers, employed during the hot season to pull the great fans used to cool houses, who would do their monotonous work from the verandah and who apparently tended to fall asleep while on the job. Most households also employed a *bheestie* to fetch and carry water for the house. In a household with horses a *syce* was required to look after each horse, while grasscuts would cut grass for them. Similarly, if cows were kept a cow-man was hired, if fowls, a fowl-man. *Malis* cared for the garden. Better off establishments also hired *jhampannies*, footmen who carried sedan chairs for their employers, *chuprassies*, who acted as messengers and *chowkidars*, who were watchmen. The *dhobie* was the washerman and was the source of much complaint and the butt of many jokes for his brutal treatment of his employer's clothes. EHA provided a mocking sketch of this servant:

> Day after day he has stood before that great black stone and wreaked his rage upon shirt and trouser and coat, and coat and trouser and shirt. Then he has wrung them as if he were wringing the necks of poultry, and fixed them on his drying line with thorns and spikes, and finally he has taken the battered garments to his torture chamber and ploughed them with his iron, longwise and crosswise and slantwise, and dropped glowing cinders on their tenderest places. Son has succeeded father through countless generations in cultivating his passion for destruction, until it has become the monstrous growth we see and shudder at in the *Dhobie*.[88]

At the bottom of the servant hierarchy in Anglo-Indian households was the *mehter*, or sweeper, described by Steel and Gardiner as 'a savage with a reed

[86] Dr R. Riddell, *Indian Domestic Economy*, 6.
[87] E.M. Collingham, *Imperial Bodies*, 103.
[88] EHA [E.H. Aitken] quoted in Margaret Macmillan, *Women of the Raj*, 149.

broom'.[89] The sweeper was invariably of low caste. It was their task to sweep and perform 'other menial offices, which no other servant will, on any consideration, put his hand to' such as emptying and cleaning the thunderbox and dealing with refuse.[90]

As deference givers, servants were important within the lavish ceremonial display through which India's conquerors sought to establish their political legitimacy as rulers in the late eighteenth and early nineteenth centuries. Anglo-Indian households employed large numbers of servants, often many more than they would have been able to afford in England. In Edward Braddon's words: 'The active and handy housemaid who cleans the house, washes a child or two, does the marketing, cooks the dinner, waits at table, and performs other offices, is represented in India by some ten individual specimens of menial humanity.'[91] Fanny Parks listed fifty-seven servants as necessary to cater for the needs of a private family while she was living in Cawnpore in the earlier nineteenth century. She was however the wife of the Acting Collector, a man of significant status. Other Anglo-Indians of this period wrote of employing significantly fewer servants than Fanny Parks, but still considerably more than they would have been able to afford in England. In the 1830s Julia Maitland wrote that she kept 'fewer than many people ... altogether twenty seven,' while Emma Walter recorded in her journal in 1839 that she had nineteen servants, not more than she needed.[92] Julia Maitland poked fun at the extravagance:

> I have an ayah (or lady's maid), and a tailor (for the ayah cannot work); and A- has a boy: also two muddles – one to sweep my room and another to bring water. There is one man to lay the cloth, another to bring in dinner, another to light the candles, and others to wait at table. Every horse has a man and a maid to himself – the maid cuts grass for him; and every dog has a boy. I inquired whether the cat had any servants, but I found that she was allowed to wait upon herself; and as she seemed the only person in the establishment capable of doing I respected her accordingly.[93]

Numbers of servants employed in Anglo-Indian households do appear to have declined somewhat as the century progressed, but still remained far higher than in the English counterparts. Servants remained as important an indicator

---

[89] F.A. Steel and G. Gardiner, *The Complete Indian Housekeeper and Cook*, ix.
[90] Edward Braddon, *Life in India* (London: Longmans, Green and Co., 1872), 114.
[91] Edward Braddon, *Life in India*, 113.
[92] [Julia Maitland], 'A Lady' *Letters from Madras*, 51; 28 November 1839, Journal of Emma Walter, MSS/Eur/B265/1, IOR.
[93] [Julia Maitland], 'A Lady' *Letters from Madras*, 18.

of status for the sahib as they had for the nabob. In 1873 Lady Mary Hobhouse had around thirty servants to cater for her and her husband's daily requirements, while most manuals recommended approximately thirteen servants to cater for a household in India, with extra servants to care for children as required.[94] As one author claimed in 1882, echoing the view expressed in the anthology cited earlier in this chapter, it was 'one of the social follies of Indian life … that you must keep three [servants] to do the work of one'.[95]

The number of servants one employed was important in representing one's significance and magnificence, not only to other Englishmen, but also to Indians. Servants both facilitated the pampered lifestyles of nineteenth-century Anglo-Indians and formed a symbolic barrier distinguishing them from the country and people amongst whom, and at whose expense, they lived. Furthermore, the employment of many servants placed the Anglo-Indian at the centre of a nexus of patronage within the Indian community, adding to his social and cultural capital.[96] The 1881 Census report on Madras suggested that domestic servant-keeping had not been usual in indigenous Indian households: 'It is not the custom to keep servants for domestic purposes. It is the custom among the landed gentry to have numerous retainers; but these are generally tenants. They perform many offices, and often receive consideration in grain and marks of honour, but they are not domestic servants.'[97] The implication was that domestic service, in its colonial form, had been developed by the colonizing British. Certainly, during this period the domestic servant was identified as a 'socially marginal figure, and domestic service as an institution that was prominent in the production and reproduction of social hierarchies, distinctions and inequalities'.[98] In terms of establishing status via prestige, it was not only individual prestige that was on display, but also, by association, that of the British Company, and later nation, represented by the Anglo-Indian. The perceived need to maintain prestige in Indian eyes was to remain an important factor structuring the relationship between servants and employers and their relation to Indian and English identities.[99] For Englishmen and -women the domestic sphere was the heart of civilization and the place where characters were made and broken. This idea had

---

[94] See for example the recommendation in *Indian Household Management* by Mrs Eliot James, 44–6, also An Anglo-Indian, *Indian Outfits and Establishments*, 49.

[95] An Anglo-Indian, *Indian Outfits and Establishments*, 49.

[96] E.M. Collingham, *Imperial Bodies*, 19–21.

[97] *Report on the Census of British India taken on the 17 February 1881*, Vol. I, 391.

[98] Nitin Sinha and Nitin Varma, 'Introduction' in *Servants' Pasts*, 4.

[99] David Cannadine discusses the centrality of 'prestige' to imperial self-perception in *Ornamentalism*. David Cannadine, *Ornamentalism. How the British Saw Their Empire* (London; Penguin, 2001).

imperial significance: it was central to the making of both metropole and colony. Across imperial space, people learned their social place through their relation to service. In India, service became a part of the way in which the colonizers displayed the racial and social hierarchies underpinning British notions of civilization both to colonial subjects and to themselves.

Conclusion

The domestic service relationship that was familiar to British imperial migrants was reconfigured through colonialism, and fed into the making of colonial place in India. The servant-employer relationship in colonial India was essential to the development of colonial domesticity, through which management of the colonial home was constituted as critical to the imperial civilizing project. White women attempted to manage their encounter with India through their relations with their Indian servants in the nineteenth-century Anglo-Indian home. However, these efforts were complicated by the particular circumstances of the Indian context. These women positioned the home at the centre of the imperial civilizing project, using the language of imperial governance to describe domestic organization, configuring domestic ideology to develop a specifically Anglo-Indian domesticity. It was in the domestic sphere, however, that the limits of this process were most clearly revealed. Through their explanation and definition of Indian servant roles Anglo-Indians represented an encounter that implicitly acknowledged Indian agency, even while they explicitly claimed triumph over it. As we will see in Chapter 4, Indian domestic servants complicated efforts to recreate England within the private sphere.

3

Intimate knowledge and the servant-employer relationship in Britain

Running a household in the nineteenth-century metrople, even a modest one, took considerable work. Servants' labour was essential to the smooth functioning of a huge number of households, from the aristocratic country pile to the simple farmhouse, and from the upper middle-class townhouse to the humbler artisan's home. As Davidoff, Doolittle, Fink and Holden have written, 'the majority of the population had the experience of either having been "in service" [or] living in a household with servants.'[1] This was particularly true for women, who were designated the custodians of the domestic sphere in the nineteenth century. As was discussed in Chapter 1, domestic service was the largest employer of women throughout our period, and the second largest employer of men and women after agricultural labour. The relation between servant and master and/ or mistress was fundamental within the Victorian social world.

Servants and their employers conducted their relations within households in ways that followed broad conventions linked to status, but there were important variations from household to household. While the law set out basic principles for an employer's responsibilities and advice manuals outlined rules of conduct for employer-servant relations, the way the relationship actually operated within homes was varied. A range of factors interacted to influence how servant-employer relations and obligations were differently structured within households across the period. These factors included the social status and gender of the employer, the gender of the servant, the age of the servant, the number of servants in the household, the location of the household, the architecture of the household, wider discourses relating to servant-employer relations and perhaps most importantly the personal proclivities of the employer. However, despite variation broad themes do emerge. The unique intimacy and mutual dependence

---

[1] Leonore Davidoff, Megan Doolittle, Janet Fink and Katherine Holden, *The Family Story. Blood, Contract and Intimacy 1830–1960* (London: Pearson, 1999), 158.

of the relationship between servants and their employers produced not only variations in experience but also similarities across households. Certain areas of tension surface and resurface in memoirs and letters throughout the period, and are the result of asymmetries of power and knowledge embedded within the servant-employer relationship. It is the private side of this relationship with which this chapter is concerned.

The master-servant relationship had long been an intrinsic part of the English social world. However, the late nineteenth century saw a shift in the social certainties that had underpinned its structure. Franchise extensions in 1867 and 1884 responded to claims, articulated by working-class men, to masculinity, morality, property in labour, independence and rights to citizenship. Feminists and socialists, amongst others, challenged pre-existing notions of social hierarchy and its meanings, using the expanding press to reach increasingly literate audiences, thanks to the late nineteenth-century expansion of educational provision. Their challenges to normative class and gender structures prompted shifts in liberal and conservative political ideologies, as party politics adapted to compete for millions of new votes. Developments in science, the publication of the findings of social investigators and the demands of imperial wars highlighted health, poverty and the fitness of the British people as issues of public concern. Alternative employments began to become available for increasingly educated young lower- and working-class men and women, both in Britain and in its expanding empire. Political and social theorists developed novel ideas about work, race, gender relations, class and social responsibility. Through these changes, British society developed new social hierarchies.

The writers of advice manuals, journal and newspaper articles and novels, as well as public speakers and local gossips, articulated refined ideas about what constituted propriety and respectability and defined behaviours associated with these ideas in the second half of the nineteenth century. These ideas were associated with the rules of 'Society', but had an impact well beyond its boundaries. Membership of 'Society' was structured by formalized behaviours such as the rituals of calling, At Home and chaperonage.[2] These rules embodied the belief that a certain social order was central to 'civilization'. Servants' work was central to the performance of such rituals. Servants maintained the spaces and the 'elaborate physical plant' in and with which the rituals took place.[3] Servants were also active in the actual execution

---

[2]   See Leonore Davidoff, *The Best Circles. Society Etiquette and the Season* (London: The Cresset Library, 1986), Chapter 3.
[3]   See Leonore Davidoff, *The Best Circles*, 88.

of social rituals as they ferried cards between callers and so on. Furthermore, servants' position as excluded observers of their employers' elaborate social performance enhanced both their difference and their employers' sense of the moral value of their own behaviour, in that observance of it taught the servants about respectability.

The wider articulation of ideas about respectability and propriety, such as the notion that one should keep to a strict timetable for meal times, work times, social times and so on, constituted an ongoing effort to consolidate new social hierarchies in a period of rapid social-change. Defining appropriate relations between servants and employers was a functional part of this process. However, the interdependence that characterized the relationships between servants and their employers complicated distinctions of status difference, even while the overt meanings of the servant-employer relationship pointed towards the closure of social boundaries. This was because the master/servant relationship involved work and intimacies that implicitly challenged structures of social difference. The servant was the outsider in the family home. The servant was the lower-class resident of a middle-class house. She worked in the sacred domestic sphere for a wage. She was an individual with a character who performed personal tasks for her employer and upon whom her employers depended. All these differences were dependent on culturally constructed social categories which were subject to change over time.

Defined as dependants in a range of discourses from the legal to the religious, servants' difference from the families whose lives they maintained was crucial within the structure of the relationship. Servants' difference was given meaning through the concrete practices of their employment – the work they did day in and day out – and through the operation of certain ideas, rituals and behaviours connected with that work. It was in the constant effort to achieve the closure of social boundaries through enforcing difference of dress, differences in movement and behaviour that employers' anxiety towards their servants was most visible. It was in the areas where the limits of acceptable behaviour for servants were defined that the artificiality of their difference, and deference, was most psychologically challenging. Tensions echo in the records left by both servants and employers over issues of dress, of honesty, of childcare, of obedience, of sociability, of secrets. This is not to say that servants could not have genuinely affectionate or straightforward relationships with their employers, but that the dynamics of power and dependence that characterized the relationship tended to complicate it.

It is at times hard to precisely define in which direction dependence flowed in some relationships between servants and employers, and where the boundaries of family inclusion lay.[4] Categorical ambiguities were exactly what employers were trying to address in their insistence on behavioural rituals that distinctly differentiated between family member and family employee. Rituals exist to substitute tangible differences for intangible similarities. Behavioural rituals, learned from childhood by both employer and servant, situated the servant and employer in a specific kind of relationship. The structure of this relationship was in line with wider thinking about gender, class and race relations and served the purpose of shoring up not only the employer's individual authority but also that of the echelon she/he saw herself/himself belonging to, at the same time bolstering the security of that belonging.

As the nineteenth century progressed the separation of work from home, the withdrawal of women from labour, even within the home and the drawing of tighter boundaries around who was, and who was not, to be included in the family were fundamental features of the development of a definitively middle-class ideal of respectable domesticity. The ideology of separate spheres discussed in Chapter 1 gave moral weight to the process by which domestic life was secluded. Within this ideology home became 'the place of Peace; the shelter, not only from all injury, but from all terror, doubt and division', clearly distinguished from the busy and brutal outside world.[5] Home was the site of the family – increasingly narrowly defined – which became ideally a morally, rather than economically productive unit.

The moral ideology of separate spheres intertwined with more prosaic motivations behind the distinction between public and private. The exclusivity of domestic privacy was linked to affluence. Only the financially successful could really afford to seclude their family through devices such as designating certain rooms for entertaining, or using servants to undertake domestic labour and to mediate between family members and guests or tradespeople or lower servants.[6] For a lot of families strictly separate spheres remained little more than an ideal to aspire to. However, there were other ways through which the worlds of labour, money, dirt, disorder and sweat could be differentiated from the 'temple of the hearth', not least through the architectural organization of a house. Although in 1851 many more middle-class families lived over the shop or right

[4] Leonore Davidoff, Megan Doolittle, Janet Fink and Katherine Holden, *The Family Story*, 161.
[5] John Ruskin, *Sesame and Lilies*, 1864 pocket edn (London: George Allen 1906).
[6] Leonore Davidoff, *Worlds Between* (Cambridge: Polity, 1995), 24.

next to their place of work than did not, the trend towards a separation of working from family life was clear.[7] In the second half of the nineteenth century, houses were increasingly designed to suit domestic, rather than business, purposes, with rooms designated for specific activities such as entertaining, dressing, eating and so on.[8] A part of this process was the shift towards employing servants to do the work that in earlier decades might have been done by kin.

The metropolitan domestic house became more commonly a place of conspicuous consumption, the site of the display of affluence that secured and denoted a family's social status within a carefully graded hierarchy. The need to display wealth in order to establish social status resulted in a proliferation of furnishings, decorations, trinkets, valuables and even rooms within houses, all of which required considerable labour to be kept clean and tidy according to the dictates of 'respectability'. This display was not only for the benefit of visitors to the house, but also reflected the family's status back to its members. Portraits and large ornate mirrors in which the family sat surrounded by the paraphernalia of gentility literally served this purpose.

Embedded in the expulsion of, or at least effort to fence off, working from domestic life was the powerful notion that the domestic sphere was rightly the preserve of women who should have as little to do with earning or labour (excluding childbirth) as the family could afford. Respectable middle-class masculinity in the nineteenth century necessitated an entirely dependent wife and family. A non-earning wife indicated an affluent family and a family in which the wife could delegate household work entirely to servants was doing nicely indeed. Affluence, and the domestic lifestyle it afforded, underpinned class status, as the advice book writer Sarah Ellis indicated when she stated that 'gentlemen may employ their hours of business in almost any degrading occupation and, if they have the means of supporting a respectable establishment at home, may be gentlemen still'.[9]

The link between affluence, domesticity, class and gender also resulted in the definition of degrees of femininity. The ideally domesticated mistress took on a function that the ideology, constructing her role as 'Angel of the House' to use Coventry Patmore's trite phrase, has failed to disguise. As Davidoff has

---

[7] Leonore Davidoff and Catherine Hall, *Family Fortunes. Men and Women of the English Middle Class 1780–1850*, 2nd edn (London: Routledge, 2002), 231–2.

[8] Vanessa Parker, *The English House in the Nineteenth Century* (London: Historical Association pamphlet, 1970), 20; John Tosh, *A Man's Place. Masculinity and the Middle-Class Home in Victorian England* (New Haven and London: Yale University Press, 1999), 21.

[9] Sarah Ellis, *The Women of England* (London: Fisher and Son, 1839), 331.

written, 'the wife-mother-house-mistress image often merged with the physical symbol of the house so that it became difficult to visualize the woman as having a separate identity from the house; in a sense she *became* the house'.[10] To serve this illustrative function, both mistress and home ideally should be free from the polluting taint of work and its associated dirt and disorder. Ladylike lily-white hands could only belong to those women who didn't use them for cleaning, cookery and childcare. In this way domesticity became a prism through which femininity was classed and classing. Although the ideal was hard to achieve, within a culture that linked affluence to morality and social power, the need to approximate the ideal could be pressing, particularly for those who felt the insecurity of their status. However, the private and public spheres could never be kept absolutely separate. The 'outside' world of labour, money and dirt got into even the most secluded households, usually through the back door via the medium employed specifically to keep it at bay – domestic servants.

Hiring and the cash nexus

Despite, or rather, because of, the gendered and classed distinction between the domestic and outside worlds, paid work was important within a middle-class home. All the trappings of respectable domesticity, not least the filth it produced, required constant attention. If the mistress would be socially compromised by such work, and the master emasculated by it, then the labour of domestic servants was a necessity, not only materially to maintain a household, but also to protect servant employers from the unpleasantness of life in a rarefied environment that suited their social pretensions.[11] Employing a domestic servant was seen by many who desired to be thought of as middle-class as a way of indicating such status. Lilian Westall remembered that in her first 'place' her employers 'didn't seem to have much money themselves; he was a clerk of some sort, but they liked the idea of having a "nurse-maid" and made me buy a cap, collar, cuffs and an apron. Then the mistress took me to have a photograph taken with the children grouped around me'.[12] Servants occupying certain roles indicated degrees of status difference within the 'middle-class' category. For

---

[10] Leonore Davidoff, *Worlds Between*, 52.
[11] Leonore Davidoff, *Worlds Between*, 24.
[12] Lilian Westall in John Burnett (ed.), *Useful Toil: Autobiographies of Working People from the 1820s– the 1920s* (London: Allen Lane, 1974), 216.

example, as with *jhampannies* in India, as the nineteenth century progressed, liveried footman tended to occupy an ornamental rather than a functional role. According to John Burnett, 'when streets became safer and transport easier in Victorian times the footman's place became very much a sinecure and he degenerated into an ornamental parasite'.[13] Certainly Louisa Bain seems to have seen the employment of a footman as a snobbishly ostentatious display of status, noting in her diary in the summer of 1869:

> This afternoon to our astonishment we had a visit from Mrs Smith-Bosanquet: what could have possessed her to show us such an uncalled for civility? She made herself very agreeable, and we were amused by her footman setting open our gate, but the coachman doubted whether the drive would accommodate anything so sublime as one of the Squire's carriages, so she had to walk up to the door.[14]

The systems by which servants came to their places were largely informal. Though respectable and reliable registry offices for servants did exist, these tended to be seen as a last resort by potential employers as they carried a reputation for attracting the lowest quality of servant, or being a front for pimps.[15] Servants and employers did advertise in newspapers in increasing numbers as the century progressed and many employers hired girls from institutions such as workhouses, orphanages and industrial schools – the 'bargain basements for servants in the nineteenth century'.[16] However, diaries, letters, autobiographies and remembrances suggest that it was also common for servants and employers to find each other through personal networks. Edith Hanran knew her first employers because '[a]ll my sisters – four sisters – went to the same job when they first left school'.[17] Hannah Cullwick found a place on one occasion because a fellow servant, Ellen, 'knew of a couple just married & on their tour for a month as wanted two servants – the sister was to engage 'em'.[18] Jane Carlyle sometimes found girls through her friends, claiming on one occasion to be 'under great obligations to Geraldine's old Miss Darby, for having hunted up this girl and

[13] John Burnett (ed.), *Useful Toil*, 14.
[14] Louisa Bain's Diary, August 14 1869, in James. S. Bain, *A Bookseller Looks Back. The Story of the Bains* (London: Macmillan, 1940).
[15] Pamela Horn, *The Rise and Fall of the Victorian Servant*, 47–8.
[16] Prochaska, F.K., 'Female Philanthropy and Domestic Service in Victorian England', 82.
[17] Edith Hanran, interviewed by Paul and Thea Thompson for 'Family Life and Work Experience before 1918', Essex University Oral Archive.
[18] 'Hannah's Places' Box 98 (14) Munby Collection, Wren Library, Trinity College, Cambridge University.

taken much trouble to "suit me" in a situation that was really very desolate, my state of weakness at the time considered'.[19]

On another occasion Jane engaged 'a little girl of the neighbourhood … She is known to me as an honest, truthful, industrious little girl'.[20] Clergymen and tradespeople could also be useful in communicating information about places between servants and employers.[21] Hannah Cullwick described meeting a potential employer at 'a Revd Clark's, who turns out to be a friend of Mr Borland's'.[22] Indeed, in a letter to the *Times* in 1863 a 'Clergyman's Wife' argued that 'clergymen, school teachers, &c' had a social responsibility to 'impress upon the young the advantages of service and the miseries of improvident marriages'.[23] In such a formulation service became more than a job: it was the means by which young working-class girls could be saved from themselves.

The demands of the domestic ideal in which the middle-class family lived in cosy seclusion necessitated servants' segregation from the rest of the household. Because servants worked, they contradicted the ideology that dictated that respectable middle-class femininity and the domestic sphere should be defined by freedom from the taint of work and the cash nexus. There were ways in which the effect of this taint could be minimized in relation to the employment of domestic servants. If married, the master of the house was responsible for hiring and firing servants; establishing or ending a contract with an individual was necessarily his responsibility for both legal and ideological reasons. However, it was usually the mistress of the house who determined when and which servants were engaged or dismissed. This separation of duties ensured that the lady of the house remained unsullied by the 'business' of hiring and firing, while the master did not need to concern himself with the 'feminine' issues of domestic management. Also, some commentators suggested that employing servants was a philanthropic act: mistresses were constructed as having 'a duty towards them of helping them to become *useful* women'.[24] This was a duty essential not only to the future welfare of the servants themselves, but also to 'the comfort and well-being of our whole domestic life, which in England lies so much within

[19] Letter to Thomas Carlyle, 2 September 1850 in J.A. Froude (ed.), *Letters and Memorials of Jane Welsh Carlyle*, Vol. II (London: Longmans and Co, 1883), 129–30.
[20] Letter to Mrs Russell, 20 October 1862 in J.A. Froude (ed.), *Letters and Memorials of Jane Welsh Carlyle*, Vol. III, 131.
[21] Pamela Horn, The Rise and Fall of the Victorian Maidservant, 44–5.
[22] 'A Servant's Life: 1866–1872' Box 98 (17) Munby Collection, Wren Library, Trinity College, Cambridge University.
[23] 'A Clergyman's Wife', Letter, *The Times*, 30 November 1863, 10.
[24] Lady Baker, *Our Responsibilities and Difficulties as Mistresses of Young Servants* (London: Hatchard, 1887), 5.

doors'.[25] By contrast, managing an Anglo-Indian household was constructed as part of the process by which the British consolidated their imperial power through control of the 'native'. Nevertheless, in both cases, the power dynamic of the servant-employer relationship was crucial in situating subordinates, whether racial or class, endorsing the authority of their 'superiors' for a greater purpose – national or imperial security.

The formulation of servant-employing as philanthropic duty elided the fact that service constituted paid labour within the home.[26] Jane Carlyle preferred to think that her servants cared for her out of a natural sense of respect and love rather than because they were paid. In one letter to her husband she described being tempted to re-engage a favourite, though incompetent, servant: 'I am glad … that I had the fortitude to resist her tears and her request to be taken back as cook … Still it is gratifying to feel that one's kindness to the girl has not been all lost on her, for she really loves us both passionately'.[27] In another letter, she claimed that 'my maid nurses me with an alacrity and kindness that could not be bought with any money'.[28] Though it is unlikely that the maid would have been such a good nurse if she were unpaid, her acting in the capacity of nurse answers a need in Jane that necessarily could not be included in the terms of a contract. Jane's requirements of her servants included an unspoken request that they serve not only her physical, but also her emotional demands. In a sense, Jane's servants were paid to pretend they weren't paid.

Domestic servants were engaged to perform tasks for which they received remuneration. The gender division of labour in dealing with this was usually clear-cut. In her diary Louisa Bain, the wife of a London bookseller, discussed the problem of her servants' wages:

> This evening have had a talk with my maids, Carah and Emma, and find that they neither of them wish to leave me, but think the wages so much less than they could have elsewhere. Emma had £12 in her last place and Carah has been offered £16, while I only give ten and twelve guineas. As I know Papa will not give more I propose allowing them ¼ lb. of tea weekly, this will be equal to £1:6:0d. per annum each, and with sugar, and 1/-s. per week Beer money which

---

[25] A Mistress and a Mother, *At Home* (London: Macintosh and Co, 1874), 3.

[26] This was problematic for menservants' masculinity. For menservants, their status as dependants prevented them from completely achieving adult male status as their exclusion from franchise extensions in the late nineteenth century indicated.

[27] Letter to Thomas Carlyle, 17 September 1860 in J.A. Froude (ed.), *Letters and Memorials of Jane Welsh Carlyle*, Vol. III (London: Longmans, 1883), 61.

[28] Letter to Thomas Carlyle, 24 September 1847 in J.A. Froude (ed.), *Letters and Memorials of Jane Welsh Carlyle*, Vol. II, 9.

they have always had, will bring their wages up to what they will be content with, so I hope we shall have no change till they both marry.[29]

Mrs Bain was in a position where it was up to her to negotiate with her servants, but within financial parameters set by her husband (Papa). Mrs Bain managed the process by which the servants' remuneration was arranged, but was unable to alter the cash payment they received other than through substituting goods for cash. Though it was not unusual for servants' wages to be supplemented in this way, Mrs Bain had no control over the servants' actual wage, despite the fact she was clearly balancing the household budget carefully and perhaps had greater knowledge of its workings and the demands on it than her husband. It was not ideal for a middle-class wife or daughter to be involved in the cash nexus in the home, although of course many women were. For Mrs Bain, as a married 'lady', to have dealt directly with the cash payment of servants' wages was inappropriate to her class and gender status. However, Mrs Bain was able to pay her servants 'in kind', in a manner in which they might have been more commonly remunerated for their work fifty years earlier. In Mrs Bain's case, we may be seeing evidence of the tension caused by the transition to different, capital-based kinds of payment relations, with older forms of payment persisting under the guise of men controlling money. This change matched the shift towards more formalized employer-servant relationships in the second half of the nineteenth century.

The issue of commissions and perquisites was a tricky one for nineteenth-century servant employers. Seen as a traditional entitlement by servants, employers often complained that it constituted theft. In February 1865 there was 'considerable excitement in Leeds, chiefly among the working classes of various grades, owing to a female servant having been sent to the borough gaol and imprisoned therein for having purloined some 2lb of dripping … when Mrs Chorley [her mistress] charged her with purloining the dripping she claimed it as her perquisite'. Eliza Stafford, the cook in question, became a working-class heroine. According to *The Times*, while Dr Chorley was 'frequently mobbed in the streets, and was assailed with vituperative exclamations of a threatening character … [l]arge placards were posted throughout the town, calling upon the public to give Mrs Stafford a joyous oration when she came out of gaol'. In the end, on leaving the gaol, Mrs Stafford slipped away to Scarborough at an earlier hour than expected by the crowd, so instead they went to Dr Chorley's house 'and

---

[29] Louisa Bain's Diary, 31 January 1863, in James. S. Bain, *A Bookseller Looks Back. The Story of the Bains*.

one of them carried a long pole, at the top of which was fixed a doctor's bottle and an old dripping pan'.[30] A riot ensued at which several of the demonstrators were trampled and a policeman broke his wrist. In this case the tension over the right to a perk spread beyond the confines of the private sphere and became an issue of public and class concern. Notably, the behaviour of the crowd in this situation was reminiscent of the 'rough music' or 'skimmington rides' with which communities in England had traditionally meted out customary justice and regulated social behaviour since medieval times.[31]

As with Mrs Bain's method of paying her servants in kind, Eliza Stafford's case points to the existence of an economy which did not revolve around cash and which the local community felt bound to defend. The furore over Eliza Stafford's case shows how shifts in ideas about economic relations could create tension around notions of appropriate behaviours for servants and their employers, and how these tensions could resonate with wider class antagonisms.

Drudgery, dependence and the tensions of intimacy

The following sections consider the tension between the variable demands made on servants by their employers and servants' ideas about the limits of acceptable expectation. These sections draw on evidence from a range of households: from households with a single servant, to households employing two or three servants, to households with staffs numbering twenty or more. It was only in the houses of the most wealthy that a large domestic staff was employed. The vast majority of households rarely employed more than three servants and frequently fewer than that. Clearly none of these households can be taken as representative of generalities of experience. Rather, the intimacy of the servant-employer relationship engendered varied possibilities for the conduct of employer-servant relations.

Drudgery

Nineteenth-century bourgeois British households were organized according to social rules that were understood to underpin 'civilization', which itself was a

---

[30] 23 Feb 1865, *The Times*.

[31] Stephen Banks, *Informal Justice in England and Wales, 1760–1900* (Basingstoke: Palgrave, 2010), chapter 8.

concept underpinned by the exploitations of Empire. These rules and rituals were not questioned; observing them was a duty, not a personal choice. Ceremonial behaviours surrounded major life event such as birth, marriage and death, but also more quotidian routines of calling and dining. Servants were central in the performance of all these rituals. They admitted callers to houses, and used specific methods and manners when cleaning, or serving food. Servants ordered the spaces in which their employers observed rituals both social and personal such as the parlour, the dining room and the bathroom. The material work that servants did afforded their employers the time and appropriate space to act their own parts in the cultural play.

The link between the rules and rituals structuring 'Society' and ideas about what constituted 'civilized' life justified an elaboration of daily living that produced much domestic labour for servants. Household work in our period was highly labour-intensive and required strength and stamina. As Leonore Davidoff and Ruth Hawthorn have shown, a jug of bath water weighed around 30lbs and would often have been carried up many flights of stairs.[32] Without the modern appliances we have come to take for granted today, the tasks of scrubbing floors, beating carpets, blackleading stoves, cleaning windows, preparing food, hauling coal and water up and down stairs, tending fires and polishing wood, silver and brass, not to mention being constantly available to the family to run errands, answer doors and perform any other personal services, could constitute drudgery indeed.

For the maids-of-all-work, or general servants – by far the most numerous category of servant throughout our period – who frequently worked alone in households up and down the country, the work could be backbreaking. General servants were expected to perform all the formal duties and chores that in a larger household might be performed by two or three servants, with only the occasional assistance of a charwoman or 'step-girl', if that.[33] The following extract from the diary of Hannah Cullwick which describes a day in her life as a maid-of-all-work in 1860 gives some indication as to how hard general servants were expected to work, even in houses where more than one servant might be employed. Hannah would usually rise at around 6.30 am and rarely got to bed before 11 pm:

> Saturday 14 July Opened the shutters & lighted the kitchen fire. Shook my sooty things in the dusthole & emptied the soot there. Swept & dusted the rooms &

---

[32] Leonore Davidoff and Ruth Hawthorn, *A Day in the Life of a Victorian Domestic Servant*, 78
[33] Frank E. Huggett, *Life below Stairs*, 106.

the hall. Laid the hearth & got breakfast up. Clean'd 2 pairs of boots. Made the beds & emptied the slops. Clean'd & wash'd the breakfast things up. Clean'd the plate; clean'd the knives & got dinner up. Clean'd away. Clean'd the kitchen up; unpack'd a hamper. Took two chickens to Mrs Brewer's & brought the message back. Made a tart & pick'd & gutted two ducks & roasted them. Clean'd the steps & flags on my knees. Wash'd up in the scullery. Clean'd the pantry on my knees & scour'd the tables. Scrubbed the flags around the house & clean'd the window sills. Got tea at 9 for the master & Mrs Warwick in my dirt, but Ann carried it up. Clean'd the privy & passage & scullery floor on my knees. Wash'd the dog & clean'd the sinks down.[34]

Hannah had been doing heavy physical work since the age of twelve. At the age of thirty she stood almost five feet eight inches tall, weighed eleven stone and the girth around the bicep of her right arm was thirteen and three quarter inches, a quarter inch thicker than the girth of her neck.[35]

The work required of servants could vary widely. This added to the sense of the relation between servant and mistress or master as being of a different order from that between employees and employers in other trades and professions. There were no fixed hours and for many mistresses and masters of smaller households, no fixed limits to the work expected of a servant. In farming households, the servants were often expected to work in the dairy. One Norfolk servant remembered having to help with the butter making, standing on a stool because she was too small to reach the churn, after which she

had to wash up all the pans … It was then getting well into the afternoon, and it was time for their tea and mine. I got their tea ready in the dining-room and mine in the kitchen. When I had finished tea and washed up, there were faggots of sticks to get for the fire in the morning. Then I had to go all round the fields to collect the eggs, then see they were all clean and rolled in paper to take to the market.[36]

Similarly, Catherine Bailey's day began at 6 am with milk deliveries. After she had had a cup of tea she 'had to take the milk out, in cans, round the village green. Cold weather, frosty, snow, or whatever it was, I had to go … Not in a big hand cart, or anything, they were the milk cans. Used to cut my poor little

[34] '1860' Box 98 (13) Munby Collection, Wren Library, Trinity College, Cambridge University.

[35] 'Hannah Cullwick. Servant of all work. Her dimensions at the age of thirty'. Box 110 (18) Munby Collection, Wren Library, Trinity College, Cambridge University.

[36] 'My First Job', essay kept at Essex County Record Office quoted in Pamela Horn, *The Rise and Fall of the Victorian Servant*, 60.

fingers.'[37] Catherine was employed in the household of a butcher around the turn of the century, and alongside her usual cleaning, dairy and childcare duties which filled her day until 9 pm, she was also required to 'make pork cheese, at 10, 12 o'clock at night, for the butchers, and the lard.'[38]

Though the employment of residential indoor menservants was in long-term decline in England throughout the second half of the nineteenth century, a significant number of households did employ males in a single-handed capacity alongside female servants, though their numbers were far less than in India, where service was dominated by men. Kitchen-boys, foot-boys or hall-boys were at the bottom of the male servant hierarchy and might be expected to undertake a range of tasks such as cleaning boots and waiting on other servants and the family. Of his days as a foot-boy in a local squire's house in 1870 William Lanceley remembered he had to rise at 6 am and

> light the servants' hall fire, clean the young ladies' boots, the butler's, housekeeper's, cook's and ladies'-maids', often twenty pairs altogether, trim the lamps (I had thirty-five to look after, there being no gas or electric light in the district in those days), and all this had to be got through by 7.30; then lay up the hall breakfast, get it in, and clear up afterwards ... My day's work followed on with cleaning knives, house-keeper's room, silver, windows, and mirrors; lay up the servant's hall dinner; get it in and out and wash up the things, except dishes and plates; help to carry up luncheon; wash up in the pantry; carry up the dinner to the dining-room and, when extra people dined, wait at table; lay up the servants' hall supper; clear it out and wash up. This brought bedtime after a day's work of sixteen hours.[39]

In some households an older single-handed male servant might be kept alongside female servants. Aged thirty, William Tayler said in the 1830s of his place with the widow Mrs Prinsep that he was 'the only manservant kept here' though there were also 'three maidservants, very good quiet sort of bodys.'[40] Such a servant could combine the roles of footman and butler.[41] William Tayler, though entitled 'footman', did such work in the Prinsep household – alongside cleaning knives and taking care of the lamps he 'opned the door when any visitor

[37] Catherine Bailey, interviewed by Paul and Thea Thompson for 'Family Life and Work Experience before 1918', Essex University Oral Archive.

[38] Catherine Bailey, 'Family Life and Work Experience before 1918'.

[39] William Lanceley, *From Hall-Boy to House-Steward* (London: Edward Arnold and Co, 1925) in John Burnett (ed.), *Useful Toil*, 187.

[40] 31 January 1837 in Dorothy Wise (ed.), *Diary of William Tayler, Footman, 1837* (London: St Marylebone Society Publications Group, 1962) extract in John Burnett, *Useful Toil*, 175–6.

[41] Pamela Horn, *The Rise and Fall of the Victorian Servant*, 88.

came … layed the cloth for dinner, took the dinner up at six o'clock, waited at dinner' and accompanied his mistress when she went out. He seemed generally happy with his position, but still expressed a desire for 'rather more liberty', describing a servant's life as being 'something like that of a bird shut up in a cage. The bird is well housed and well fed but is deprived of liberty, and liberty is the dearest and sweetes [sic] object of all Englishmen'.[42] Perhaps because of, and for, his gender security, William Tayler happily told his female employers off when he felt they made unreasonable demands; in one diary entry he writes:

> Been out with the carriage this afternoon with Miss P. She kept me out longer than she aught to of done, therefore I gave her a little row for it. I hope it will do her good. I served the old lady the same way the other day and it did her a deal of good, and I have no doubt that it will act the same in this case.[43]

William Tayler wrote his diary in 1837, earlier than most of the other servants evidenced in this chapter. The liberty he took in chastising his employer may have been unusual and may have been because his employer was a woman. It is hard to imagine William Lanceley, who described being six months in one master's employ 'before he [the master] spoke to me [Lanceley]', telling his employer off.[44] However, Tayler's experience does indicate the variable possibilities for servant's self-expression in the servant-employer relationship.

Dependence and independence

The fact that there were technically no limits to what a master or mistress could demand of a servant meant that tensions often arose over employers' expectations. Servants had little formal bargaining power but as many mistresses were aware, they had the ability to disrupt a household effectively if they felt their employers had gone too far in their demands.

The division of roles between servants could lead to frustration when a servant was required to do anything extraneous to his or her usual duties. Jane Carlyle complained about this after helping Lady Ashburton to dress some dolls which were to be gifts for local children at Christmastime in 1851:

[42] 30 December 1837 in Dorothy Wise (ed.), *Diary of William Tayler, Footman, 1837*, extract in John Burnett (ed.), *Useful Toil*, 185.

[43] May nineteenth 1837 in Dorothy Wise (ed.), *Diary of William Tayler, Footman, 1837*, extract in John Burnett (ed.), *Useful Toil*, 182.

[44] William Lanceley, *From Hall-Boy to House-Steward* in John Burnett (ed.), *Useful Toil*, p189.

The very footmen won't *carry the dolls* backwards and forwards! When told to bring one they simply disappear and no doll comes!- I remarked on this with some impatience yesterday, and Lady A. answered, 'Perfectly true, Mrs Carlyle – they *won't bring the doll!* – I know it as well as you do – but what would you have me do? – turn all the servants men and women out of the house on account of these dolls? For *it would* come to *that* – if I made a point of their *doing anything in the doll line!* Perhaps it would be the right thing to do – but then what should we do next week without servants when all the company come?' Such is the slavery the grandest people live under *to what they call* their '*inferiors*'.[45]

The phrase 'to what they call their inferiors' suggests Jane recognized the superficiality of servants' deference, while the use of the word 'slavery' points towards the potentially powerless dependence of employers on their servants. Jane Carlyle was ambivalent to the point of jealousy about Lady Ashburton, with whom Thomas Carlyle was fascinated. In a letter to Helen Welsh Jane wrote bitterly that 'her Ladyship's will is become the law of this house! – even her *whims* are as imperative as the ten commandments!'[46] In the letter to Mrs Russell quoted above, Jane uses her opinion of Lady Ashburton's relationship to her servants as a way of having a dig at Lady Ashburton herself. The unsaid implication is that the less grand Jane is not enslaved to the whim of her domestics. In this sense Jane and Lady Ashburton's different relationships with their servants were a part of the way Jane understood the relationship between herself and Lady Ashburton.

Some employers appear to have thought that refusals by servants to undertake certain tasks were the result of a kind of snobbery on the part of servants. William Lanceley certainly expressed snobbish attitudes in his memoir, writing that there was 'a quotation among old servants on the good breeding of the old aristocracy' which ran 'You may break, you may shatter the vase as you will/But the scent of roses will cling to it still'. Another quotation described 'our new society': 'You may rub up and polish and dress as you will/But the style of the plebian clings to him still.'[47] Lanceley had worked up through the ranks of service in upper-class households and his prejudices probably reflected those of his employers. But it also seems likely that this was part of the way in which he invested meaning in work that was taken for granted and even demeaned within wider society. As

---

[45] Letter 6 December 1851 in Leonard Huxley (ed.), *Jane Welsh Carlyle: Letters to Her Family, 1839–1863* (London: John Murray, 1924), 353–4.

[46] Jane Carlyle, Letter 7 November 1846 in Alan and Mary McQueen Simpson (eds.), *I Too Am Here. Selections from the Letters of Jane Welsh Carlyle* (Cambridge: Cambridge University, 1977) 227.

[47] William Lanceley, *From Hall-Boy to House-Steward* in John Burnett (ed.), *Useful Toil*, 192.

Hannah Cullwick wrote in 1864: 'the lowest work is honourable in itself & the ... drudge is honourable too ... But how often poor servants have to hear the scorn & harsh words & proud looks from them above her which to my mind is very wicked & unkind & certainly most disheartening to a young wench'.[48]

In Lanceley's quotations, the inability of 'new society' to escape its distasteful 'plebian' origins, while 'good breeding' would always smell of roses to a servant's experienced eye, evinces both snobbery and also a sense that the servant stands outside this class relationship and can judge it. By distinguishing between types of employers in this way, servants assumed a position as arbiters of class. Lanceley gives this quotation as a saying 'among old servants' – therefore experienced, knowledgeable servants. In both of Lanceley's quotations the employer is represented through the metaphor of household work – it is through the servant's work that the 'plebian' attempts to disguise his origins, but the servant knows the truth. In this way the servant could invest meaning, agency and independence into his position. The quotations also imply servants in 'better' households associated themselves with their employers' status, using it to construct a social hierarchy outside the household, between households. Hannah Cullwick's diaries and accounts of her life suggest that the status of an employer might affect the value of a servant's character. At one point she describes an offer of a place being retracted by one would-be mistress because of the nature of Hannah's current place of employment: 'when she found it a lodging house & the Missus *not* a lady she didn't like to take me, for I got a letter saying I sh'd not suit her'.[49]

Refusing to do certain jobs may also have been a way in which the work that was done by servants could be brought to their employers' notice. In the extract from Jane's letter quoted above, which describes Lady Ashburton's predicament with the dolls, Lady Ashburton acknowledged her dependence on her servants. The servants refused to do 'anything in the doll line' and that refusal made clear their necessity to their mistress 'when all the company come'. In this case servants refusing to do a job forced their mistress to contemplate the effect of bending them to her will and she realized her need for them. To avoid unpleasantness William Lanceley advised employers to 'explain as fully as possible the duties they are expected to undertake, and don't add, "Of course, you may be called

[48] 'A Maid of All Work's Diary 1864' Box 98 (15) Munby Collection, Wren Library, Trinity College, Cambridge University.
[49] 'A Servant's Life, 1866–72' Box 98 (17) Munby Collection, Wren Library, Trinity College, Cambridge University.

upon for some other little things". Most servants will take that as something you don't care to speak about.'[50]

Servants also gave meaning to the work they did by investing pride in a job well done. Some even saw their responsibility to the things they cared for as being as important as their responsibility to the people they served. An aged housemaid who had worked in the same household for thirty years was

> always proud to relate that for twenty-five years she had been in charge of the best dinner service and nothing had been broken or chipped. She would allow no one to handle the plates and dishes, but washed and wiped them herself and she alone would carry them to the dining-room door and wait there to bring them back to the house-maid's pantry where they were washed.[51]

There were several ways in which domestic servants could revenge themselves on employers they felt badly treated by. Spoiling food was one method, though it could go horribly wrong, as Eliza Smalley discovered when she put some mercury in her mistress's coffee in revenge for having been falsely accused of killing a fowl. 'I did not think it would have killed her, I only thought it would have made her badly,' Eliza told the constable who arrested her.[52] One cook claimed that '[s]ervants that feel they're being put upon can make it hard in the house in various ways like not rushing to answer bells, sullen dumb insolence and petty irritations to make up for what you're not getting.'[53] Jane Carlyle was irritated by such behaviour in one of her housemaids, who took

> a position in the House which was quite preposterous; domineering towards the cook, and impertinent towards me! picking and choosing at her *work* – in fact not behaving like a *servant* at all, but like a *lady*, who, for a caprice, or a wager, or anything except wages and board, – was condescending to exercise light functions in the house, *provided* you kept her in good humour with gifts and praises.[54]

Servants could also vote with their feet, leaving situations where they were unhappy. Catherine Bailey left her first place after a week: 'I couldn't do it, it was too heavy for me' she remembered.[55] One of Jane Carlyle's servants, when

---

[50] William Lanceley, *From Hall-Boy to House-Steward* in John Burnett (ed.), *Useful Toil*, 191.
[51] William Lanceley, *From Hall-Boy to House-Steward* in John Burnett (ed.), *Useful Toil*, 187.
[52] 15 November 1850 *The Times*.
[53] Margaret Powell, *Below Stairs* (London: Pan, 1968), 156.
[54] Letter 20 October 1862 in Alan and Mary McQueen Simpson (eds.), *I Too Am Here. Selections from the Letters of Jane Welsh Carlyle*, 147.
[55] Catherine Bailey, interviewed for Paul and Thea Thompson 'Family Life and Work Experience before 1918'.

her housekeeping skills were criticized 'declared "it was to be hoped I would get a person to keep my house cleaner than she had done; as she meant to leave that day month!"'[56] Another of Jane's servants left her in the lurch, provoking the following outburst, in which Jane expressed her sense of powerlessness through a reference to 'a Negro eating pumpkins' – this racist stereotype apparently being a preoccupation in the Carlyle household:

> My maid Elizabeth whom I had allowed to get the upper hand with me, lead [*sic*] me such a devil of a life after Mr C's departure, that I finally convinced myself I should be better as a Negro eating pumpkins than the so-called *mistress* of that young person – and so I gave her notice to quit at the end of the month, whereupon she would not wait till the end of the month, but rushed off in a day! leaving me with no servant, a house in a most "abnormal" condition, a visitor (Miss Jewsbury) expected for some days, and my own health all "gone to smithers" – But so long as one keeps alive one struggles thro better or worse, so, now, so now I have got things straight again, or nearly so, and have realized myself a country-girl for a servant, who has a temper as sweet as barley-sugar, but knows no more of cooking than an unfledged dove. And I am trying to teach her, God help me![57]

Here Jane also expresses a common preference for country girls as servants. Amongst urban mistresses, girls from rural areas had a reputation for docility and obedience relative to city girls. In this way ideas about the effects of urban living on class and gender identities were articulated through ideas about servant character.

One of the issues that seems to have riled many servants centred on their employers expecting too much and taking what was done for granted. William Lanceley highlighted this, pointing towards the servant's possession of privileged knowledge within the household: 'Ladies who are constantly finding fault with their servants, and pouring out their woes over five o'clock tea, would not feel flattered if they heard the remarks passed on them by the very people who so sympathized with them when relating the same.' Lanceley went on to threaten that '[i]f overheard by servants, they, in their turn will not fail to put the establishment on the black list and warn others not to go after a

---

[56] Letter October 1856 in Alan and Mary McQueen Simpson (eds.), *I Too Am Here. Selections from the Letters of Jane Welsh Carlyle*, 142.
[57] Letter 19 September 1850. Townsend Scudder (ed.), *Letters of Jane Welsh Carlyle to Joseph Neuberg 1848–1862* (Oxford: Oxford University Press, 1931), 16.

vacant situation there.'[58] The possible existence of such a 'black list' was a pre-occupation of many letters from servant employers to *The Times*, as we will see in Chapter 6.

Servants could also mark the limits of acceptable behaviour by leaving places where they felt their right to a personal life or expression of personal identity was overly restricted. This may have been the case with Linda Wilson, a servant in the employ of Mr Claxton, a farmer of Stoke Holy Cross, Norfolk. In February 1857 Linda absconded with 'nine 10 L notes belonging to her master, and having adopted male attire succeeded in getting quite away'.[59] The girl assumed the character of 'a "fast" young man' and 'travelled twice by railway from London to Edinburgh, and laid in a liberal supply of clothes, two church services and other books'.[60] Eventually they landed up in Great Yarmouth, where, 'still playing the part she had undertaken, she incurred a considerable tavern bill, bought cigars, and indulged in the usual diversions of youth'.[61] It wasn't long before they were apprehended by police on a charge of robbing their master when it was discovered that 'the foolish girl had dissipated nearly all her ill-gotten money'.[62] Though we can only speculate as to why Linda Wilson did this, it would seem that they sought an identity and freedom denied to them as a girl, and especially as a servant girl in 1857. It seems safe to say that the 'usual diversions of youth' in which they apparently indulged would certainly not have been usual for most young farm skivvies.

Religion was often problematic – to ensure religious conformity many employers insisted on servants' attendance at family prayers. This could cause difficulties when a servant's religion was different from that of her employer. Henry Mayhew interviewed a Catholic ex-servant who had left service partly because her employers 'was always running down my religion, and did all they could to hinder my ever going to Mass'.[63] Servants also left places because they were not allowed to dress as they pleased in their time off. 'Dress is another bogy', wrote William Lanceley, 'Most servants have sisters and brothers in business houses, especially those whose homes are in London, and they like to meet their own kin on something like the same footing … although [one household] was

---

[58] William Lanceley, *From Hall-Boy to House-Steward* in John Burnett (ed.), *Useful Toil*, 192.
[59] *The Times*, 5 February 1857, 6.
[60] *The Times*, 5 February 1857, 6.
[61] *The Times*, 5 February 1857, 6.
[62] *The Times*, 5 February 1857, 6.
[63] Peter Quennell (ed.), *Mayhew's Characters* (London: Spring Books, 1951), 149.

a most comfortable place, two years was about the longest servants stayed in it. They left for no other reason than the restriction in dress.'[64]

Abandonment by a servant could be of significant inconvenience to an employer as Jane Carlyle noted: 'I shall have to be training a new servant into the ways of the house (when I have got her) at a season of the year when it will be the most uphill work for her and me.'[65] Where leaving constituted a breach of contract, employers could and some did take their servants to court. This was another way in which the content of the 'private sphere' could leak into the public world, as the limits of acceptable behaviour in the employer-servant relationship were put to public judgement in the theatre of the courtroom.

The tensions of intimacy

From the moment she woke in the morning to the moment her head hit the pillow at night a domestic servant's time belonged to her employer. As Davidoff, Doolittle, Fink and Holden have written, '[t]he personal control of the servant's labour and time singled out the relationship and coloured the contract, as did the intimate nature of the work, caring for the bodies and the personal possessions of the employer and household'.[66] This intimate work could and often did involve more than just cleaning duties. Servants could have more intimate knowledge of the bodies of the family members they worked for than family members had of each other. In contrast with the physical distance maintained between servants and employers in the dining room and the parlour, in the bedroom and bathroom servants shared a bodily intimacy with their employers that still did not necessarily undermine their sense of social difference. Indeed, the physical differences between servants and employers were perhaps most evident in these moments. Differences in skin tone, in size and in smell did much to enhance, rather than collapse, perceptions of social difference.

In many households servants performed emotional work, sometimes relieving members of the household of the stress of dealing with children or ageing relatives, and in other cases providing emotional support to neurotic mistresses. Rose Allen was told by one would-be mistress that her 'duties would

---

[64] William Lanceley, *From Hall-Boy to House-Steward* in John Burnett (ed.), *Useful Toil*, 192.
[65] Letter October 1856 in Alan and Mary McQueen Simpson (eds.), *I Too Am Here. Selections from the Letters of Jane Welsh Carlyle*, 142.
[66] Leonore Davidoff, Megan Doolittle, Janet Fink and Katherine Holden, *The Family Story*, 165.

include sitting with your work in the room when Mr Bennett has the gout; I hardly ever do, he's so violent, and he requires someone at such times whom he can scold and abuse as he likes'.[67] Gertrude Lloyd leaned heavily on one of her nursemaids, Charlotte Scott, who according to Gertrude was 'such a superior, nice, quiet girl'.[68] Charlotte came to replace nurse Mary Cottrill who left after two and a half years with the family. Gertrude parted with Mary 'with not much regret for though fond of Baby, she spoils him, and is no comfort to <u>me</u> personally'.[69] Though the nurse was ostensibly engaged to care for the baby, it was her failure to provide comfort to her mistress that irked Gertrude.

Jane Carlyle often attempted to draw emotional sustenance from her relationship with her servants, though only rarely with any long-term success. Jane seems not to have known how to negotiate the boundaries between the servants' and her own territory. Several of her servants were frustrated by her 'interference' and gave notice. As well as noting her servants' appearance, as seems to have been fairly common amongst mistresses, Jane also noted whether they were 'clever' or not and spoke of slow or dim-witted servants with contempt, referring to one as a 'helpless, ill-trained, low-minded goose' and another as an 'Old Half-Dead Slowcoach'.[70] Jane seems to have wanted her servants to be more than employees – she enjoyed the intimacy of her relations with her servants and relished their grief when she was especially sick and their gratefulness when she was kind to them. Nevertheless, she was clear about the structure of authority in her household, and her entitlement as a white, middle-class woman to 'rule': 'I arrived yesterday, much in the state I expected, but also with a little "monarch of all I survey" feeling … In my life I think I never did so enjoy giving orders and being waited upon as last night, and being asked what I wanted and getting it!'[71]

Jane remained childless throughout her life and this fact may not be irrelevant in her apparent need for some kind of emotional connection with her servants. One girl in particular, Charlotte, she described as 'quite a jewel of a servant. Far more like an adopted child than a London maid-of-all-work'.[72] This turn of phrase points towards the paradox at the heart of Jane's relationship with Charlotte: on the one hand Charlotte was a servant Jane had employed to do

---

[67] Rose Allen, *Autobiography of Rose Allen* (London: Longman, 1847), 98–9.
[68] Gertrude Lloyd, 'Biography of Gerald Braithwaite Lloyd', 30 July 1888.
[69] Gertrude Lloyd, 'Biography of Gerald Braithwaite Lloyd', 29 July 1888.
[70] Letter 27 July 1852 in Alexander Carlyle, *New Letters and Memorials of Jane Welsh Carlyle* (London: John Lane, 1903), 38; Alan and Mary McQueen Simpson (eds.), *I Too Am Here. Selections from the Letters of Jane Welsh Carlyle*, 128.
[71] Letter 2 October 1847, J.A Froude (ed.), *Letters and Memorials of Jane Welsh Carlyle*, Vol. II, p11.
[72] Letter September 1852 in J.A Froude (ed.), *Letters and Memorials of Jane Welsh Carlyle*, Vol. II, 387.

work in her household. On the other Jane saw her as a surrogate child, and it was this, rather than her domestic skill, that made her 'a jewel of a servant' in Jane's eyes. Here, we can see how affect might shape the 'good servant' as a category of labour.

In fact, despite Jane's enjoyment of the household having 'something of the sound and character of a nursery', Charlotte's 'born tendency to muddle' meant she lasted only three years in the house.[73] Though Jane continued to regard her with affection and kept in touch with her long after she left Cheyne Row, Charlotte's inefficiency as a servant outweighed her value as 'adopted child'. In one letter Jane wrote that 'Charlotte, poor foolish thing! is still hanging on at her 'mother's.'[74] By putting the word 'mother' in inverted commas Jane implied that Charlotte's mother wasn't real. Is that what Jane desired? Perhaps the fact Charlotte already had a mother of her own meant that Jane could never really occupy that role in Charlotte's life and this meant her relationship with Jane could never be wholly satisfactory.

At other times Jane enjoyed being 'mothered' by her servants. In one letter to her husband she described her new servant as 'a good nurse, very quiet and kindly, and with the sense to do things without being told. I have not had my clothes folded neatly up, and the room tidied, and my wants anticipated in this way since I had no longer any mother to nurse me.'[75] Servants were often a comfort to Jane during her frequent illnesses:

> I took quite ill in the middle of the night – colic and such headache! ... If it had not been for Fanny's kindness, who, when all else that she could do failed, fairly took to crying and sobbing over me, I think I must have died of the horror and desolation of the thing ... Fanny is the best comfort I have had, so willing to flyover the moon for me and always making light of her discomforts.[76]

Servants were also useful in marital relations. Jane Carlyle trusted her servant's reports of her husband's welfare more than those from him, writing in a letter while away from home that '[m]y stay is determined by the accounts I get of Mr C from himself, and (still more dependably) from my housemaid Maria'.[77] Releasing women from the concerns of childcare, cookery and cleaning meant

---

[73] Letter 8 December 1860, J.A Froude (ed.), *Letters and Memorials of Jane Welsh Carlyle*, Vol. III, 67.

[74] Letter 19 October 1860, J.A Froude (ed.), *Letters and Memorials of Jane Welsh Carlyle*, Vol. III, 63–4.

[75] Letter 17 September 1860 in J.A Froude (ed.), *Letters and Memorials of Jane Welsh Carlyle*, Vol. III, 60–1.

[76] Jane Carlyle, Letter to Thomas Carlyle, September 1852 in J.A Froude (ed.), *Letters and Memorials of Jane Welsh Carlyle*, Vol. II, 183–6.

[77] Letter 14 August 1862 in J.A Froude (ed.), *Letters and Memorials of Jane Welsh Carlyle*, Vol. III, 111.

they could concentrate on being good wives, though the continued popularity of brothels and the proliferation of sexually transmitted diseases suggests not all men concentrated so hard on being good husbands. Indeed, the men of some households used their servants sexually. Some servants, like Sarah Jenkins of Llanelli who was seduced by her employer's son, entered into such relationships in the usually vain hope that it would lead to marriage.[78] Other servants were raped or assaulted, like Philander Kerry, a Stowmarket servant whose employer, the shopkeeper Edward Rust, ordered her to fetch water for him to wash, then undressed and confronted the girl who was in the bedroom, making his bed. Rust 'used the prerogatives of a master' to create a situation that would normalize his sexual appropriation of her; Philander's work, particularly bathing her master, involved such bodily intimacy that the step from demanding personal to sexual service was an easy one for her employer to take.[79]

Servants were often young girls. The 1871 census shows that nearly one in three housemaids was under the age of twenty and in many households servants were isolated from support networks of friends and family. Placed in the 'private sphere' and legally defined as dependants of their master, the formalities structuring other relationships between employers and employees were absent in the master-servant relationship. This made servants particularly vulnerable to those employers who believed their rights as master included helping themselves to their servants' bodies. Employers who behaved in this way took absolute possession of their servants' bodies – having employed them, they behaved as if they owned them. Though this was rarely spoken about other than in the context of the courtroom, it is likely that it was not an infrequent occurrence.

Intimacy can lead to insecurity, particularly when an intimate is not completely trusted. Servants possessed intimate knowledge of their employers' lives, working as they did within the most private areas of the private sphere. Most employers appear to have known little about their servants' personal lives; in letters and memoirs mistresses rarely mention a servant's family or friends, unless the mistress is inconvenienced by them falling sick or wishing to marry a servant. This is not to say that employers were not aware of their servants' connections to other worlds. In fact, masters and mistresses were aware of such connections and were rather afraid of them. This anxiety in part drove employers' enforcement of rituals of deference and strict rules of behaviour for

---

[78] Russell Davies, 'In a Broken Dream: Some Aspects of Sexual Behaviour and the Dilemmas of the Unmarried Mother in South-west Wales 1887–1914', *Llafur* 3 (1983), 26.

[79] Case cited in Shani D'Cruze, *Crimes of Outrage. Sex, Violence and Victorian Working Women* (London: UCL Press, 1998), 89.

servants. Even though employers had an apparent monopoly on overt power, the asymmetry of knowledge in the relationship was weighted in the servant's favour. Servants' maintenance of this asymmetry – the refusal to allow their employers access to their own private lives – may be thought of as an act of (possibly unconscious) agency.

Although servants were central to middle-class lifestyle and self-image, the idealization of a specifically middle-class secluded family existence meant that servants could be seen as alien within the house, representing a dangerous conduit to the world of poverty and dirt beyond its civilization. Thackeray described such fears in characteristically emotive language:

> In your house and mine there are mysteries unknown to us. I am not going into the horrid question of 'followers'. I don't mean cousins from the country, love-stricken policemen, or gentlemen in mufti from Knightsbridge Barracks; but people who have an occult right on the premises: the uncovenanted servants of the house; grey women who are seen at evening with baskets flitting about area railings; dingy shawls which drop you furtive curtsies in your neighbourhood; demure little jacks, who start up from behind boxes in the pantry ... Then again those *servi servorum* have dependants in the vast, silent, poverty-stricken world outside your comfortable kitchen fire, in the world of darkness, and hunger, and miserable cold, and dank, flagged cellars, and huddled straw, and rags, in which pale children are swarming.[80]

Anthea Trodd has noted that in Victorian crime novels in the second half of the nineteenth century, servants 'appear as spies and blackmailers, or as witnesses, exposing to the outside world through their distraught behaviour the secret their employers are capable of concealing'.[81] Employers' fears could be justified. Jane Carlyle described catching one of her maids 'listening at the door; and the second morning I came upon her reading one of my Letters! And in every little box, drawer and corner I found *traces* of her prying.'[82]

Servants' relationships with their own families and followers were a source of particular tension for employers. Some employers were afraid of the privacy of the family being breached by gossip leaking from the house. For example, Jane Carlyle was careful about what she said in front of one of her servants 'knowing

---

[80] W.M. Thackeray, 'On a Chalk-Mark on the Door', *Roundabout Papers* (London, 1876) quoted in Anthea Trodd, 'Household Spies: The Servants and the Plot in Victorian Fiction', *Literature and History* 13, 2 (1987), 178.

[81] Anthea Trodd, 'Household Spies: The Servants and the Plot in Victorian Fiction', 178.

[82] Jane Carlyle, Letter 27 July 1852 in Alexander Carlyle, *New Letters and Memorials of Jane Welsh Carlyle*, 38.

that she carried everything to her Mother'.[83] For other employers, external loyalties
to family or friends always had to come second to loyalty to the employing family.
Whether this was simply a result of employers' lack of consideration or part of a
conscious effort to enforce an order of priority onto servants that would ensure the
employer's control is not clear. Whatever, Hannah Cullwick was denied permission
to visit her dying parents. Her account of her 'Places', written in 1872, poignantly
reads: 'So I never saw them again, for they died of a fever just a fortnight 'twixt each
other & my Missis wouldn't let me go. They died on the same day and at the same
hour as one another, only a fortnight between – on a Saturday at ten o'clock in the
morning'.[84] Hannah was fourteen years old. Harriet Rogers, housekeeper at Erddig
in Wrexham, found it difficult not to disappoint her friends, damaging her relations
with them:

> So often have we looked forward to the pleasure of your visit but as often as we
> have looked we have been disappointed and for what reason? First because Miss
> Rogers had not the courage to ask Mrs Yorke for a week's leave ... the longer you
> remain satisfied with so little liberty the longer you shall be ... We have made up
> our minds that if you do not come and see us, we will never call again.[85]

Followers were a great problem for employers. They represented another
connection with the world beyond the house and family and advice books
recommended that servants' meetings with followers be carefully regulated.
Many employers specified that no followers were allowed and breaking this
rule could cause significant upset. For example, the future wife of the second
Philip Yorke of Erddig noted in her diary that her father was outraged on finding
their cook speaking to her suitor at the back door.[86] For an employer in a settled
household followers were a potential nuisance – a servant who married a suitor
would either leave service, or if she or he stayed in service would have a demand
on her or his time that might inconvenience the employer, as was the case with
Louisa Bain's neighbours:

> Our neighbours, two maiden ladies, have for some time had the wife of their man
> as a temporary cook, and the other evening the good woman was thoughtless

---

[83] Letter January 1863 in Alan and Mary McQueen Simpson (eds.), *I Too Am Here. Selections from the Letters of Jane Welsh Carlyle*, 151.

[84] 'Hannah's Places' Box 98 (14) Munby Collection, Wren Library, Trinity College, Cambridge University.

[85] Letter from J.C. Maddocks to Harriet Rogers, 28 July 1861, quoted in Merlin Waterson, *The Servant's Hall. A Domestic History of Erddig* (London: Routledge, 1980), 85.

[86] Merlin Waterson, *The Servant's Hall. A Domestic History of Erddig*, 85.

enough to give birth to a baby which was not expected for some time. After a few days the old ladies left home on a visit, leaving the invalid to recover at her leisure, and as both man and wife are great favourites they will be inclined to overlook the liberty taken by the mother and child.[87]

Advice manuals and articles expressed a general concern that followers could lead a servant down a vice-ridden path to disaster for both servant and family. It was feared by many that servants would make unfortunate matches and end up in unhappy marriages or worse, that they might bring misfortune into the house by allowing thieving ne'er-do-wells and seducers over its threshold.

Jane Carlyle's sense of outrage and violation on discovering that one of her servants, Mary, had given birth to an illegitimate child in the crockery pantry while Carlyle was taking tea in the next room 'with Miss Jewsbury talking to him!!! Just a thin small door between them!' is palpable.[88] It is unclear whether Jane was more outraged by the illegitimate birth or the fact that it happened in the room next door to the one in which Carlyle was entertaining a guest. Perhaps, to the childless Jane, there was a sting in the fact that her servant had, by having a baby in the house, brought her fecundity and external sexual life into it. It is evident that more than anything, Jane was upset by the deception. She was angry at her exclusion from knowledge of these events until a much later date and deeply hurt and humiliated by the by-now-obvious falseness of her servant's affection for her. 'Now, my Dear,' she wrote to her friend Mrs Russell,

> if you had seen the creature Mary you would just as soon have suspected the Virgin Mary of such things! But I have investigated, and find it all true. For two years I have been cheated and made a fool of, and laughed at for my softness, by this half idiotic-looking woman; and while she was *crying* up in my room, moaning out: 'What would become of her if I died?' and witnessing in me as sad a spectacle of human agony as could have been anywhere seen; she was giving suppers to men and women downstairs; laughing and swearing – oh I can't go on. It is too disgusting![89]

Jane's sense of vulnerability in relation to her servants is clear. Mary had betrayed Jane's trust and it was this, rather than the scandal of illegitimacy, that

---

[87] Louisa Bain's Diary 22 October 1874 in James. S. Bain, *A Bookseller Looks Back. The Story of the Bains*.

[88] Letter 12 November 1864, Alan and Mary McQueen Simpson (eds.), *I Too Am Here. Selections from the Letters of Jane Welsh Carlyle*, 156.

[89] Letter 12 Nov 1864, Alan and Mary McQueen Simpson (eds.), *I Too Am Here. Selections from the Letters of Jane Welsh Carlyle*, 156.

had upset Jane the most. Once again it is clear that in Jane Carlyle's case the needs of the mistress included more than just a demand for physical service.

'Class pride and discomfort with the cash nexus' may have contributed to employers' preference for their servants to be as segregated as possible.[90] Servants' presence in the household constituted a point at which the domesticated and working worlds could bleed into each other. As such, their work had to be routinized so that it caused as little disruption to the family as possible. Servants moved through the houses they worked in differently from their employers. They entered and exited the house through different routes; they used different staircases; they slept in rooms that should, according to one advice book writer, be minimally furnished to 'resemble the homes of their youth, and to be merely places where they lie down to sleep as heavily as they can.'[91] Lilian Westall remembered such a bleak bedroom:

> My room was in the attic. There was a little iron bed in the corner, a wooden chair and a washstand. It was a cold, bare, utterly cheerless room. At night I used to climb the dark stairs to the gloomy top of the house, go over to my bed, put the candle on the chair, fall on my knees, say my prayers and crawl into bed too tired to wash.[92]

Anthea Trodd has noted that in Victorian novels a servant out of place in a house could signal a disruption to the order of life. She gives the example of Wilkie Collins' *The Moonstone* in which the maid Rosanna's 'distracted appearances in places where servants should not be, such as the library and the billiard room, offer the most visible clue to the mysterious derangement of the household.'[93]

Domestic servants protected their employers from defilement, by dealing with the rough, dirty and polluting elements of life.[94] However, servants could also be seen as carriers of pollution as they mediated between dirt and cleanliness, indoors and outdoors, the working and the middle classes. As Davidoff points out, 'those closest to defiling and arduous activities were, whenever possible to be kept out of sight. In great houses their existence was denied.'[95] In the household of the tenth Duke of Bedford, to 'cross his path, unless he wished to see you, was little short of a crime, and any of the women servants who met him after twelve

---

[90] John Tosh, *A Man's Place. Masculinity and the Middle-Class Home in Victorian England*, 47.

[91] Mrs J.E. Panton, *From Kitchen to Garrett* (London: Ward and Downey, 1893).

[92] Lilian Westall in John Burnett (ed.), *Useful Toil*, 216.

[93] Anthea Trodd, 'Household Spies: The Servants and the Plot in Victorian Fiction', 182.

[94] Leonore Davidoff, *Worlds Between*, 24–5.

[95] Leonore Davidoff, *Worlds Between*, 25.

o'clock in the day, when their duties might be supposed to be done,' could be dismissed as a result.[96]

In the minority of more affluent houses the domestic work would be divided between a number of different servants, whose roles were distinct, complementary and organized according to a strict service hierarchy, which an ambitious servant would aim to climb. This hierarchy was 'an exact copy of the order of precedence "above stairs"; an unwritten code, it presumably originated in aristocratic households and spread by example to become the accepted pattern in Victorian times, doubtless approved by employers as inculcating a proper respect for rank and authority'.[97] In households such as this lower servants protected even the upper servants from defiling activities. Lower servants would deal with the scullery, the slops and the chamberpots, the degradation associated with such activities contributing to the sense of their lowly status. The upper servants then mediated between the lower servants and the family.[98] As Mrs C.S. Peel wrote, the head servants

> were regarded by the under-servants, shut away in their own quarters and never permitted to be seen in the front part of the house after the family and their guests had left their bedrooms, almost as kings and queens. Only the head servants, body servants, and those in attendance on the sitting rooms, or dining room, would be even likely to know their employers by sight.[99]

Servants' contact with family members needed to be controlled, particularly with regard to children. The polluting influence of a servant could include influencing children's behaviour and attitudes in ways unapproved by the child's parents. As we will see, this was also a concern for Anglo-Indian employers in India. In both sites of empire – metropolitan and colonial – middle-class white English supremacy was authorized through a particular kind of comportment. In her diary Gertrude Lloyd described feeling 'horrified' at her 'little gentle boy' who was 'lately so very disobedient & speaks rudely to me & very to C & puts his tongue out & called Miss Taylor here "old Fatty"! … Emma (cook) at home teaches him to say all sorts of queer things, she goes out to him in the garden and plays with him'.[100] Charles Dickens articulated anxiety about the influence servants could have on children in his essay 'Nurse's Stories' in which he

[96] quoted in Pamela Horn, *The Rise and Fall of the Victorian Servant*, 24.
[97] John Burnett (ed.), *Useful Toil*, 150.
[98] Leonore Davidoff, *Worlds Between*, 25.
[99] Mrs C.S. Peel, 'Homes and Habits' in G.M.Young (ed.), *Early Victorian England* (Oxford: Oxford University Press, 1934), 81–2 quoted in Pamela Horn, *The Rise and Fall of the Victorian Servant*, 24.
[100] Gertrude Lloyd, Biography of Gerald Braithwaite Lloyd, July 1890.

stated: 'if we all knew our own minds (in a more enlarged sense than the popular acceptation of that phrase), I suspect we should find our nurses responsible for most of the dark corners we are forced to go back to, against our wills'.[101]

Domestic servants' intimacy with the children they served was threatening to some employers. Part of the resentment expressed by women such as Gertrude Lloyd was caused by their fear of being usurped by the servant. Gertrude wrote rather wistfully about the time she spent with her one and a half year old son: 'I have him from 7.15 to 45 in our bed & downstairs from 9.40 to 10.30 & again from 2 till 2.45 & then he comes in the drawing room from 5.15 to 5.45 when he is undressed – so altogether I see plenty of our son and heir'. The time totalled two hours and thirty-five minutes out of an entire day. The baby spent the rest of the time with his nursemaid. This is indicative of the intimacy of the position nursemaids occupied, and of their functional role in family relations, which in itself may have produced ambivalence in mistresses. Insecurity about parenting is clearly expressed in Gertrude's diary. Of course, other mistresses welcomed a servant acting as intermediary between them and their children. Lucy Hitchman, nursemaid to Lousia Yorke's children, wrote to tell her absent mistress that she and the children were 'pleased to hear how much you are enjoying your visits',

> I hope you will be as pleased with your little son, when you return he seems to have grown, even in the short time of your absence, he walks <u>all the way along</u> the nursery passage now from one nursery to the other & so carefully just like a little bird, using his hands to balance his little self instead of wings.[102]

Rather than express bitterness or ambivalence that she was missing out on her children's first steps, Louisa Yorke seemed happy with Lucy's care of her sons, writing in her diary: 'We like Lucy, the nurse, so much. She is young, only 26, but so careful with the little boy'.[103]

While many middle-class families would not have employed a maid specifically as nurse, servants' diaries and reminiscences show that childcare was often a part of the housemaid or maid-of-all-work's duties. For example, Hannah Cullwick frequently noted in her diary of 1860 when working for the Jackson family as a maid-of-all-work that she 'took the children in the garden'

---

[101] Charles Dickens, 'Nurse's Stories' in *An Uncommercial Traveller* (New York: George Munro, 1884), 106.

[102] Undated letter from Lucy Hitchman to Louisa Yorke, Erddig MSS/D/E/2831, Clwyd County Record Office, Hawarden.

[103] Louisa Yorke's diary 30 July 1903, Erddig MSS D/E/2816, Clwyd County Record Office, Hawarden.

and 'took care of the children & put them to bed'.[104] Even while distancing rituals were employed to shut the other servants out of the inner sanctum of the family, the maid's influence was ever-present within the relationship between middle-class parent and child. The maid's role was important in the making of the identities of middle-class mothers, fathers and children, and to the process of the relationship between them. The work of the nursemaid and the release it afforded parents was necessarily implicated in the way in which their roles were gendered and classed. Moreover, through relations with servants middle-class children learned a 'habit of command' that was imagined to be important for people of their status in the imperial metropole.

Masters and mistresses in the nineteenth and early twentieth centuries certainly bore a general suspicion towards their servants' possession of intimate knowledge of the family and its foibles. They felt threatened by their servants as a potential conduit, polluting the family with the dirt, disorder and degradation of the world beyond the family, and releasing into that world the secrets and knowledge gleaned from their intimate work within the house. If servants' difference, their connections to other worlds, their loyalties to their own friends and families were perceived as liabilities for their employers, the enforcement of strict rules in some households constituted an effort to secure control over servants and their links to areas potentially beyond their employers' power. Servants were expected to be quiet and to express their subservience through their body language. Catherine Bailey remembered of her first place that her mistress wouldn't let her maids 'work together. She would not. Didn't like talk, you see …. You couldn't be alone and talk. Never left you alone, you know. You mustn't talk'.[105] Such a rule could exacerbate feelings of loneliness in young domestic servants such as Stanley Wilson Bailey, who recalled

> the loneliness, I mean to say every night you was put in a special back room you see and – you had nobody to speak to, you had no – I mean you was treated as a boy you know. You were shoved up in a corner. There was no – there was no companionship. And a boy in those days wanted a companionship. So I scarpered. Yes. So did me sister, she was sent out to service. One of the big nobs up in Stamford Hill … My sister was sent up there, she come – she come home after a week.[106]

---

[104] 15, 18, 29 July 1860 in '1860 A Few Fragments', Box 98, Munby Collection, Wren Library, Trinity College, Cambridge University.

[105] Catherine Bailey, interviewed by Paul and Thea Thompson for 'Family Life and Work Experience before 1918'.

[106] Mr Stanley Wilson Bailey, interviewed by Paul and Thea Thompson for 'Family Life and Work Experience before 1918'.

Catherine Bailey was one of two maids employed in the household of a butcher, and the mistress worked alongside them both. The gendered and classed ideal of the non-working mistress who managed, rather than worked in, the household was little more than a dream for many wives. This tension between the ideal and the reality may have contributed to the often ambivalent and sometimes downright hostile and even abusive attitude mistresses could exhibit towards their servants, evidenced in a steady stream of court cases throughout our period (we will consider this in Chapter 5). However, more frequently, mistresses' need to endorse their power and superiority over their servants manifested in the enforcement of rules of behaviour for them. These rituals of deference worked towards establishing the employers' authority over their servants, while marking the difference between the domestic and working worlds. The rationale underpinning deference rituals was linked to the concept of 'Society' and the duty to uphold the practices of what was perceived to be the 'civilized' world. Certain etiquettes such as the rituals of dining and mourning constituted the implementation of these beliefs. Servants were central to this process, both in terms of their physical work and the performance of submission to their employers that shaped the way that work was done. For example, servants remained silent while a family dined, moving forward to the table to serve food or respond to demands, speaking only when spoken to, keeping eyes downcast and body movements minimal while they completed their tasks. Even in modest households such rituals were observed insofar as possible.

Rituals of deference marked class and gender distinctions, and the relations of power those distinctions organized. By behaving in servile ways, domestic servants gave their employers a sense of superiority regardless of their individual quality of character. 'The superior was thus guaranteed a minimum of deference even if he was "alone" in his own home, i.e. with only his servant or servants':

> Servants stood when spoken to and kept their eyes cast down, they moved out of a room backwards, curtsied to their betters and were generally expected to efface themselves; doing their work and moving about the house so as not to be visible or audible to their employers … In the street, servants, male or female, walked a few paces behind their master or mistress.[107]

---

[107] Leonore Davidoff, *Worlds Between*, 24, 112.

Deference rituals were one way employers made servants embody subservience. In India perceived differences in the colour of skin also marked out who was the master and who was the servant. In Britain uniforms distinguished the servant from the family, signifying the employers' authority by making servants look the same as each other, interchangeable, on display in much the same way as the furnishings.[108] The notion of a uniform for servants had been in development from the early nineteenth century and by the 1860s there was a recognized uniform for female domestic servants.[109] This was, as Catherine Bailey remembered, 'a print dress and a white apron and cap. Then in the afternoon it was a black dress, little starched apron and cap.'[110]

In a similar way to the common custom of changing a servant's name to something that was easy for the employer to remember, uniforms undermined servants' individuality. Discomfort with servants' expression of individuality through dress was linked to their connection to other worlds, as it pointed towards an alternative existence for servants, an existence outside the household that did not revolve around, nor was primarily loyal to, the house and family, but concerned the servant's own pleasure. By dressing as they pleased in their time off, servants threw off a persona adopted for work and insisted on by their employers, and took on one of their own choosing. This told masters and mistresses that their servants were not completely controlled and suggested that the deference shown during working hours was bought rather than a genuine expression of subordination. Some servants attempted to adapt their uniforms by adding ribbon or lace to their caps – a practice frowned upon by advice book writers like Mrs Motherley who advised servants that a 'gaudily-dressed servant looks, at best, like a coarse and vulgar lady'.[111] Louisa Bain associated her housemaid's appearance with her personality, remarking in her diary that the maid had 'a large crinoline that almost sweeps one into the ashes. Have suggested to her that it is too large for our small rooms ... but I fancy people with such crisp, wavy hair as she has are generally obstinate.'[112]

[108] Like Liz Stanley I take 'uniform' to include 'hair, speech and demeanour', Liz Stanley (ed.) *The Diaries of Hannah Cullwick* (New Jersey: Virago, 1984), 32.

[109] John Burnett (ed.), *Useful Toil*, 171–2.

[110] Catherine Bailey, interviewed by Paul and Thea Thompson for 'Family Life and Work Experience before 1918'.

[111] Mrs Motherley, *The Servant's Behaviour Book* (London: Bell and Daldy, 1859), 87.

[112] Louisa Bain's Diary November 1865 in in James. S. Bain, *A Bookseller Looks Back. The Story of the Bains*.

Conclusion

The nostalgic image of the faithful retainer or nanny permeates many memoirs. There were employers who looked on their servants as family members, but the experience of Nora Blewett, who used to 'love being with my mistress there in the daytime. Cos she used to chat away as if she was my mother to me,' was rare.[113] The definition of who should be included in 'the family' was a shifting and troublesome one through the nineteenth century.[114] Servants were legally dependants of the household and its master. They were a part of the household in that they worked for the family and the family was responsible for feeding and training them. Domestic ideology constructed the orderly domestic sphere as a pedagogic place at the heart of morality, society and empire. Ideally service would prove a useful preparation for young lower-class girls, teaching them useful skills and their place within a social hierarchy. In this ideological context, by teaching working-class women how to be servants many employers saw themselves as encouraging working-class people more generally towards suitably respectable and subservient roles. Certainly, the *Sydenham and Penge Gazette* of 1892 was sure of the natural order of relations between servants and employers, claiming that 'the highly educated class or "head" of the social body should occupy itself in doing *its* proper work of *thinking* for the welfare of the hands and feet that serve it'.[115] The problem was that those hands and feet often seemed to have minds of their own.

---

[113] Nora Blewett interviewed by Paul and Thea Thompson for 'Family Life and Work Experience before 1918'.

[114] Leonore Davidoff, Megan Doolittle, Janet Fink and Katherine Holden, *The Family Story*, 160–1.

[115] quoted in Leonore Davidoff, Megan Doolittle, Janet Fink and Katherine Holden, *The Family Story*, 166.

4

Colonizing the private sphere: Making a home from home in colonial India

Domesticity was an important part of the apparatus of coloniality. As in Britain, the colonial household in India was conceived as a key site for the making of 'civilization'. This 'civilization', of course, was a specifically British imperial invention that interacted with the organization of domestic relationships and practices. The colonial home was a place for the exercise of imperial authority, and ideally for the making of Britons and Indians into colonizer and colonized according to the 'rule of colonial difference'.[1] But the politics of dependence within Anglo-Indian colonial households were not necessarily so straightforward. As in the metropole, the liminal status of Indian servants afforded them a degree of agency, and their intimate knowledge of their employers both enhanced and disrupted the certainties of categories of difference associated with race, gender and class. This ambivalence of power was a part of the complex coloniality of the household: colonialism was a process that encompassed and transformed the identities of both Britons and Indians, perhaps nowhere more clearly than in the intimate relations of home. The rigor of 'domesticity' could provide a way of managing the anxieties this process could provoke. In this chapter we will consider some of the ways British employers tried to understand and control the effect Indian servants had on their lives.

By the mid-nineteenth century, 'race' had captured the imagination of the British public. Race had emerged in the late eighteenth and early nineteenth centuries as method of categorizing humans according to their physical appearance. It was not a neutral system of categorization: it emerged in the context of the development of globalizing networks of trade, most importantly

---

[1] Partha Chatterjee, *The Nation and Its Fragments: Colonial and Post-Colonial Histories* (Princeton: Princeton University Press, 1993), 10. See also Alison Blunt 'Imperial Geographies of Home: British Domesticity in India 1886–1925', *Transactions of the Institute of British Geographers*, 24, 4 (1999): 421–40.

that of the Atlantic slave trade. The profits from trade such as in enslaved people and opium, and that with captive colonial markets such as India, financed the industrialization of Britain, its extraction of resources from its empire and its development as a modern capitalist economy. As a concept and a system of social organization 'race' justified the oppression and exploitation by Europeans, for profit, of millions of people all over the world, even while people in Europe – especially Britain – were styling themselves as the arbiters of morality within, and the bringers of civilization to, the societies they colonized or otherwise exploited.[2]

By the mid-nineteenth century, the racist views of men like Robert Knox, Thomas Carlyle and Charles Dickens had gained popularity, spreading easily as result of cheap printing and increased literacy.[3] Racial difference offered a convenient explanation for the restiveness of colonized people, which in India in 1857 erupted into widespread rebellion. Race and gender intersected: racisms borrowed from gender stereotypes to give meaning to their content.[4] Class also interacted unevenly with racial thinking. It differentiated whiteness. It also shaped perspectives as to which colonized people might be incorporated into the administration of colonial governance, and debates as to how more generally the 'native' population should be governed. Some British officials believed elite Indian men should be provided with an English education, so that they could then serve the colonial government. Others took an uncompromisingly authoritarian approach and focussed on inculcating habits of industry and frugality in lower-status Indian people, believing poverty to be rooted in indigenous ignorance and sinfulness.[5] Moreover, the classing of race was gendered. For example, in the case of the Ilbert Bill controversy of 1883, when Anglo-Indian society convulsed with anxiety at the prospect of Indian judges trying Europeans in criminal cases in the *mofussil* (rural areas), savage sexuality as well as vindictive maliciousness was suggested as typical of both 'low-class' Indian servants and as evidence of the 'true' nature of all Indians.[6]

---

[2]   F.C. Dussart, 'Liberty, History and the Making of Whiteness', *Medium*, 5 June 2020. https://medium.com/@f.c.dussart/liberty-history-and-the-making-of-whiteness-2bda0ea94954

[3]   See for example Thomas Carlyle, 'Occasional Discourse on the Negro Question', *Fraser's Magazine for Town and Country*, XL (1849): 670–9; Charles Dickens, 'The Noble Savage', *Household Words*, 7, 168 (1853): 337–9; Robert Knox, *The Races of Man. A Fragment* (Philadelphia: Lea and Blanchard, 1850).

[4]   See Mrinalini Sinha, *Colonial Masculinity. The 'Manly Englishman' and the 'Effeminate Bengali' in the Late Nineteenth Century* (Manchester: Manchester University Press, 1995).

[5]   See Clive Dewey, *Anglo-Indian Attitudes: The Mind of the Civil Service* (London: Hambledon, 1993).

[6]   Fae Dussart '"To Glut a Menial's Grudge" Domestic Servants and the Ilbert Bill Controversy of 1883', *The Journal of Colonialism and Colonial History*, 14, 1 (2013), n.p.

Anglo-Indians' identities as Anglo-Indians, and their connection to Englishness, were structured by their superiority over Indians, symbolized by their retention of racial privileges and on a microcosmic scale by their absolute control over their households, staffed by adult male native servants. Perceived threats to racial superiority were often evidenced by claims that native servants were becoming insolent, and that this was caused by disregard by the official class of the vulnerabilities of their non-official compatriots. For example, in the context of the Ilbert Bill controversy a member of the Viceroy's Council, Gibbs, wrote to the then Viceroy, Lord Ripon, to inform him that he had been told that the feeling against the Bill was 'not really caused by the Bill' but was 'the result of the measures taken during the past three or four years all over the *Mofussil*'.[7] According to Gibbs' letter, Anglo-Indians in the *Mofussil* felt 'that the Government are determined to put down the European, and raise the native to the detriment of the former' and that they complained that

> their native servants are not respectful, as they used to be, and that among that class, as well as generally among the great portion of the native urban population, the idea had sprung up, and is openly stated that your Lordship came out simply to 'put the native on the gadi' (throne) as they say, and benefit them at the cost of the Europeans.[8]

Servants were often used to evidence the barbarity of 'the Indian', throughout the nineteenth century, across the shift from Company to Crown control of the colony. Anglo-Indian attitudes towards servants did reflect the wider feelings of antipathy towards Indian people that were consolidated by the uprising of 1857–8, but this was not a profound or sudden shift. British ideas about servants were remarkably consistent, not only across time, but also across space. Characteristics associated with servants in metropolitan Britain, such as a tendency for dishonesty, were also attributed to Indian servants. Under Company rule domestic servants had been seen by many employers as a necessary evil, and they continued to be a source of complaint after the establishment of Crown control of India. The fact that there does not seem to have been any great change in attitudes towards servants before and after 1857 may be due to the peculiar intimacies and anxieties of the servant-employer relationship. Some servants were loyal to their employers during the uprising, risking their own lives for

---

[7] Letter from Gibbs to Ripon, 23 March 1883, *The Marquis of Ripon. Correspondence with Persons in India 1883*, BP 7/6, 173.

[8] Letter from Gibbs to Ripon, March 23 1883, *The Marquis of Ripon, Correspondence with Persons in India, 1883*, BP 7/6, 173.

those of the families they served; others turned on or abandoned the families and individuals they worked for. Since many employers appear to have mistrusted their servants as a matter of course, perhaps those who 'betrayed' them simply confirmed pre-existing ideas about the untrustworthiness of servants, ideas that were then mapped onto the character of 'the native' more generally.[9] As for those who were loyal, their loyalty could be seen in the context of ties to the family, developed through service, which overrode other allegiances to community or kin. Such servants proved the effectiveness of domesticity as part of the apparatus of imperial governance and contributed to a different kind of racialization that appears throughout representations of life under the Raj: that of the subservient native and benevolent master.

The problem of caste

The class categories by which society in nineteenth-century England was increasingly stratified were transformed in the Indian colonial context. Social rank depended on official position on the whole, and military families ranked below those in which the husband held a government position.[10] Status in the metropole was of relatively little consequence in determining social ranking in early nineteenth-century India, but the signifiers of high rank were similar nonetheless. As one commentator put it, India provided the opportunity for 'clerks' and 'pedlars' to sit on 'the thrones of Aurangzebe'.[11] Early nineteenth-century images of Anglo-Indians attended by retinues of servants display references to stereotypes of the indulged European aristocrat and the court of the 'oriental' prince. Englishness was re-defined in India, as a uniquely Anglo-Indian way of life endorsed European power in an 'Indian idiom'.[12] Eliza Fay described Madras society as characterized by 'Asiatic splendour, combined with

---

[9]   The common use of the generic word 'native' not only had the effect of homogenizing Indian people within the subcontinent, but also with colonized peoples who were also called 'natives' in other sites of Empire.

[10] Although it is important to note that those who worked for the civil service or became army officers would most likely be drawn from the middle class. Collingham has suggested that 'they came from a circumscribed section of the traditional middle class' and 'among both civilians and army officers the aristocracy, small-scale businessmen, artisans and men of the new entrepreneurial middle class, were under-represented'. E.M. Collingham, *Imperial Bodies* (Cambridge: Polity, 2001), 20; Of course, due their whiteness, those working-class men who occupied the lowest ranks of Anglo-Indian society always had the edge on most Indians.

[11] James M.Holzman, quoted by E.M. Collingham, *Imperial Bodies*, 21.

[12] Javeed Majeed, *Ungoverned Imaginings. James Mill's 'The History of British India' and Orientalism* (Oxford: Oxford University Press, 1992), 22.

European taste exhibited around you on every side, under the forms of flowing drapery, stately palanquins, elegant carriages, innumerable servants, and all the pomp and circumstance of luxurious ease and unbounded wealth'.[13] As discussed in Chapter 2, the large numbers of servants employed by the British were an important status symbol, assisting Englishmen, mostly of modest beginnings, in usurping and mimicking the lives of elites both Indian and English:

> The Anglo-Indian did not carry his own chattah (an umbrella traditionally signifying royalty), this was carried by a chattah bearer; if he stirred more than a few yards out of doors he was relieved of the necessity of walking by the use of his palanquin; washing and dressing required little exertion on his part as he was ministered to by a bevy of attendants.[14]

Anglo-Indians were aware that such large numbers of servants would seem 'ridiculous, not to say extravagant' to families and friends in England and the complaint that it was 'not a matter of choice, but of necessity' was a common one throughout the nineteenth century.[15] The most frequent explanation throughout the century given for this 'necessity' was that it was a product of caste restrictions upon servants' activities, which were believed to 'render the occupations of all perfectly distinct'.[16] As Minnie Wood wrote to her mother in 1857: 'Each department has a Servant of a <u>caste</u> which does <u>not</u> permit them to do anything else consequently it <u>obliges</u> one to keep more than one would wish.'[17] However, the scholars and administrators of the eighteenth and early nineteenth centuries were to a large extent responsible for the rigid categories of behaviour associated with caste that determined servants' occupations. Part of the process by which India's laws and 'traditions' were codified and categorized involved cataloguing castes and their associated occupations, including those of domestic servants, fixing in text and image as rules what had been relatively flexible relations between caste and occupation.[18] Nicholas B. Dirks has controversially written, '[c]aste ... is a colonial construction, reminiscent only in some ways

---

[13] Mrs Eliza Fay, *Original Letters from India (1779–1815)* (London: Hogarth, 1925), 162.

[14] E.M. Collingham, *Imperial Bodies*, 22.

[15] Mrs Eliot James, *Indian Household Management* (London: Ward, Lock and Co, 1879), 46; Mrs Murray Mitchell, *In India: Sketches of Indian Life and Travel from Letters and Journals* (London: T. Nelson and Sons, 1876), 71.

[16] Thomas Williamson, *The East India Vade-Mecum; or Complete Guide to Gentlemen Intended for the Civil, Military or Naval Service of the Honourable East India Company*, Vol. I (London: Black, Parry and Kingsbury, 1810), 181.

[17] 10 March 1857, Letters of Maria Lydia Wood, MSS/Eur/B210, India Office Records, Asia Pacific and African Collections, British Library (hereafter IOR). Emphasis as in original.

[18] E.M. Collingham, *Imperial Bodies*, 18; See also Nicholas B. Dirks, 'Castes of Mind', *Representations*, 37 (1992): 56–78 for further discussion of this process.

of the social forms that preceded colonial intervention.[19] It was not in servants'
interest to challenge the British belief that caste restrictions were fixed, because
the decline of the Mughal aristocracy meant that many servants needed work,
and the differentiation of tasks ensured employment for the greatest number.[20]
Also, the assertion of caste arguably provided a way for servants to resist the
absolutism of their employers' authority. Indeed many writers appear to have
felt that servants asserted caste restrictions simply to irritate their employers,
as Edward Braddon's words suggest: 'Caste or custom forbids that the Indian
servant should make himself generally useful and live in the esteem of his fellow
men, and so he is generally useless.'[21]

The caste system was a major source of both confusion and irritation for
English employers, despite the fact that it provided a justification for Anglo-
Indians to keep the number of servants they believed the maintenance of prestige
required. Often Indian servants, on the basis of their caste designation, would
only perform certain tasks. Minnie Wood, referring to servants' observation
of caste, claimed it required an 'excellent temper to stand all their nonsense'.
'Actually,' she wrote, 'the other day I ordered my Table Attendant to bring me the
Drawing Room Lamp to clean as I take charge of them & he refused saying he
would lose caste. Fool. I got so angry & after a hard battle got my way but they
really are enough to drive one mad.'[22]

In their effort to construct themselves as a modernizing force by defining
an ancient, yet primitive, India, successive generations of Anglo-Indians
referred to the caste system frustrating their domestic lives as an example of the
primitive irrationality of Indians, as compared to the clear, sober rationality of
the Englishman. The demarcation of service occupations by caste also served
as a signifier of servants' ethnic difference, which fed their employers' racial
prejudice, not only against Indian servants, but against the race they were
perceived to represent, regardless of whether they were Hindus or Muslims or
Christians:

> We are now almost crazy about our table attendants. They are so impertinent
> and give me so much trouble that I declare I feel inclined to kill them all, the
> beasts! ... As to ever liking the country, that is quite out of the question. One

---

[19] Nicholas B. Dirks, 'The Original Caste: Power, History and Hierarchy in South Asia' in McKim
    Marriott (ed.), *India through Hindu Categories* (New Delhi: Sage, 1990), 74.
[20] E.M. Collingham, *Imperial Bodies*, 18.
[21] Edward Braddon, *Life in India* (London: Longmans, Green and Co., 1872), 113.
[22] Letter, 10 March 1857, Letters of Maria Lydia Wood, MSS/Eur/B210 IOR.

feels quite differently now, even I who have been so short a time here, now begin
to see the creatures one has to deal with. I think they are a nasty, stinking, dirty
race and nothing more can be said of them.[23]

Dress and display

As the emphasis of British involvement in India shifted from orientalist to
anglicist principles, Anglo-Indians' dress altered. The flamboyant costume of
the nabob gave way to the more sober and standardized suit that identified
the sahib, reflecting clothing trends in England. In this way Anglo-Indians
came to wear metropolitan identifications literally on their sleeves, distancing
themselves through their clothing from 'oriental' influence.[24] Sartorial interests
extended beyond Anglo-Indians' own attire to that of their servants, although
beyond the cummerbund and turban, Anglo-Indian writers rarely discuss
imposing a uniform on their servants, though there are references to liveries
for *jhampannies* (footmen). Mary Hobhouse claimed her husband's were
'about the most sensational jhampannies in Simla, being clothed in maroon
and two shades of yellow. One gentleman here (Mr Haliburton) has got up his
as sailors, with the name of the house on their caps. This is quite an "idea," and
I envy him'.[25]

Concern with servants' attire in advice manuals seems to have focussed
on cleanliness. The author of *Morning Hours in India* claimed that it was 'a
positive insult to his master and mistress for any servant to enter their presence
in soiled clothing. Household servants should invariably be required to wear
their cummerbund, when in attendance on their master or mistress'.[26] However,
despite the emphasis on sartorial simplicity and cleanliness rather than oriental
grandeur in advice manuals many Anglo-Indians noted the clothes worn by
their servants and appear to have enjoyed the spectacle of 'a turbaned sultan-like
creature behind every chair'.[27] In the 1830s Julia Maitland described 'beautiful
barefooted peons, with handsome turbans, strutting' behind '[s]ome old Anglo-
Indians' who 'think themselves too grand to walk in their gardens without their

---

[23] Letter 19 December 1857, Letters of Maria Lydia Wood, MSS/Eur/B210 IOR.
[24] See E.M. Collingham, *Imperial Bodies*, 60–6 for further discussion of this process.
[25] Mary Hobhouse *Letters from India* (Edinburgh: printed for private circulation, 1906), 126.
[26] Elizabeth Garrett, *Morning Hours in India* (London: Trubner and Co., 1887), 30.
[27] [Julia Maitland], 'A Lady' *Letters from Madras during the Years 1836–1839* (London: John Murray,
    1846), 24.

servants'.[28] Such enjoyment continued throughout the nineteenth century. In the 1870s Mrs Mitchell noted her bearer's clothing with approval:

> He was clad in cool white; a fresh-starched calico coat, loose trousers, which looked like a petticoat, a flat turban, and a bright scarlet shawl wound round his waist in numerous folds. This garment is called a cummerbund, and the bright bit of colour had the happiest effect. As we entered he made a profound salaam – the very picture of a servant![29]

Although many employers bemoaned the fact their Indian servants did not behave like English servants, they enjoyed their Indian servants dressing in a manner that reflected their 'Indianness'. The 'rows of swarthy domestics, clothed in spotless white, who stand like so many statues behind their masters' chairs' contributed to the colonizers' sense of imperial magnificence and superiority, even throughout the period when efforts were being made to anglicize some Indian people.[30] Perceived as 'sultan-like' creatures, the servants arguably symbolized the subjugated Orient, disciplined by English authority.

The problem of proximity

It is easier to find more Anglo-Indian comment on servants in sources relating to the second half of the nineteenth century. This may be due to the fact that as the century progressed, and the British government assumed direct control of India, more women travelled there and wrote about their experiences of Indian domestic life, contributing to the popular advice literature genre, as well as novels and private, personal writings. In India, local culture intersected with colonizer desires and demands to produce a colonial expression of domesticity. Colonial households employed domestic workers whose labour, though connected to a pre-colonial past in some of its practices, was also shaped by the colonial present.

As Anglo-Indians moved towards what Elizabeth Collingham has called a less 'indianized' way of life in the early nineteenth century, so they noted with disapproval their servants' intrusion into that life.[31] There appears to have been growing uneasiness well before 1857 with the proximity of servants to British individuals and families in India. The openness of the Anglo-Indian bungalow

---

[28] [Julia Maitland], 'A Lady' *Letters from Madras*, 25.
[29] Mrs Murray Mitchell, *In India: Sketches of Indian Life and Travel from Letters and Journals*, 69.
[30] Mrs Murray Mitchell, *In India: Sketches of Indian Life and Travel from Letters and Journals*, 136.
[31] The word 'indianized' is E.M. Collingham's.

as compared to the metropolitan house meant that employers and servants could not avoid encountering one another.[32] The Indian servant's presence was thus seen as more invasive than his English counterpart's, which many employers, such as Emma Roberts, found irritating: 'None of the inferior domestics keep themselves, as in England, in the background ... and in Bengal, where the lower orders of palanquin-bearers wear very little clothing, it is not very agreeable to a female stranger to see them walk into drawing-rooms, and employ themselves in dusting books or other occupations of like nature.'[33] Here, Roberts uses the nomenclature of English domestic place – 'drawing rooms', and the work it required – 'dusting of books' – to emphasize the discomfort she feels at her male Indian servants' unsettling of the behavioural norms she expects in such places. These were norms that defined her femininity and elite status. By highlighting their disruption, Roberts refurbished her claim to a white, elite Englishness that she understood through a filter of gender and class.

Frederick Shore 'had bells hung in all the rooms in the house, after the English fashion' in order to ensure some kind of privacy for his wife and himself, and he described the servant as a 'sort of spy, and by no means an inattentive observer of all that passes in the private apartment of his mistress.'[34] Frederick Shore and his wife felt threatened not only by their servant's intrusion but also by the fact that he was male – as well as being described as a 'spy', he is described as an 'observer' of his mistress – a voyeur. Similarly, Dr Riddell claimed that '[c]uriosity ... is another of his [the native's] peculiarities ... They ... endeavour to find out all that concerns you.'[35] Anglo-Indian masters and mistresses could find servants' interest in them discomfiting, particularly given the employers often were external to their servants' lives, and knew little of them. This was something reflected by spatial arrangements; servants would cross multiple thresholds into and within Anglo-Indian households in the course of their work, while their own homes remained places their employers did not, and perhaps could not visit. As Minnie Wood described to her mother:

> Your servants with their families live in your compound in mud houses & pens, but that is all, you do not feed them or have anything to do with them, only

---

[32] See E.M. Collingham, *Imperial Bodies*, 99–102 for a discussion of the implications of the organization of the bungalow for private life in India.

[33] Emma Roberts, *Scenes and Characteristics of Hindoostan, with Sketches of Anglo-Indian Society*, Vol. I (London: W. H. Allen, 1837), 7–8.

[34] Frederick John Shore Collection, 23 December 1833, MSS/Eur/E307/5 IOR; Frederick John Shore, *Notes on Indian Affairs*, Vol. II (London: John W. Parker, 1837), 513.

[35] Dr R. Riddell, *Indian Domestic Economy and Receipt Book*, 7th edn (London: Thacker and Spink, 1871), 9.

allow 1 hour & a half each day for their Khana or dinner which is the only meal of which they ever partake & as to touching anything from off our table, that is unheard of, they generally have the same thing, rice or lentils, over & over again each year.[36]

The proximity of servants within Anglo-Indian households could extend from being an irritation to being a threat for some memsahibs, particularly during and after the uprising of 1857. Minnie Wood, in a letter to her mother written during the uprising, wrote that '[o]ne has to put up with so much now from one's servants. They are most insolent, and think nothing of telling you that soon we shall all be in the service of the King of Delhi.'[37] Following the uprising imperial domesticity was seen as critical to the success of British rule: '[I]mages of British women with their servants embodied imperial power on a domestic scale and stood in stark contrast to the domestic defilement and desertion of servants that had characterized many accounts of the uprising.'[38] This was quite a responsibility. Sequestered in their homes, with little company other than servants whose difference they felt so keenly, and whose 'civilization' they were responsible for, many women appear to have felt isolated and vulnerable, which may go some way to account for both their antipathy towards and their attachment to their servants.

Indian domestic servants and Anglo-Indian children

As in England, the anxiety some employers felt about servants was often articulated in terms of their influence on children.[39] The threat servants posed to children was generally not seen as a physical one. Indeed, in advice manuals, Indian servants are recommended for their devotedness to and 'unwearying patience and gentleness' with children.[40] Rather, the danger tended to be

---

[36] Letter to her mother 27 March 1857, Letters of Maria Lydia Wood, MSS/Eur/B210/A, IOR.

[37] Letter, 22 July 1857, Letters of Maria Lydia Wood, MSS/Eur/B210, IOR.

[38] Alison Blunt, 'Imperial Geographies of Home', 427.

[39] See Elizabeth Buettner's discussion of children and servants in her *Empire Families* (Oxford: Oxford University Press, 2004), 36–45 and also Indrani Sen's important article 'Colonial Domesticities, Contentious Interactions: Ayahs, Wet-nurses and Memsahibs in Colonial India', *Indian Journal of Gender Studies*, 16, 3 (2009): 299–328.

[40] 'A Lady Resident', *The Englishwoman in India* (London: Smith, Elder and Co,1864), 61. For further examples see Elizabeth Garrett, *Morning Hours in India* (London: L. Upcott Gill, 1882), 72; An Anglo-Indian, *Indian Outfits and Establishments,* 47; Mrs Eliot James, *Indian Household Management,* 46; Mrs Murray Mitchell, *In India: Sketches of Indian Life and Travel from Letters and Journals,* 68.

articulated in terms of a threat to children's identity as English, rather than as a concern for their physical well-being. The author of *A Domestic Guide to Mothers in India* warned mothers to beware of their 'native servants' who, if allowed too much contact with English children would 'instil all kinds of poisonous ideas into their young minds. Being heathens themselves, they see no harm in teaching them all the dogmas and obscenity of their religion'.[41] Furthermore, according to this author, the 'native servants are very fond of [deception]; and if children are left much to them, we see them grow cunning, deceitful and tellers of falsehoods'.[42] Similarly, Elizabeth Garrett advised that in India 'great patience is needed in training our children in habits of truthfulness. Their surroundings, alas! are generally a hindrance, rather than a help in such lessons'.[43] Parents were also counselled to make sure their children's linguistic development was not tainted by their acquiring local dialects from servants 'as with the language they are almost certain to imbibe ideas and knowledge most prejudicial to them in every way'.[44] According to Florence Marryat, 'the conversation of the natives, as a rule, is too filthy to be imagined, which always gave me a great horror of permitting my children to pick up the Tamil language from their ayahs'.[45] As in the metropole, the subtext to such antipathy may have been jealousy, or anxiety that the children might in some way be lost to their parents, perhaps in terms of their belief in the embodied differences of race, gender and class that underpinned the imperial enterprise. Nevertheless, despite the dislike of English children having contact with 'heathens', employers were often reluctant to hire Christian servants or English servants.[46] Several employers seem to have thought Christian servants were opportunistic, professing Christianity only to gain some advantage. As 'Lady Resident' recommended to her readers:

> As much as possible, secure for your servants a set of unmitigated heathens. Converts are usually arrant humbugs; Catholics little better; indeed, the domestics who have robbed and cheated us during our sojourn in India, have with one exception been Christians and I have resolved never to engage another knowing him to be 'master's caste'.[47]

[41] 'A Medical Practitioner', *A Domestic Guide to Mothers in India* (Bombay: American Mission Press, 1848), 49.

[42] 'A Medical Practitioner', *A Domestic Guide to Mothers in India*, 62.

[43] Elizabeth Garrett, *Morning Hours in India*, 112.

[44] A Lady Resident, *The Englishwoman in India*, 106.

[45] Florence Marryat, '*Gup*' *Sketches of Anglo-Indian Life and Character* (London: Reprinted from Temple Bar, 1868), 55.

[46] Indrani Sen, 'Colonial Domesticities, Contentious Interactions', 316.

[47] 'A Lady Resident', *The Englishwoman in India*, 55.

As Nupur Chaudhuri has suggested, this response to Christian servants may have been due to the fact that sharing a common faith may have brought servants too close to their employers for comfort.[48] Although many employers seem to have been irritated by their servant's difference, difference was perhaps more comfortable than similarity, particularly in matters of faith. Though employers would have usually shared their Christian faith with their servants in England, in India it may have threatened to undermine the systems of difference that legitimized British colonial authority and exploitation. Mrs Mitchell's comment in one of her letters lends support to this interpretation: 'The bearer is a Christian, and an old servant of Mr D., a small, keen-eyed, dark Madrassi, with a towering mass of white turban, and full of springy activity. It is nice to have a Christian servant, but this man looks perhaps rather too clever.'[49]

Not all employers felt threatened by their servants. In the 1830s Julia Maitland described one servant's attentions to his mistresses as follows: 'Then creeps in, perhaps, some old wizen, skinny brownie, looking like a superannuated thread-paper, who twiddles after them for a little while, and then creeps out again as softly as a black cat, and sits down cross-legged in the verandah till "Mistress please to call again"'.[50] While her words and tone are both patronizing and racist, Julia Maitland also distinguished herself from the lazy and indulged 'real Indian ladies' who 'lie on a sofa, and, if they drop their handkerchief, they just lower their voices and say, "Boy!"' There is no sense her servants pose any threat to her.[51] Rather, she sees them as infantile, 'like babies in their ways'.[52] Maitland was writing at the time when the British were shifting away from 'orientalist' practices of government, and here constituted herself as an independent and competent Englishwoman, in contrast to both her domestic servants and other Anglo-Indian mistresses, who she implied had been corrupted by their residence in India.

Often male bearers would undertake the duties of childcare; indeed, it was widely seen as a part of their duties to look after the children, once they had reached a certain age. Nupur Chaudhuri, in her article 'Memsahibs and Their Servants in Nineteenth-century India', argues that:

---

[48] Nupur Chaudhuri, 'Memsahibs and Their Servants in Nineteenth-century India', *Women's History Review*, 3, 4 (1994), 552.

[49] Mrs Murray Mitchell, *In India: Sketches of Indian Life and Travel from Letters and Journals*, 69.

[50] [Julia Maitland] 'A Lady' *Letters from Madras*, 18–19.

[51] [Julia Maitland] 'A Lady' *Letters from Madras*, 18.

[52] [Julia Maitland] 'A Lady' *Letters from Madras*, 21.

Since domestic jobs were perceived in Britain as women's work, in the eyes of the memsahibs these Indian male domestics were placed in the domestic sphere that belonged to women. The inability of these indigenous men to extricate themselves from menial household work marked them as inferior to British male servants and placed them on a level with British female servants.[53]

Chaudhuri's observation points towards the knotty dynamics of gender, class and caste at play in the workings of the relationship between memsahibs and their male servants. Rather than some kind of equivalence between English female and Indian male servants, it would in fact seem that it was their gender and racial difference to English female servants that was problematic for mistresses, and that this problem was not resolved by their being 'placed on a level with British female servants'. While it seems to be true that many Englishwomen saw Indian as inferior to English servants, this seems to have been less to do with their being men doing 'women's work' as it was to do with their being perceived as lower-class Indian males who had access to the private lives of their employers. Their maleness added to the threat of their 'otherness'. Moreover, male servants' resistance to mistresses' control seems to have been articulated around a resistance to their authority on the basis of their gender. For example, it was often stated by women that they had problems being understood by servants, and that they needed their husbands to dictate their orders to ensure they were obeyed. Minnie Wood wrote in a letter to her mother that

> I quite dread book-keeping as I have no power over the servants … & the accounts I have to get my husband to translate every morning'while A Lady Resident claimed that 'One bad trait … is the frequency with which they disregard the comfort and convenience of ladies, often their express orders, unless most directly enforced by the master'.[54] Similarly, Mary Hobhouse wrote in 1872 that 'tis difficult to make the male servants respect womankind'.[55]

Male servants' resistance to female authority is also a recurring theme in many of the transcripts of interviews, held in the IOR's oral archives, with people who lived in colonial India. Edith Dixon remembered the bearer in her house 'would have thrown me to the jackals, if it lay between saving [me] and ….the little Lordship my small brother'.[56] Women's willingness to use their husbands

[53] Nupur Chaudhuri, 'Memsahibs and Their Servants in Nineteenth-century India', 553.
[54] March 10 1857, Letters of Maria Lydia Wood, MSS/Eur/B210/A, IOR; 'A Lady Resident', *Englishwoman in India*, 60.
[55] Mary Hobhouse, *Letters from India 1872–1877*, 9.
[56] Edith Dixon, MSS.Eur.T26, IOR.

to bolster their authority may suggest they tacitly acknowledged their male servants' implicit challenge.

While it does seem to be case that servants were frequently characterized as childishly immature, servile, stupid, dirty, indolent, dishonest and likened to animals, they do not appear to have been feminized or described as effeminate by British writers in the same way as middle-class so-called '*baboos*' were. Elizabeth Garrett, in her advice book *Morning Hours in India*, wrote that:

> After the child is three or four months old he should be carried by the <u>bearer</u>. The child will feel much safer than in a woman's arms … Hindoo <u>bearers</u> become much attached to the children of whom they have care, and take a great pride in their young charges. For boys, after they are six or eight months old, they are undoubtedly the best nurses.[57]

The reference to the strength of the male, as opposed to the female servant, and the implication that male children are better cared for by one of their own sex suggests that the male servant can bring usefully masculine qualities to the role of 'nurse'. Furthermore, the figure of the threatening servant was not always a vindictive female. In 1883, during the period of social unrest that surrounded the Ilbert Bill controversy, the Magistrate of Howrah, E.V. Westmacott, wrote in a report to the Lt.-Governor of Bengal: 'I do not suppose the *Baboos* who are agitating and leading the anti-European tendencies of Government are likely to indulge in rape or murder of Europeans, but I see very clearly what is the outcome of the *Baboo* agitation, when translated into language, intelligible to themselves by natives of the lower classes.'[58] The threat here was articulated in terms of the 'lower classes' (by which he meant servants', having previously referred to their increased 'insubordination') potentially rampant male sexuality. Of course, genteel masculinity was supposedly characterized by restraint, but these were Indian servants under discussion and therefore not seen by colonizers to be genteel. While English female servants were also seen by servant-employers as posing a potential sexual threat, it was figured in a significantly different way. As discussed in Chapter 1, the perceived weapon of English female servants was temptation, rather than aggression, the latter being commonly understood to be a characteristic associated with the masculine psyche. This is not to say that

---

[57] Elizabeth Garrett, *Morning Hours in India*, 80.

[58] Rivers Thompson to Ripon, *Ripon Papers: Letters of Rivers Thompson*, Vol. 54, 17, June 1883. See Fae Dussart, '"To Glut a Menial's Grudge": Domestic Servants and the Ilbert Bill Controversy of 1883', *Journal of Colonialism and Colonial History*, 14, 1 (2013), n.p. for an account of the functional role ascribed to domestic servants in the controversy.

ideas about gender did not play their role in structuring the way in which male Indian servants were characterized, simply that the way in which such ideas worked was complex and ambivalent. As Nitin Sinha and Nitin Varma have noted, the nineteenth century was marked by 'a growing degree of menialization of domestic servants and domestic work. Servants were identified as a distinct social group, performing menial household tasks, which was seen as a function of their lower class and caste status and their marginal position in a feudal culture of authority and subordination.'[59] Indian servants' masculinity was framed by their low status in hierarchies of class and caste.

Infantilization and violence

As Ann Laura Stoler has written, the representation of racialized Others as child-like was one that 'conveniently provided a moral justification for imperial policies of tutelage, discipline and specific paternalistic and materialistic strategies of custodial control.'[60] The idea that Indian servants were effectively children endured throughout the nineteenth century. In the bible of Indian housekeeping, *The Complete Indian Housekeeper and Cook* (1898), the authors claimed that '[t]he Indian servant is a child in everything save age.'[61] They went beyond simply describing the Indian servant as a child and suggested he or she 'should be treated as a child'.[62] To this end, the authors claimed that in training their servants they 'adopted castor oil as an ultimatum in all obstinate cases, on the ground that there must be some physical cause for inability to learn or remember'.[63]

The description of Indian servants as children also resonated with the notion that the servant-employer relationship in Britain was ideally paternalistic. Advice manual writers in India recommended caring for one's Indian servants in a paternalistic way in order to inspire loyalty. Provided one was kind and firm with them 'they will prove in many little ways, by many little actions, many little attentions, that they fully appreciate your kindness, and endeavour, in their

[59] Nitin Sinha and Nitin Varma, 'Introduction' in Nitin Sinha and Nitin Varma (eds.), *Servants' Pasts. Late-Eighteenth to Twentieth Century South Asia*, Vol. 2 (Hyderabad: Black Swan Pvt Ltd, 2019), 3.
[60] Ann, Laura Stoler, *Race and the Education of Desire: Foucault's History of Sexuality and the Colonial Order of Things* (Durham: Duke University Press, 1995), 150.
[61] F.A. Steel and G. Gardiner, *The Complete Indian Housekeeper and Cook* (London: W. Heinemann, 1898), 2.
[62] F.A. Steel and G. Gardiner, *The Complete Indian Housekeeper and Cook*, 2.
[63] F.A. Steel and G. Gardiner, *The Complete Indian Housekeeper and Cook*, 3.

way, to repay it. In being kind, draw the line, do not overdo it … do not allow them to mistake kindness for weakness'.[64] This echoed the metropolitan manual author 'A Practical Mistress', quoted in Chapter 1, who claimed that 'Servants – as well as children – require to be managed with *kindness* and *firmness*. The greatest "kindness" we can exercise towards them is to endeavour, by a mild rein, to keep them in the path of duty'.[65] Certainly many employers had close and affectionate relationships with their servants, particularly with bearers and ayahs. After her bearer supported her when her mother died, Lady Wilson wrote to a friend: 'Of the sympathy shown us in times of sickness and sorrow by those of our own household, most Memsahibs can speak with feeling … sometimes such things mean a great deal to us.'[66]

However, the idea that Indian servants were dependants within a household was problematic. While styled as children in their attitudes and behaviour, they were not dependent within the household in the same way as English servants were. First, they were mostly male. Second, they were often married with families of their own, who often lived within the compound and who were dependent on them. Third, they worked for a wage, where servants in England might be paid in kind. Nevertheless, Indian servants were repeatedly referred to both angrily and with affection as children, in texts ranging from household manuals, to missionary writings and personal letters and diaries. Such a construction provided a way in which mistresses could reassure themselves that they were not only superior to, but also authoritative over their servants. It was a way of denying their dependence on the servants, which was certainly a source of anxiety for many mistresses. Anne Wilson described feeling 'baffled impotence' after her first experience of Anglo-Indian housekeeping.[67] Minnie Wood described frustration in a letter to her mother:

> As regards Servants my life has been worried out by Ayahs, I have had no less than <u>four</u>, since my arrival in Jhelum & am not yet suited, they are a thousand times worse than English Servants, <u>you</u> I am sure would never stand them, they perfectly spoil one's temper for they are such fools without a grain of sense & yet to do without them is impossible.[68]

[64] Mrs Eliot James, *Indian Household Management*, 43.
[65] 'A Practical Mistress of the Household', *Domestic Servants as They Are and as They Ought to Be* (Brighton: W. Tweedie Simpson, 1859), 4.
[66] Lady Wilson (Anne C. Macleod), *Letters from India* (Edinburgh: William Blackwood, 1911), 284–5.
[67] Lady Wilson (Anne C. Macleod), *Letters from India*, 5.
[68] Letter March 1857, Letters of Maria Lydia Wood, MSS/Eur/B210 IOR.

Viewing servants as children was common amongst employers in England as well as India, but in India the attitude took on a different tone. In England servants' childlike status was enshrined in the law, where they were defined as dependants, rather than employees. The fact that most English servants were young women enhanced the idea that they were childishly vulnerable. In India, however, this was not the case. As well as being represented as infantile, Indian servants were frequently described as if they were domesticated animals: often frustrating, sometimes threatening, occasionally amusing and generally dumb. Julia Maitland claimed her servants 'lie on their mats, strewing the floor like cats and dogs', while Florence Marryat employed a similarly derogatory and reductionist metaphor: 'there is something in being driven by a human (but anything but humane) monkey … which is distasteful to a mind prejudiced in favour of English customs and manners'.[69] Even Mary Hobhouse, usually relatively sympathetic to her household staff, claimed her servants were like 'dogs or children in the way they respect any personal order'.[70]

By describing their servants as children or domesticated animals, mistresses attempted to neutralize the sexual and physical power of the male servants, circumventing the problem of their gender and rendering them theoretically powerless and dependent (while allowing the possibility they were inherently sinful). In this respect the common habit of calling an adult male servant 'boy' is revealing. Likening servants to children connected them obliquely to 'helpless' females and similarly infantilized 'dependent' others, without making explicit comparisons that could undermine the classed, white feminine identity of the memsahib. This helped secure her imperial authority, eliding her own subjection to white patriarchal power.

Efforts were made to anglicize mainly high-caste Indians, redefining them according to metropolitan standards as 'native gentlemen', differentiated from lower-class Indians through their respectable 'English' education and collaboration with the ruling bureaucracy.[71] Despite this, most Anglo-Indians also saw all Indians as fundamentally racially inferior to the British. Julia Maitland bemoaned the 'rudeness and contempt' with which Indians were treated by their British rulers, writing that '[t]hese natives are a cringing set, and

---

[69] [Julia Maitland] 'A Lady' *Letters from Madras*, 35; Florence Marryat, *'Gup' Sketches of Anglo-Indian Life and Character*, 14.

[70] Mary Hobhouse, *Letters from India*, 40.

[71] Susan Bayly, 'The Evolution of Colonial Cultures: Nineteenth Century Asia' in Andrew Porter (ed.), *The Oxford History of the British Empire. The Nineteenth Century* (Oxford: Oxford University Press, 1999), 452; Robin J. Moore, 'Imperial India, 1858–1914' in Andrew Porter (ed.), *The Oxford History of the British Empire. The Nineteenth Century* (Oxford: Oxford University Press, 1999), 431.

behave to us English as if they were the dirt under our feet; and indeed we give them reason to suppose we consider them as such'.[72] Similarly, Mary Hobhouse described Indians as 'slavish people, all whose habits and instincts, good or bad, seem of a servile nature'.[73] Colesworthy Grant acknowledged the effect that relations with servants could have on colonizer perceptions of Indian character, writing that 'the want of principle so unhappily prevailing amongst the very class with whom Europeans in Calcutta have the most dealings, strikes at one of the most vital points in a man's affections ... The feelings thus engendered toward the servants extend themselves to the people at large'.[74]

Some Anglo-Indians sanctioned violence as a means to keeping Indian servants under control, claiming it was in line with indigenous practices of rule. 'Of course', stated an editorial in *The Pioneer*, 'cuffs and stripes, and all kinds of corporeal maltreatment are recognized in India by Indians as well as Europeans, as more in accordance with the natural fitness of things than such phenomena would be thought in Europe'.[75] Admittedly, many Anglo-Indians, such as Mary Hobhouse, found the use of violence unnecessary and offensive:

> This behaviour to natives is one of the things that make one a little sick here sometimes. I read quite a commonplace report of an officer the other day, whose servant had not filled up his lamp sufficiently with oil. He sent for the man, who was unwilling to come, and then twice threw a knife at him, and the man was severely wounded and taken to hospital – the officer fined fifteen rupees. 'In the very same paper was a letter saying, 'India was going to the dogs since the enactment by which servants were allowed to bring actions against their masters'.[76]

Mary was the wife of Arthur Hobhouse, a senior government official. Both she and her husband had more liberal attitudes than many of their peers in terms of the practice of colonial government, something that appears to be reflected in Mary Hobhouse's generally sympathetic attitude towards her Indian servants.

In July 1876 a case took place in which a *syce* (a groom/footman – a lower servant), having failed to bring a carriage to the front door of his English employer's house on time, was beaten by his employer and subsequently died. The employer, Mr Fuller, was sentenced to a fine of thirty rupees. Concerned by

[72] [Julia Maitland] 'A Lady' *Letters from Madras*, 20.
[73] Mary Hobhouse, *Letters from India*, 64.
[74] Colesworthy Grant, *An Anglo Indian Domestic Sketch* (Calcutta: Thacker and Spink, 1862), 90.
[75] Editorial, Wed July 19 1876, *The Pioneer*.
[76] Mary Hobhouse, *Letters from India*, 129.

the leniency of the sentence, Lord Lytton, then Viceroy, issued a Minute in which he expressed disapproval of Anglo-Indians' inclination to control their servants with violence, and at the Courts' tendencies to punish such offenders lightly. According to Mary Hobhouse this raised

> a howl of indignation from the Anglo-Indian press, who all look upon beating as the right and proper way of treating servants. One man writes this morning to say, 'I wish Lord Lytton would tell me what I am to do when my servants bring breakfast a quarter of an hour late'. We, Arthur and myself, always say 'what would you do if an English servant was at fault?' but this is considered a ludicrous and inappropriate sentiment.[77]

Although beating servants was generally frowned upon in Anglo-Indian society, many Anglo-Indians believed it occasionally unavoidable, and certainly understandable. This contrasts the situation in Britain, where two highly publicized cases of employer cruelty to servant-girls in the mid-nineteenth century provoked a general public outcry and prompted the passage of the Apprentices and Servants Act in 1851. The fact that Indian servants as well as being Indian were also usually male was probably relevant to their employers' belief that they sometimes needed physical chastisement in order to inculcate necessary subservience. As an editorial in the *Pioneer* stated in response to Lytton's Minute: 'the truth is … that there is hardly a large household in India which could be kept in decent order by strictly legal means' and advised 'every European here' to 'take care that he never strikes a servant in a way that can possibly have more than a superficial effect'.[78] Florence Marryat suggested that Anglo-Indian employers were driven to violence by their servants' lack of appreciation of how lucky they were: 'their usual behaviour is so aggravating that … I cannot wonder at any one losing control of their temper when with them; but in general they serve you well as long as it suits their convenience to do so, and when it does not no amount of past kindness and indulgence will secure you from the effects of their ingratitude'.[79] Furthermore, those people (including the government) who did disapprove of violence tended to do so not because beating servants was bad for the servant as much as it brutalized the employer and was 'so injurious to the honour of British rule, and so damaging to the reputation of British justice in this country'.[80] We will return to the Fuller

---

[77] Mary Hobhouse, *Letters from India*, 252.
[78] Editorial, July 19 1876, *The Pioneer*.
[79] Florence Marryat, *'Gup' Sketches of Anglo-Indian Life and Character*, 31–2.
[80] 'Moffusilite', Letter to *The Englishman*, 26 July 1876.

case and the legitimacy of employer violence towards servants in metropole and colony in Chapter 5.

Stereotypes and intimacy

In England deference rituals recommended by advice manual writers such as Mrs Motherly, together with the directive that servants should be neither seen nor heard, combined to reduce servants to an existence in which their value was defined only by their fulfilment of a service role. Indian servants underwent similar processes of depersonalization but in their case, these processes were connected to racial stereotypes. John Kaye's remark provides an example of extreme depersonalization: 'one is wont to get wondrously indifferent to these black automata, and after a few months one learns to think of them no more than of the chairs and the tables.'[81] This was not entirely true. Employers thought about their servants a lot, particularly about their irritating or invasive characteristics. Certain characteristics were associated with some of the different servant roles. For example, the *khansamah* (table servant) was seen as a cheat, who 'carries on an avowed system of plunder' and whose dishonesty was incurable.[82] '[I]t is manifestly hopeless to attempt to reform the khansamah', wrote one correspondent to *The Englishman*, 'He has been spoilt beyond redemption by a long and undisturbed career of plunder and must be lopped off from our household establishments like a rotten branch.'[83] Bearers, however, were generally characterized as 'a hardworking and very trusty class of people.'[84] As discussed in Chapter 2, servant occupations in India were associated with colonizer perceptions of the hierarchy of caste (even relationally for Muslim and Christian servants who could perform 'untouchable' tasks), and it may be the case that class-based English ideas about servant character had absorbed some caste prejudices.

Many of the negative characteristics attributed to servants in England, such as tendencies to dishonesty and to taking illicit perquisites, were also attributed to Indian servants. Rather than being confined to servants however, they were cited as evidence of inherent defects in Indian character. For example, 'A Lady

---

[81] John Kaye, *Peregrine Pultuney; or Life in India*, II (1884), 141.
[82] Letter, *The Englishman*, April 23 1883.
[83] Letter, *The Englishman*, April 21 1883.
[84] Dr R. Riddell, *Indian Domestic Economy and Receipt Book*, 8.

Resident' claimed from her experience with servants that 'a native never speaks the truth except by accident, and really this is hardly an exaggeration'.[85] Similarly, Dr Riddell generalized from a discussion of servant character, claiming that 'Cunning and double-dealing characterize the Native and are some of his principal faults'.[86] Florence Marryat went further, claiming that 'Both men and women are inveterate liars and it is impossible to place dependence on anything that they say'.[87] The identity of 'the servant' thus worked as a conceptual device for colonizers through which differences of race might be constituted, and colonial class and gender identities were also worked out.

Generalizations were not always negative. Many employers testify in letters and manuals to servants' loyalty and in particular, to their kindness when their employers fell ill. Dr Riddell wrote that '[i]n sickness they will take the greatest care of you, doing for you services that a European seldom ever will', while Lady Resident claimed the 'extreme lightness and delicacy of touch which characterizes the native, makes the ayah often a very great comfort'. Bertie Maynard wrote in a letter home that he found 'the servants very good when one is at all unwell'.[88] Some writers even spoke out against Indian servants' poor reputation. The author of *Indian Outfits* suggested that 'grumbling against servants is a national fault amongst us' and claimed that new arrivals in India 'will be told that natives are everything that is bad and cannot be trusted'.[89] However, she advised that she had 'seen a good deal of native servants, and I know no reason why, from my experience of them, they should not be trusted quite as much as others of their class'.[90] Mrs Eliot James similarly claimed that new arrivals in India would be led to 'believe that, of all the race of servants, Indian ones are undoubtedly the worst' but advised her readers not to 'judge too hastily'.[91] In her view 'we might have been singularly fortunate in our dependents. Certainly I am inclined to think – nay more, I firmly believe – that the native race are grossly belied'.[92] Nevertheless, despite her defence of Indian servants Mrs Eliot James still equated 'the native race' with 'the race of servants', suggesting that she did not think of Indians in

[85] 'A Lady Resident', *The Englishwoman in India*, 59.
[86] Dr R. Riddell, *Indian Domestic Economy and Receipt Book*, 9.
[87] Florence Marryat, *'Gup' Sketches of Anglo-Indian Life and Character*, 36.
[88] Dr R. Riddell, *Indian Domestic Economy and Receipt Book*, 8; 'A Lady Resident', *The Englishwoman in India*, 53; Katherine Lethbridge (ed.), *Letters from East and West* (Devon: Merlin, 1990), 24.
[89] An Anglo-Indian, *Indian Outfits and Establishments*, 49; 46.
[90] An Anglo-Indian, *Indian Outfits and Establishments*, 47.
[91] Mrs Eliot James, *Indian Household Management*, 43.
[92] Mrs Eliot James, *Indian Household Management*, 43.

any other capacity and elsewhere in her book she reinstated the prejudice that Indian servants 'tell stories' because ''tis their nature to'.[93]

Despite the shift towards establishing racial distance between Anglo-Indian and Indian people in the nineteenth century, intimacy between servants and employers persisted in many households. The gentle brown hand and jangling bracelets of a soft-footed ayah were recurrent, if stereotyped, images in the rememberings of Anglo-Indian children.[94] The combination of warmth and stereotype in such memories indicates the way in which the peculiar intimacy of the relationship between servants and employers was framed by the servant's 'Indian-ness'. It speaks of the way in which the servant might have acted as a medium through which India could flow into the most private recesses of Anglo-Indians' material and psychological existence, no matter how much they tried overtly to prevent it from doing so.

Ayahs were necessarily physically intimate and often emotionally intimate with the people they worked for. Memsahibs often expressed fondness for their ayahs. For example, Emily Eden described her gravely ill ayah Rosina as 'a good affectionate old body' and said that she had 'done nothing but cry about her' while she was unwell.[95] This intimacy could have sexual dimensions. Though ideally a 'desexualized and maternalized figure past her sexual prime', Satysikha Chakraborty's research has shown that in the earlier decades of the nineteenth century at least, ayahs may have previously been the *bibis* of European men, women who had been excommunicated from their communities as a result of cohabiting with European men.[96]

By generalizing pejoratively about Indian character from their experience as mistresses of Indian servants, Anglo-Indian women could make a claim to personal authority over their households. They could also claim agency in the imperial venture, implicitly endorsing the moral legitimacy of British colonialism as progress towards civilization. However, alongside generalizations, there were variations in Anglo-Indian attitudes towards Indian people. Although negative ideas abounded and experience interacted with public discourse to reinforce them, encounters with Indian servants being part of this experience, it is simplistic to suggest that a widely disseminated and effective idea of 'the Indian in general'

---

[93] Mrs Eliot James, *Indian Household Management*, 43.

[94] See for example the oral history accounts in Charles Allen, *Plain Tales of the Raj* (London: Century, 1985)

[95] Emily Eden quoted in Nitin Varma, 'The Many Lives of Ayah. Life Trajectories of Female Servants in Early Nineteenth Century India' in Nitin Sinha and Nitin Varma (eds.), *Servants' Pasts*, 102.

[96] Satyasikha Chakraborty, 'From *Bibis* to *Ayahs*. Sexual Labour, Domestic Labour and the Moral Politics of Empire' in Nitin Sinha and Nitin Varma (eds.), *Servants' Pasts*, 65–6.

was uniquely drawn from memsahibs' relationship with their servants. Within a broad context in which anything English was considered to be superior to anything Indian, there were variations and contradictions in responses to Indian people, including servants. Certainly there were general ideas about Indian servants that interacted with ideas about 'native character', but the one did not necessarily produce the other.

Conclusion

The relationship between servants and employers was fraught with tension. Even employers who valued and defended Indian servants evidenced some prejudices which were similar to those expressed by others who apparently hated their servants. Elizabeth Collingham has suggested that the new attitude of the British towards India diverged into two behavioural trends – put crudely, the conciliatory and the condemnatory.[97] However, I would argue that this distinction oversimplifies the responses of Englishmen and women to Indian people. One of the distinctive features of the writings of Anglo-Indians on India is the variability of their responses to their Indian servants, even while references are made to a homogeneous 'native character' in the descriptions of servants. For example, writers of manuals and letters often testified to the general dishonesty of Indian servants and then recommended some of them for their trustworthiness. Anglo-Indians were aware of such variability and new arrivals could be confused by the inconsistency in the advice they received. Mary Hobhouse wrote in a letter that 'Mr C's dictum as to these servants is "Trust them entirely and look into nothing yourself"; and the same evening Mr W. said to me, "look into everything; be firm and patient – never indulgent".[98] Shortly after her arrival in India, Anne Wilson also noted the range of opinion, and tentatively drew her own general conclusion: 'Servants differ greatly in different parts of the country, and their employers' opinions of them as a class vary as widely, ranging from enthusiasm to despair. Take them as a whole, I think I find them as yet distinctly trying.'[99]

The dependence of Englishwomen, particularly those white women living isolated lives in the *mofussil,* on their Indian servants, and the inscrutability

---

[97] E.M. Collingham, *Imperial Bodies*, 56–9.
[98] Mary Hobhouse, *Letters from India*, 49.
[99] Lady Wilson (Anne C. Macleod), *Letters from India*, 10–11.

of the culture to which those servants belonged was a source of confusion for employers in India. Despite the derogatory reductionism which writers employed to justify putative English superiority, the ambivalence of their writings bears witness to such confusion. The unfamiliarity of Indian servants – their skin colour, their caste system, their habit of squatting and sleeping in the afternoon, their 'oriental' dress, their language, their gender – observation of such features contributed to an ambivalent idea of Indian character in Anglo-Indian minds. 'I realise that I am face to face with a sphinx who is not dumb, but who remains an eternal enigma', wrote Anne Wilson revealingly in one of her letters home.[100] The writers of letters and manuals interpreted what they saw of their servants in the context of a country that mystified them, and thus produced ambivalent, racialized notions of Indian character for an English-speaking readership across imperial space.

[100] Lady Wilson (Anne C. Macleod), *Letters from India*, 87.

Violence, domestic authority and the politics of imperial governance

In earlier chapters, some of the subversive ways in which servants could resist the totality of their employers' authority were discussed. Domestic servants' connections to other worlds, whether to working-class friends and family in Britain or to Indian society in India, could appear inscrutable and discomfiting to their employers. This was despite (or perhaps because of) the fact that, especially in India, these connections were essential to the functioning of not only the household, but also the empire. Servants mediated between above and below stairs, public and private, domestic and marketplace, indigenous and colonial, working and middle or upper class, administering much of the essential traffic between these interdependent sectors and cultures. Although the balance of power in the servant-employer relationship was weighted in the employers' favour in both India and Britain, the dependence of the employer on the servant created a space in which small acts of servant resistance to over-bearing employers were possible. Offended servants could spoil food, deliberately fail to hear or understand instructions, spread gossip and generally sabotage the smooth running of the household. However, such methods constituted revenge or resistance, rather than justice. At times, a servant or an institution representing servants' interests would seek public sanction as to what a servant's rights were and where the limits of acceptable behaviour on the employers' part should be drawn. Domestic servants stood in the dock in nineteenth-century courts in both India and Britain, often on charges of petty larceny or breach of contract and not infrequently on charges of prostitution, infanticide, concealment of birth and even murder. However, they also occasionally brought prosecutions against their employers, sometimes for assault. This section considers some occasions when employers in India and in Britain stood in the dock, prosecuted by servants, or by other authorities on behalf of servants.

Court cases are of interest as the courtroom was a 'functional site of power for the contested formation of ... social identities'[1] and a place in which representations of private experience were publicly judged. Although the balance of power in the servant-employer relationship was overwhelmingly in favour of the employers in both metropole and colony, servants in both sites used the courtroom as a space in which to publicly contest the limits of their employer's authority. Servants did not always win their cases, but the fact that the cases were brought for judgement at all bears examination. Comparing metropole and colony reveals the specificity of constructions of 'violence' within the master/ mistress-servant relationship. Such constructions intersected with dominant discourses of gender, race and class in the second half of the nineteenth century to produce differentiated ideas about what the relative rights and responsibilities of servants and employers were across imperial space. The relative status of servants and their employers, in relation to discourses of gender, race, class and domesticity, shaped the process and outcomes of the court cases in each site, and their representation in the contemporary press.

The print media in India and Britain varied considerably. Britain's *The Times* newspaper was a national daily directed at middle- and upper-class readers of a conservative bent. It was thus the mouthpiece of employers of servants rather than servants themselves. The colonial newspapers considered here, including *The Pioneer*, *The Englishman*, *Indian Daily News* and *The Civil and Military Gazette*, were regional papers, though the uniformity in the major news stories their editors chose to cover is often striking.[2] These were geared to the tastes of a specifically Anglo-Indian readership and reflected the concerns of a white population who considered themselves as a pioneering minority at times threatened by the Indian colonial subjects they lived amongst. There were of course nuances to this attitude: ideas about how Britons should conduct relations with Indian people ranged from the conciliatory to the autocratic. However, there appears to have been little doubt in most Britons' minds as to their greater degree of 'civilization' relative to Indian colonial subjects.

Alan Lester has suggested that colonial newspapers were important in connecting disparate colonizing communities in different sites of empire with one another and with the metropole, encouraging a sense of shared

---

[1]   Shani D'Cruze, *Crimes of Outrage. Sex, Violence and Victorian Working Women* (London: Routledge, 1998), 4–5.
[2]   During the period covered in this chapter *The Pioneer* was published from Allahabad, *The Englishman* and *Indian Daily News* from Calcutta and *The Civil and Military Gazette* from Lahore and Simla.

purpose and identity.[3] At the same time, British (and Indian) subjects rarely conformed to homogenous constructions and often openly challenged them in line with wider debates over the moral purpose of imperialism, and the relative rights of individuals within its contested hierarchies. Like all culturally constructed categories of human difference, as well as having hazy borders, 'White' in colonial India was complicated by other kinds of difference: factors such as length of stay in India and nature of residence (domiciled or non-domiciled), degree of affluence/poverty, relation to government (official or non-official, or military), rural/urban residence, perspective on the practice of colonialism, all fractured the coherence of whiteness.[4] The colonial newspapers discussed here thus were important in connecting communities *within* the colony, as well as between colonies, responding to and reflecting the anxieties of colonizers and helping to constitute a dominant and homogenous white 'Anglo-Indian' identity as distinct from and as superior to, 'the Indian'.

The master/mistress-servant relationship was essential within the imperial formation of Britain and India, and to the hierarchies of difference that underpinned the progress of both capitalism and colonialism as they manifested in both metropole and colony in the nineteenth century. In India, following the transfer of control of the subcontinental colony from the East India Company to the Crown, the Queen's proclamation of 1858 had committed the Government of India, in theory, to a policy of racial equality:

> We hold ourselves bound to the natives of our Indian territories by the same obligations of duty which bind us to all our other subjects ... We declare it to be Our Royal Will and Pleasure ... that all shall enjoy the equal and impartial protection of the Law.[5]

However, the preservation of certain privileges for Anglo-Indians in India contradicted such apparently inclusive aims. In the second half of the nineteenth century it was increasingly clear to the colonial authorities that 'continued British political and economic exploitation of India depended on the maintenance of

---

[3] Alan Lester, *Imperial Networks. Creating Identities in Nineteenth-Century South Africa and Britain* (London: Routledge, 2001), 6.

[4] For critiques of 'whiteness' in colonial India see Satoshi Mizutani, *The Meaning of White: Race, Class, and the 'Domiciled Community' in British India 1858–1930* (Oxford: Oxford University Press, 2012) and Harald Fischer-Tiné, *Low and Licentious Europeans: Race, Class, and 'White Subalternity' in Colonial India* (New Delhi: Orient BlackSwan, 2009).

[5] *Proclamation by the Queen in Council to the Princes, Chiefs and the People of India,* (Allahabad: Governor General, 1 November 1858), 1–3.

certain exclusive racial privileges for European British subjects in India.[6] India was of very real economic importance to Britain. The challenge to Britain's economic dominance from other European nations and the huge increase in Britain's financial investments abroad in the second half of the nineteenth century put the colonial authorities in a difficult predicament, compromised by liberal aspirations and the political and economic exigencies of the moment. Furthermore, educated Indians were beginning to organize politically. By the mid-1870s, politically conscious Bengalis had begun touring India to promote regional solidarity.[7] Nascent Indian nationalism and Anglo-Indian anxiety about the security of British control of India formed the backdrop to the representations considered here of cases of assault by Anglo-Indian employers on their Indian servants.

In Britain meanwhile, feminists and members of the growing labour movement were developing new ideas about the rights of women and workers. This fed into employer anxieties about their authority over their servants. As we have discussed in previous chapters, in the final decades of the nineteenth century the 'Servant Problem' was a common theme in newspapers and journals and encompassed both what servant employers saw as an increasing scarcity of servants and their perceived uppitiness.

As was discussed in Chapter 1, domestic servants in Britain were largely employed in upper- and middle-class households, although significant numbers of artisan and respectable working-class households employed a single general servant or maid-of-all-work. According to Mrs Nassau Senior's 1874 report on the education of girls in pauper schools for the Local Government Board: '[t]he low rate of wages given to these girls ... makes them sought after by many people who, a few years ago, would have done their own housework, whose income does not permit them to keep a superior servant, and who often look on their little servant as a mere drudge.'[8] Indeed, the plight of such girls, when abused by their employers, frequently made it into the pages of the newspapers. It is difficult to say whether this was a true reflection of life in families who were more 'rough' than 'respectable', or merely an editorial response to the prejudicial expectations of *The Times* readership. Certainly, orphan pauper girls

---

[6] Mrinalini Sinha, *Colonial Masculinity. The 'Manly Englishman' and the 'Effeminate Bengali' in the Late Nineteenth Century* (Manchester: Manchester University Press, 1995), 39.

[7] Christine Dobbin, 'The Ilbert Bill: A Study of Anglo Indian Opinion in India, 1883', *Historical Studies Australia and New Zealand*, 13, 45 (Oct 1965), 93.

[8] Local Government Board, *Third Annual Report: Report by Mrs Nassau Senior on the Education of Girls in Pauper Schools, PP*, XXV (1874), 338.

appear to have been particularly vulnerable to poor treatment wherever they worked. In terms of India, the prevalence of adult male Indian domestic servants in Anglo-Indian households skewed the politics of dependence which framed metropolitan domestic service, affecting the representation in colonial texts of employer violence towards servants.

Assault and neglect

As part of the evangelical drive to reform manners in the early nineteenth century, ideal respectable living entailed a retreat from physical violence. Judicial and official tolerance of a widening definition of violent behaviour diminished through the course of the nineteenth century in both Britain and India. Self-control was coming to be seen as a defining characteristic of Englishmen in both metropole and colony. This characteristic was central to the making of bourgeois Britishness, as it joined the 'governing of a population to new interventions in the governing of the self'.[9] It was part of a wider humane perspective on governance that influenced political discourse in the nineteenth century, and which emerged from a synthesis of Enlightenment philosophy, evangelical morality and engagement with different cultures facilitated by globalizing technologies of mobility and communication.[10] Influential philanthropists and humanitarians highlighted the vulnerabilities of other colonial subjects and urged the state to acknowledge these both at home and abroad.[11] In India, whereas the 'relationship between many Anglo-Indian masters and Indian servants in the early nineteenth century appears to have been characterized by casual brutality', as the nineteenth century progressed such behaviour was, at least publicly, seen as damaging to the authority of the British.[12] Advice manuals published from the 1840s onwards advised Anglo-Indian employers to be firm with their servants without resorting to physical

---

[9]   A.L. Stoler, 'Cultivating Bourgeois Bodies and Racial Selves' in Catherine Hall (ed.), *Cultures of Empire. A Reader* (Manchester: Manchester University Press, 2000), 88.

[10] See Alan Lester and Fae Dussart, *Colonization and the Origins of Humanitarian Governance. Protecting Aborigines across the Nineteenth Century British Empire* (Cambridge: Cambridge University Press, 2014).

[11] See Alan Lester, *Imperial Networks: Creating Identities in Nineteenth-Century South Africa and Britain* (London: Routledge, 2001); Elizabeth Elbourne, 'The Sin of the Settler: The 1835–36 Select Committee on Aborigines and Debates over Virtue and Conquest in the Early Nineteenth-Century British White Settler Empire', *Journal of Colonialism and Colonial History*, 4, 3 (2003). doi:10.1353/cch.2004.0003.

[12] E.M.Collingham, *Imperial Bodies* (Cambridge: Polity, 2001), 109, 110.

chastisement, which was increasingly seen as 'un-British and unlikely to yield the desired result'.[13] Elizabeth Collingham has suggested that violent behaviour created an inappropriate 'intimacy between the Indian and his assailant'.[14] In contrast advice manuals published in Britain in the second half of the nineteenth century do not tend to mention the issue of physical chastisement at all, perhaps because it was (erroneously) assumed that masters and mistresses would not be inclined to strike British servants, or perhaps because in Britain racial consanguinity between employer and servant made the use of physical chastisement less problematic than in India.

Contrary to the myth of an imperialism characterized by British decency, racist violence continued to be an everyday part of colonial life in India: an ubiquitous adjunct to imperial power, despite high-minded ideals.[15] In spite of the advice against using violence to discipline servants in India, it appears that the practice was fairly common in both lower- and upper-class households. Some Anglo-Indians criticized the use of violence. For example, Constance Frederica Gordon Cumming wrote in 1884 that 'to see an Englishman fly into a passion with a native and strike a man who dares not hit him back, is humiliating indeed. If not cowardly, it certainly is horribly derogatory to British dignity, and quite the most painful sight you are likely to witness'.[16] A person's view on how to treat Indian servants could stand as a proxy for their perspective on the purpose, morality and practice of imperial rule. The newly installed Viceroy, Robert Bulwer-Lytton, asserted in 1876: 'Our greatest danger in India is from the whites' who claimed 'absolute liberty to outrage in every way the feelings of a vast alien population [and] resent the slightest control on the part either of the Government at home or the Government in India.'[17] Lytton's clear distinction between 'our' interests and 'the whites' who endangered them was indicative of the way Britishness could be differentiated across imperial space, articulated through the performance and policing of conduct towards indigenous peoples, and coded through race – in this case, whiteness. As Kolsky has argued, a by-product of this process was the

---

[13] Mary Procida, *Married to the Empire. Gender, Politics and Imperialism in India, 1883–1947* (Manchester: Manchester University Press, 2002), 91. See for example J.H.Stocqueler, *The Handbook of India, a Guide to the Stranger and the Traveller, and a Companion to the Resident* (1844), 198.

[14] E.M.Collingham, *Imperial Bodies*, 110.

[15] See Elizabeth Kolsky, *Colonial Justice in British India. White Violence and the Rule of Law* (Cambridge: Cambridge University Press, 2010); Jordanna Bailkin, 'The Boot and the Spleen: When Was Murder Possible in British India?', *Comparative Studies in Society and History*, 48, 2 (2006): 462–93.

[16] Indira Ghose, *Memsahibs Abroad: Writings by Women Travellers in Nineteenth Century India* (Delhi: Oxford University Press, 1998), 190.

[17] Lytton to John Morley, 24 September 1876, Private Papers, IOR, Mss/Eur/218/522/15.

expansion of the imperial state's power, as troublesome 'whites' as well as Indians became an object of its regulatory control.[18]

In courts in Britain, as the nineteenth century progressed, judges were 'increasingly seeking to set more stringent standards of self-control, refusing to tolerate kinds of violence supposedly accepted elsewhere'.[19] Nevertheless, a master's right to 'discipline' and 'chastise' his dependents was still legally endorsed in Britain. In 1845, the case of *Turner v. Mason* established that it was 'a master's province to regulate the conduct of his domestic servant' as he saw fit.[20] The provision here is somewhat ambiguous; 'regulation' can take a range of forms from physical and verbal punishment to material deprivation. This ambiguity in the servant-employer relationship became problematic in cases of abuse, because in order that a verdict might be reached it was necessary to define the limits of an employer's jurisdiction over his or her servant and to mark the boundary between legitimate physical punishment and offensive violence within the servant-employer relationship. The Apprentices and Servants Act of 1851 made no mention of physical abuse in its provisions; it merely endorsed a servant's dependent status by making employers legally obliged to supply 'necessary Food, Clothing, or Lodging' to servants under the age of eighteen. Thus, unless they were prosecuting their employers for failure to provide food, clothing or lodging as minors, if servants sought redress for physical abuse, they had to bring cases of assault for prosecution.

In India the employer-servant relationship was covered by breach of contract and breach of trust laws, which covered employer-employee relationships generally and which protected the employer rather than the employee. The servant, like any British subject, had a right to freedom from assault under the Indian Penal Code.[21] Indian servants did sometimes bring cases of assault against their employers. This appears to have happened with greater frequency in the last three decades of the nineteenth century, perhaps as a result of a greater willingness on the part of Indians to assert rights, which commentators linked to increasing political activism at this time. Indeed, in 1883 opposition to the Ilbert Bill, which sought to empower Indian judges to try Europeans in criminal cases in rural areas in India, coalesced around a fear that Indian servants would 'annoy

---

[18]   Elizabeth Kolsky, *Colonial Justice*, 6.
[19]   Martin J. Wiener, 'The Sad Story of George Hall: Adultery, Murder and the Politics of Mercy in mid-Victorian England', *Social History*, 24, 2 (1999): 190.
[20]   Cited in Pamela Horn, *The Rise and Fall of the Victorian Servant* (Stroud: Sutton, 1990), 113.
[21]   See Act XLV of 1860, Chapter XVI in *Legislative Acts of the Governor General in Council Vol. III*, IOR/V/8/119, APAC.

their employers by dragging them into court'.[22] Opponents of the Bill argued that European women would be left 'at the mercy of unscrupulous servants', and this could dangerously undermine colonial authority, as 'An Englishwoman' suggested disingenuously in a letter to *The Englishman* newspaper:

> We women may not be politicians, we may be very illogical, but we surely, some of us, have sufficient knowledge of the position of the English in India to understand that anything that weakens the prestige of our name is detrimental to our safe holding of the country.[23]

Such anxieties resulted in major changes to the bill which became law in 1884, demonstrating how the relationship between servants and masters and mistresses could have a political significance well beyond that of the household.[24]

Cases of assault brought by Indian servants against their employers did not carry the same sensational value for the Indian press as the abuse of servant girls did in British papers, due to the different gender and racial positions of Indian from British servants. In India, cases of assault brought by servants tended to feature as small entries in the 'Police' columns in Anglo-Indian newspapers, when they featured at all. In Britain, the details of cases involving the maltreatment of servant girls were often sensationally entitled with statements such as 'Disgusting Cruelty' or 'Gross Case of Cruelty'.[25] Almost every year between 1850 and 1910, two or three cases, invariably involving servant girls, were warranted sufficiently newsworthy to appear in the pages of *The Times*. The records of local newspapers suggest that less sensational prosecutions by servants were not an infrequent occurrence at petty and quarter sessions. The cases of abuse of servants appearing in the pages of the British national dailies in our period were extreme and cannot be taken as representative of the experience of most domestic servants. Such accounts fitted into the popular narrative of the poor friendless orphan child immortalized in the fiction of the period by writers such as Charles Dickens, and perhaps attracted press attention for this reason. Nonetheless, the cases discussed here were not fictional, and mapping the extremities can illustrate underlying contests relevant to the spectrum of 'appropriate' relations between employers and servants. Comparison with media treatment of cases of assault brought by Indian servants adds another dimension

---

[22] Letter from 'An Englishwoman', *The Englishman*, 14 March 1883.

[23] Letter from 'An Englishwoman', *The Englishman*, 14 March 1883.

[24] See Fae Dussart, "'To Glut a Menial's Grudge:" Domestic Servants and the Ilbert Bill Controversy of 1883', *Journal of Colonialism and Colonial History*, 14(1) for a discussion of the significance of domestic servants in the Ilbert Bill controversy.

[25] *The Times*, 12 February 1857; *The Times*, 20 September 1856.

to this spectrum, showing how the legitimacy of violence within the employer-servant relationship was differently figured across imperial space, contributing to the distinctive character of metropole and colony.

In many of the cases in Britain, an employer's brutality was precipitated by some perceived failing on the part of the servant to fulfil his or her work duties. As discussed in earlier chapters, servants' work could involve a wide range of tasks from scrubbing the floors to cleaning the silverware and from lighting the fires to bathing the children of the family. Rules of respectability dictated that servants' work was done according to a strict timetable punctuated by daily events such as mealtimes and visiting times.[26] For a general servant working alone, getting everything done on time could be difficult. Hannah Cullwick would rise at dawn and was rarely in bed before 11 pm. Failure to keep to the timetable could compromise the family's respectable status and result in punishment for the servant. In 1851 Hannah Hinton was beaten 'because she had not got the fire lighted at 7 o'clock in the morning'.[27] In 1852 Elizabeth Malcolm was beaten because she was 'stupid and slow'.[28]

Other servants were punished for perceived disobedience. Fanny Square Keys' mistress hit her because 'she did not do something she was told'.[29] Emily Fox was beaten because 'I was not strong enough to carry the boiler'.[30] Similarly, in India an employer's perception that a servant was failing to fulfil work duties could provoke violence, though the work differed. Indian servants' tasks were usually more specific as households tended to have bigger complements of servants. As discussed in Chapter 2, separate servants would be employed to cook, wait at table, fetch water, provide personal service, clean the floors and pull the fans. Breakdowns in communication, or the perception of disobedience, laziness or dishonesty could provoke an employer's anger. In 1883 a cook in Calcutta brought a case of assault against her mistress, claiming that her mistress had 'assaulted her with clenched fists' when she had declined to 'cook seven or eight dishes for a party of visitors … saying she was unable to prepare same alone'.[31]

In smaller households in Britain, the family and the servants could not avoid sharing space and work, which exacerbated tensions, sometimes resulting in

---

[26] Leonore Davidoff, *The Best Circles. Society Etiquette and the Season* (London: The Cresset Library, 1986), 35.

[27] *The Times*. 13 January 1851.

[28] *The Times*, 11 November 1852.

[29] *The Times*, 20 September 1856.

[30] *The Times*, 12 March 1866.

[31] *The Englishman*, 14 July 1883.

violence. Servants' work involved the physical performance of submission. As the advice manuals discussed in Chapter 1 indicate, employers expected their servants to be seen and not heard. Ideally they kept their eyes downcast, backed out of rooms, curtsied or touched their cap to their employers. A servant on her knees, face close to the floor she was scrubbing, assumed a physical position charged with meaning. Her posture denoted subservience, possibly sexual as well as social, which may have increased her vulnerability to physical abuse. In the case of Susan Russell, whose mistress, Ann Radcliffe, was charged and found guilty of grievous bodily harm at the Central Criminal Court in 1868, the violent presence of the mistress while the servant works is striking. In her testimony Susan, the only servant in the household, described 'cleaning a grate in a bedroom about 2 o'clock [on Sunday], and the prisoner entered the room. She was then kneeling, and the prisoner kicked her behind, being cross that she had not cleaned the stove before that time. Her master was in the room at the time, and sent her home at once'.[32]

Susan Russell also described being assaulted by her mistress while cleaning saucepans and on another occasion while cleaning knives. In cross-examination the servant described having been 'well treated up to August last, and the prisoner then began to treat her ill. She used to complain of her being dirty'. Ann Radcliffe's violent behaviour towards her servant appears to have taken place over three days. The mention of the master of the household in Susan's testimony is interesting in this context as he appears to have protected her, or at least to have removed her from violent situations: 'On the previous Friday the prisoner boxed her ears and her master sent her downstairs. Her master went out, and after that she was cleaning some saucepans in the kitchen, when the prisoner poured some water into a teacup from a kettle on the hob and threw it over her neck, which it blistered, and also her bosom'.[33] Though it is not possible to say with certainty what had provoked Ann Radcliffe's abuse of Susan, the intimacy of the violent acts in such cases reflects the proximity of master/mistress and servant and points towards emotional tensions; the mistress's fear and perhaps jealousy of, and consequent need to subjugate, the servant/Other.

In these cases the authority of an employer to 'regulate' a servant extended into a right to physically chastise a servant for not doing a job well. Indeed, in many of the cases, the employers justified their actions by drawing attention to the servant in question's faults and upheld their right to punish as they saw

[32] *The Times*, 29 February 1868.
[33] *The Times*, 29 February 1868.

fit. For example, Mr John Pemberton argued that his servant 'was deceitful and given to lying, and had other evil propensities' and defiantly claimed that 'whatever censure ... the world might pass on him, he ... would inflict corporal punishment on the girl whenever he thought she deserved it'.[34]

As in Britain, Indian servants were expected to keep to a timetable of work, and to respond promptly, appropriately attired, to their employer's calls. The formalized service of meals or teas, as a moment when Indian servants' and Anglo-Indian employers' notions of appropriate behaviour could differ, was a potential flashpoint. A servant's failure to do work on time or to behave with the requisite degree of deference or decorum could be used by Anglo-Indian employers as defence for their action. On 3 August 1883 a case was heard at a Calcutta Police Court in which a servant accused his employer, Mr Jones, of assaulting him when he pressed a demand for his wages. Mr Jones admitted striking the servant, but claimed that this had happened not because the servant demanded payment but because the servant 'neglected to bring him his tiffin, on which he remonstrated with him. The latter, however, became very insolent, whereupon he slapped him'.[35] Mr Jones was fined Rs 2, a nominal punishment which indicates ambivalence surrounding what kinds of behaviour were understood by Anglo-Indians to be legitimate within the relationship between Anglo-Indian employer and Indian servant.

Anecdotal evidence suggests that physical chastisement of servants continued to be fairly common throughout the nineteenth century. Florence Marryat described feeling

> the keenest sympathy with the action of an officer in our regiment, who, aggravated at the slow and solemn manner in which a young Mussulman in his employ was carrying a pile of plates from the luncheon-table out at his back door, jumped up, and regardless of the fate of his crockery, gave the tardy domestic such an energetic kick that he sent him flying, plates and all, down a flight of some dozen steps, into the garden, vastly astonished, I have little doubt, at the unexpected impetus which had been given to his footsteps.[36]

The casualness with which Marryat described this act of aggression and the way in which 'the fate of the crockery' was implied to be more significant than the injuries the servant might have sustained in falling down the steps suggests

---

[34] *The Times*, 11 November 1852.
[35] *The Englishman*, 4 August 1883.
[36] Florence Marryat, *'Gup' Sketches of Anglo-Indian Life and Character* (London: Reprinted from Temple Bar, 1868), 31–2, 35.

such behaviour on the part of Anglo-Indians was tolerated more in India than it might have been in Britain. It was usual for Anglo-Indian employers found guilty of assault against Indian servants to receive lenient sentences.[37] For example, in July 1876 Mr Hutchinson, a Calcutta broker, was found guilty of assaulting his servant and was fined Rs 20 as punishment for his crime. In the spring of the same year a Mr Fuller, an English Pleader at Agra, caused the death of his *syce*, Katwaroo, by striking him on the head and knocking him to the ground. It was claimed that the *syce* had suffered from an enlarged spleen, which had ruptured when he fell and caused his death. Fuller was fined only Rs 30 as punishment.[38] By contrast, in February 1868 at the Central Criminal Court in London, Ann Radcliffe was sentenced to five years penal servitude for 'cruelly ill-using and doing grievous bodily harm to one Susan Russell' her maidservant.[39]

Surprisingly the leniency of the punishment received by Mr Fuller in Agra, in the North West Provinces, did not go unchallenged. On 15 July 1876 a Minute was published in the *Supplement to the Gazette of India* in which the Governor General in Council (Lord Lytton, the Viceroy) criticized the decisions made by the Joint Magistrate of Agra, Mr Leeds, and the High Court, and argued that a fine of Rs 30 was not only an inadequate punishment for Fuller's crime, but one that damaged the reputation of British justice in India. Lytton claimed that Mr Leeds seemed 'to have viewed an assault resulting in the death of the injured man in just the same light as if it had been attended by no such result', evincing 'a most inadequate sense of the magnitude of the offence of which Mr Fuller was found guilty'.

According to Lytton, the offence was that of 'voluntarily causing hurt' which was an offence which varied in degree 'from one which is little more than nominal, to one which is so great that the Penal Code assigns to it the heavy punishment of imprisonment for a year *and* a fine of Rs 1000'. In such cases the 'amount

---

[37] See, for example, Ram Gopal Sanyal (ed.), *Record of Criminal Cases as between Europeans and Natives for the Last 60 Years* (Calcutta: J.N. Dutt, 1893), in which the author demonstrates that 'the system of administration of justice which has been established under British rule is fairly effective in the vast majority of cases. The impression, however, is widespread that it has not been equally successful in those cases, where Europeans are charged with acts of violence committed upon natives of the country', 2. Sanyal's assertion was subsequently supported by a government report, 'Return showing the number of assaults committed by Europeans on natives and by natives on Europeans in the five years 1901–1905' File no. 3445, L/P&J/6/781, APAC. See also Jordanna Bailkin, 'The Boot and the Spleen: When Was Murder Possible in British India?', *Comparative Studies in Society and History*, 48, 2 (2006) for a discussion of 'the centrality of race in constructing ideas of homicide and violence itself' and the critical nature within the politics of empire of the question of who it was possible to call violent.

[38] See *The Englishman*, 24 July 1876.

[39] *The Times*, 29 February 1868.

of hurt and the amount of provocation' were important factors in determining sentences. In Mr Fuller's case, 'while the provocation was exceedingly small, the hurt was death'. According to Lytton a fine of Rs 30 was wholly insufficient as a sentence. He considered that 'Mr Leeds has treated the offence as a merely nominal one, and has inflicted a merely nominal punishment; and that to treat such offences with practical impunity, is a very bad example and likely rather to encourage than repress them.'

Lytton also took the opportunity to express 'his abhorrence of the practice, instances of which occasionally come to light, of European masters treating their native servants in a manner in which they would not treat men of their own race'. He went on to claim that

> [t]his practice is all the more cowardly, because those who are least able to retaliate injury or insult have the strongest claim upon the forbearance and protection of their employers. But bad as it is from every point of view, it is made worse by the fact, known to all residents in India that Asiatics are subject to internal disease which often renders fatal to life even a slight external shock. The Governor General in Council considers that the habit of resorting to blows on every trifling provocation should be visited by adequate legal penalties; and that those who indulge it should reflect that they may be put in jeopardy for a serious crime.[40]

This statement, even while it condemned acts of violence towards Indian servants, constructed them as members of a physically weak race. The European, by implication, was strong and powerful and should use his power to protect, not abuse, his racial inferiors who, owing not only to their powerless position as servants but also to their physical inferiority as Indians, were more in need of protection than men of British origin. In this way the master's role was constructed as a manly, paternalistic one, in line with wider gendered and classed discourses on the ideal structure of master/servant relations across imperial space.

Lytton's Minute caused 'vehement wrath, on the part of the Anglo-Indian community, and elicited from the Anglo-Indian press … a swarm of protests and articles, attributing it to an ill-considered sentimental impulse, profound ignorance of Indian law, and reckless disregard of the majesty of the High Court'.[41]

---

[40] Letter from Arthur Howell, Esq, Officiating Secretary to the Government of India, to the Secretary to the Government of the North-Western Provinces in *Supplement to the Gazette of India*, Calcutta, Saturday 15 July 1876, no 31, p763 IOR/V/11/41, APAC.

[41] Lytton to Salisbury, 30 July 1876, *Lord Lytton. Letters Despatched. 1876* MSS Eur/E218/18, APAC.

These letters and articles revealed the ambivalence of Anglo-Indian employers as to the legitimacy of violence within the servant-employer relationship in India. Almost all letters and articles claimed to agree that 'nobody has any right to box a servant's ears in this country any more than in Europe' and that the 'brutal and cowardly habit, so common in India, of resorting to violence on the slightest provocation, and often on no provocation at all, is one that cannot be too unsparingly denounced'.[42] However, most of the letters and articles then went on to contradict themselves, making excuses for Mr Fuller's conduct and outlining justifications as to why his sentence had been fair under the circumstances. A popular point of view was that since Mr Fuller did not intend to kill the *syce*, and since the blow that killed the *syce* was probably only a slight one, the *syce's* enlarged spleen making him vulnerable to any blow, and since Mr Fuller did not know the *syce* suffered from an enlarged spleen, then a fine of 30 Rupees was a fair, even a harsh, punishment. In short, striking a servant wasn't really a significant crime, and Lytton in his position of privilege didn't understand the vulnerability of his non-official countrymen and women to their servants' antipathy.[43]

Racializing assumptions about the 'weakness' of Indian bodies did much to mitigate the charges white Britons faced when they grievously wounded or killed Indians.[44] Class prejudice also played a role, as it intersected with ideas about colonial masculinity. It was argued that it was simply impossible for white 'gentlemen' to be brutal abusers. As one letter writer to *The Pioneer* claimed, 'the English gentleman in India, of education and high feeling, never raised his hand against a native.'[45] In the Fuller case, in contrast to Fuller's testimony, three witnesses claimed that they had seen Fuller kick Katwaroo in the stomach. However, as was the case with many Indian witnesses, their testimony was dismissed by the judge, who claimed 'it is *prima facie* improbable that a European would kick his servant in the stomach.'[46] The judge did not elaborate on what it was about 'a European' that militated against him kicking servants in the stomach. We might speculate though, that Leeds assumed that European 'manners' interdicted the stomach-kicking, if not the face-slapping, of domestic

---

[42] Editorial, *The Pioneer*, 19 July 1876; Editorial, *Indian Daily News*, 21 July 1876.

[43] See for example the editorial articles in *The Pioneer*, 19 July 1876 and *The Englishman*, 24 July 1876.

[44] See Bailkin, 'The Boot and the Spleen', and Kolsky, *Colonial Justice*, for a full exploration of the 'enlarged spleen' defence.

[45] Letter to *The Pioneer*, 22 July 1876.

[46] Quoted in Bailkin, The Boot and the Spleen, 479. On the dismissal of Indian testimony see Kolsky, *Colonial Justice*.

servants. Such distinctions speak of the way in which the specificity of violent acts – where and how one person assaulted another's body – and their relative legitimacy (kicking a servant in the stomach being less acceptable than slapping his face) might be connected to the complex dynamics of gender and class as well as race in the colonial context.[47] The erasure of specific kinds of white violence within the criminal record was a part of the process through which whiteness as a category of identity gained classed and gendered content. Indeed, a letter to the Pioneer suggested that there was a 'subtle difference between corporal correction … and roughness or violence', and that 'this strange behaviour of Mr Fuller's in pulling his syce's hair blackens his case very greatly'.[48]

An editorial in *The Indian Daily News* suggested that Fuller's crime was not that serious: 'the offence of which Fuller was guilty, resulted quite accidentally from a slight exercise of personal violence.' Rather, according to this editorial, the really significant offence had been perpetrated by Lytton in criticizing Mr Leed's judgement: 'the Government resolution taken as a whole, constitutes a serious offence against the proper administration of justice in India, and an undesirable reproof of the highest judicial interpreters of the law in the country.'[49] The statement that the resolution constituted an 'undesirable reproof' of the judiciary in British India reveals that the concern here was with maintaining the prestige of the British as rulers. For the *Indian Daily News* writer, 'the proper administration of justice' presumably meant finding in favour of the Anglo-Indian. The fear underlying such an attitude as that expressed by this editorial writer was probably justified. Indian voices were increasingly vociferous in complaining about the injustices embedded in the administration of law in India. An angry letter from Kamala Kanto Ghosh, also published in the *Indian Daily News*, articulated the growing resentment felt by many Indians:

> Have you, Sir, ever heard that an Englishman was hanged or transported to the Andaman for murdering an Indian? But I doubt not you have heard of many cases, where Englishmen were found guilty of such foul deeds. Is it anarchy that such acts are being done and overlooked? Are we not men that justice will never be done to us, that our lives will be regarded like those of dogs? Are we not possessed of the same organs, same feelings, with the whiteskinned Englishmen? Why then, Sir, is justice trampled down under feet in such cases? Why then, Sir, you, who pretend to be the defender of justice, remain dumb when such

---

[47] Bailkin, The Boot and the Spleen, 487.
[48] Letter, *The Pioneer*, 9 July 1876.
[49] Editorial, *Indian Daily News*, 21 July 1876.

cases occur? The English nation are proud of their civilization, but are these the actions of civilized men?[50]

Ghosh's claim to equality with Englishmen as a man and his scornful challenging of Englishmen's claim to 'civilization' reads powerfully. Placed in the wider context of Indian nationalist frustration and anger with colonial oppression, the articulate expression of attitudes such as his in the pages of newspapers may have contributed to Anglo-Indians' sense of insecurity.

An article in the *Civil and Military Gazette* argued that the lack of any legislation protecting employers from vindictive servants was the reason employers were driven to violence because 'absence of law as between master and servant provokes occasional manslaughter as no man can manage an Indian household without an occasional blow for acts of which the law refuses to punish'. The article called for a law that would punish 'any wilful neglect of duty on the part of the servant; punish in fact the provocation to assault as being really the first blow' claiming that the master's right to 'dismissal with power to cut at most 15 days' pay' was 'no remedy'. The author went on to absolve Mr Fuller of blame for killing the *syce* by suggesting that the 'trick of throwing themselves down as the consequence of a blow which would hardly kill a fly is no novelty in India, and probably in this case it was the fall voluntarily inflicted by the syce and not the blow which caused death'.[51] Despite a nod to humanitarian concerns at the outset, the general thrust of this and other articles provoked by the Fuller case was that in Anglo-Indian households, violence was not only justified, but necessary in controlling a servant, who might otherwise 'absolutely refuse to perform the duties for which he is engaged'.[52] Such refusals were figured as snubs not only to Anglo-Indians' colonial domestic authority, but also to their imperial authority as Britons.

Despite the fact that in cases of assault brought by servants in Britain the servants failure to fulfil work duties was often cited as provocation, ambivalence over the justice of convictions and sentences appears much less marked than in India. For example, in 1868 Mary Barry charged her employer Miss Ann Turner with assault. Mary had worked for Miss Turner and her sister for just over a year and had left their employ a couple of months before bringing the charge. In her evidence Mary claimed that she 'ought to have got up at 6 in the

[50] Kamala Kanto Ghosh, Letter, *Indian Daily News*, 25 July 1876. See also the letter from 'Native' in the *Indian Daily News*, 29 July 1876.
[51] 'Master and Servant', *Civil and Military Gazette*, 22 July 1876.
[52] 'Master and Servant', *Civil and Military Gazette*, 22 July 1876.

morning, but sometimes did not, and when that occurred she was kept without her breakfast and dinner … [her mistress] had repeatedly struck her with a thin cane on her hands and shoulders, giving her two or three blows each time'. However, in cross-examination Mary revealed that she 'was very sorry when her mistress discharged her', which may have suggested to the court that her accusation was malicious. In their defence, the barrister representing Misses Turner claimed that they had hired Mary Barry after 'seeing the girl and her mother outside St Mary's Catholic Church apparently very poor' and had 'benevolently interested themselves in their welfare' by engaging the girl to work for them:

> They used their best endeavours to teach the girl the duties of a domestic servant, and were obliged to use some slight correction. She had never been treated with the least cruelty; her breakfast had been two or three times delayed, but only for an hour or so, and she never went without her dinner … the girl was in better health than when she entered the service, was well-fed and treated, and paid wages … what had been done was for the cleanliness of her own person and a desire to get her out of slovenly and bad habits. It was admitted that on one occasion two or three blows had been given on her shoulders with a light cane. She was slovenly and obstinate and needed correction.

In this evidence Mary Barry's employers asserted their right to physically punish the servant they had so benevolently taken on as their dependant and attempted to train. It is suggested that they had fulfilled their responsibility as employers – feeding and paying the girl – but that her failure to fulfil the expectations of her as a willing and obedient servant legitimized their use of physical punishment. However, while the case against them was dismissed, in his closing remarks the presiding magistrate stated clearly that there 'was an idea prevalent … that mistresses had a right to use corporal punishment. In former times such things were permitted, but that fashion had now passed away … it would have been better when they found they could do nothing with [Mary] to have sent her away'. So, although the court sympathized with Misses Turner's position, the magistrate made it clear that times had changed and employers no longer had a right to chastise their servants' bodies as they might their own child. Rather, they must dismiss her from her workplace as a failing employee. Mary Barry may not have won the damages she sought, but the assertion implicit in her accusation – that physical punishment constituted an illegitimate use of authority – had been vindicated. In contrast to the response to Lytton's words in the Fuller case in India, in Mary Barry's case there were no letters to the newspapers, no editorials, no outcry, though it must be noted that the situation may have been different if Mary Barry had won her case.[53]

Unlike in India, in Britain cases brought by servants or their representatives often pivoted upon the limits of responsibility and dependence within the employer-servant relationship. Where wages and perceived neglect of duty were flashpoints in the Indian context, food was an issue in almost all the British cases, with most of the servants complaining of receiving scanty or spoiled food and providing details in cross-examination of the food they had been given. Emily Fox claimed her employers Mr and Mrs Gumb had provided her with

> cold potatoes and cabbage for breakfast, and the same for dinner, and two or three times a week a very little meat. Sometimes I had bread and butter, and sometimes dry bread for tea ... The potatoes and cabbage were boiled in quantities which sometimes lasted me a week. They had fried potatoes and bacon for breakfast, and hot potatoes and cabbage and meat for dinner. They had tea and bread and butter. They were kept locked in the safe. My potatoes and cabbage were kept in the same safe. Mistress treated me very unkindly.[54]

We can imagine the poor girl's mouth-watering as she watched her employers enjoy their food. However, her employers' defence was that, as a pauper, the food she received in their employ 'was equal to that she had been accustomed to have in the union'.[55] Similarly, in her case against her schoolmistress employer, Eleanor Houseman testified that she

> had porridge for breakfast mixed with charcoal, and sometimes it tasted like cod liver oil. Sometimes she had fish and potatoes for dinner or tea. She never had enough to eat. She was put up into that room because Miss Scott (the prisoner) said she was not fit to be about, and because she used to steal food out of the cupboard or off the table when she was hungry.[56]

Despite a doctor testifying that the girl was seriously underweight, the defence argued that 'though it was not sumptuous food, it was such, perhaps, as a woman in her position might have to give to a servant'.[57] The implication of the defence in both these cases was that the servant's position as a servant defined the terms of her dependence and her employer's responsibility. According to the defence, the servant was not entitled to the same food as the family she lived with and

[53] *The Times,* 7 April 1868.
[54] *The Times,* 12 March 1866.
[55] *The Times,* 12 March 1866.
[56] *The Times,* 7 August 1880.
[57] *The Times,* 7 August 1880.

worked for precisely because she was a servant. As a person of inferior status she ate inferior food. The servants, by drawing attention to the distasteful or meagre food they received, were implying they had a right, within the context of their dependence, to decent food. The court was being asked to decide if these terms were reasonable or not.

The most sensational cases frequently involved young pauper servants hired out from workhouses and orphanages. The Guardians of the Poor usually brought such cases. This may be because the stigmatized status of paupers increased the likelihood of their suffering abuse at the hands of their employers, but it seems more likely that without the family and community support networks available to non-pauper servants, fewer opportunities to escape violent employers were available to pauper girls. For example, in 1856 a Mrs Grills of Steptoe, South Devon 'the wife of a respectable farmer' was charged with, and found guilty of, assaulting her fourteen-year-old pauper servant Fanny Square Keys, who had been hired from the Kingsford Union to 'tend the pigs and calves and to look after a little child'. According to Fanny's testimony she had been repeatedly violently punished by her mistress for trifling faults. However, when visited by the relieving officer, she told him 'that she was very well treated and liked her place, but she said she did this because she was so much afraid of her mistress'.[58] Similarly sixteen-year-old Sophia Jarvis, who in 1863 brought a charge of cruelty against her mistress Mrs Mary Langdon Thomas, claimed that she was always 'in company with one or other of her mistress's family and therefore had not had the opportunity of running away until the nineteenth of December'.[59] With no family to run away to when she made her escape, she went to the Industrial School of St George the Martyr at Mitcham, whence she had been hired. Though this isolation meant that pauper girls were more vulnerable to violence in their places, it may also have meant that abused pauper servants sought redress in the courts, as they could not find a resolution to their predicament other than to turn the authorities charged with their protection.

Conclusion

The greater tolerance of acts of violence towards servants in India, evidenced by the leniency of the punishments meted out to employers found guilty of

---

[58] *The Times*, 20 September 1856.
[59] *The Times*, 15 January 1863.

assault, and the lack of sympathy for the victims in such cases, as compared with the horror expressed in British newspapers at cases of abuse involving young servant girls in Britain, was linked to the gender and racial status of the servants involved. Physical chastisement of Indian servants was seen as more legitimate than that of British servants precisely because they were Indian. The opinion expressed in *The Pioneer* newspaper that 'cuffs and stripes, and all kinds of corporeal maltreatment are recognised in India by Indians as well as Europeans, as more in accordance with the natural fitness of things than such phenomena would be thought in Europe' was not a unique one amongst Anglo-Indians.[60] Furthermore, many more Indian servants were male than in Britain; the assaulted male servant did not possess the same vulnerability as the friendless, abused, young servant girl. It seems likely that the maleness of Indian servants, as compared to British maids, underwrote the racial difference upon which the legitimacy of physical chastisement was predicated.[61]

As Shani D'Cruze has argued '[t]he fact that such incidents result in court cases illustrates resistance on the part of servants ... and also a sense of outrage – that that specific assault ... was contestably an illegitimate use of authority in a society where physical chastisement of dependents (particularly children) was commonplace'.[62] Though D'Cruze is referring specifically to Britain, her statement can also be applied to the nineteenth-century Indian context. The process of the court cases represented a kind of negotiation; though the choice to go to court may not have been as rationally thought out as this, in suing their employers, the servants were implicitly asserting that the limits of acceptable behaviour on the part of their employers had been reached, and were asking the court to clarify the ambiguities in what were the servant's and what were the employer's rights within the relationship. Though the servants may have appeared powerless to protect themselves from abuse, the very fact that they brought cases for public judgement in courts constituted a significant challenge to the absolutism of their employer's authority. The fear that servants would use the courts to undermine their employers was a significant anxiety for colonial masters and mistresses.

---

[60] Editorial, *The Pioneer*, 19 July 1876.

[61] Of course there were female servants in India and male servants in Britain who would have suffered violence at the hands of their employers. However, the majority of servants in India were male in the second half of the nineteenth century and the majority of servants in Britain were female, which would be likely to have affected the way in which the limits of acceptable corporeal punishment were generally popularly drawn in the two countries.

[62] Shani D'Cruze, *Crimes of Outrage. Sex, Violence and Victorian Working Women*, 92.

Dominant ideas about the respective rights and responsibilities of servants and employers, expressed in the newspapers considered here, were developed across imperial space and owed much to the trans-imperial trope of the problematic domestic servant, who frustrated the benevolent, pedagogic efforts of his or her beleaguered master and/or mistress to 'improve' her or him, and the class or race she or he was seen to represent. Drawing on this trope, the rhetoric of moral reformation was employed by colonial and metropolitan masters and mistresses to elide their use of abuse in social control. In the metropole, the idea that domestic service should be a transformative experience, through which the 'improvement' (if not social advancement, quite the contrary, in fact) of the servant might be effected, was significant in employers' defence of abusive behaviour. In India, servant employers were more explicitly concerned with the maintenance of colonial prestige within, and beyond, the walls of the home. These employers framed their assaults upon their servants as the inevitable by-product of ruling ungrateful subjects who were unwilling to submit to the colonial yoke. In both sites, employers used abusive behaviour to endorse the construction of their class and racial status and power over the Others their servants represented.

The identification of shifts in the limits of acceptable behaviour, manifesting here in the relationship between servants and employers as it played out in the public sphere of the courtroom and in the pages of newspapers, indicates a world in flux: a colonial society threatened by indigenous nationalism, and a metropolitan patriarchal and class structure responding reluctantly to emergent ideas about work and rights. Even while violence was assumed by servant employers as an explicable, even necessary, feature of domestic mastery, tensions progressively emerged with official bodies on this issue, as the question: 'what kind of rule is legitimate?' was debated by both Indians and Europeans in different ways towards the end of the nineteenth century.

Servants' resistance to mastery in the imperial metropole

A popular Victorian saying claimed 'Servants talk about People; Gentlefolk discuss Things'.[1] One thing that is certainly true is that servants were one of the foremost 'Things' 'Gentlefolk' discussed at great length throughout our period. In newspapers, journals and books, servants were a topic of unceasing interest to nineteenth-century imperial commentators. Metropolitan servants though did sometimes reply to criticisms of their work and character. Their opinions were not frequently featured in newspaper correspondence columns (though this may have been a result of editorial bias, rather than a reflection of an unwillingness on the part of servants to write in to the papers), nor were there a large number of books published in the nineteenth century that were authored by servants. However, the fact that some servants were able to express opinions regarding their role in a public forum, such as the pages of a newspaper, is significant. Within the broad context of the Empire, it marks the greater degree of agency available to white metropolitan servants, relative to their indigenous counterparts in colonial places.

Across imperial space servants employed informal networks of communication, informing each other of places available and places to avoid amongst other things. But by writing to newspapers, metropolitan domestic servants could enter into a public and even national dialogue with the employing class, counter criticisms and make arguments both individually and as representatives of the 'servant class'. That their letters did not appear with the regularity of their employers' complaints is perhaps not as important as the fact that they appeared at all. Where servants bringing cases of assault against their employers were challenging the absolutism of their employers' authority and arguing for servants rights as human beings, in the correspondence columns of

[1] Pamela Horn, *The Rise and Fall of the Victorian Servant* (Stroud: Sutton, 1990), 128.

The Times metropolitan servants were able to make arguments for their rights as employees and suggestions as to the best ways for an employer to ensure his or her servant was willing and competent. Towards the end of the nineteenth century, some metropolitan servants felt agent enough to attempt to unionize. This chapter will consider some of the debates over servants and service that surfaced in nineteenth-century metropolitan texts and will examine servants' intervention in those debates. It will then go on to discuss servants' attempts to unionize in the later decades of the nineteenth century.

Newspaper correspondence

Newspapers were perhaps an obvious choice of forum for servants to engage in debates over their role and character. After all, throughout our period the first few pages of many newspapers, both local and national, were filled with advertisements placed by servants looking for places, or by employers looking for servants. Many servants would have been familiar with the papers for this reason. This section considers occasions when servants and service were under debate in the correspondence columns of *The Times* newspaper between 1850 and 1914. *The Times* was the newspaper of the elite (middle class and upwards). Its stance was generally conservative with a small 'c', though its editors prided themselves on their impartiality. Though not as widely read as other papers of the time, with a circulation in the 60,000s in the 1880s as compared with the *Daily Telegraph*, which had a circulation of 300,000 at the same time, it did publish the letters of domestic servants and their employers across our period, as well as editorials on 'the servant problem'.[2] Servants may have chosen to write to *The Times* precisely because it was an elite newspaper; the majority of its readership almost certainly consisted of servant employers. In a paper servants would have seen their employers reading, the correspondence column of *The Times* was a place where servants could be sure that members of the servant employing class would see their opinions.

Most letters by servants tended to be written in response to negative criticism of them in other correspondence or editorials. In the 1870s local newspapers published a number of letters, which were apparently stimulated by efforts amongst some domestic workers to unionize. The letters were often

---

[2]   George Boyce, James Curran and Pauline Wingate (eds.), *Newspaper History from the Seventeenth Century to the Present Day* (London: Constable for the Press Group of the Acton Society, 1978), 120.

entertainingly written, sometimes infused with indignation, sometimes with resigned pessimism, sometimes with biting wit. The letters from employers were also varied. Some wrote in defence of servants and some wrote in complaint, but nearly all had ideas about how to address the enduring 'servant problem' – the nature of which shifted as our period progressed. These ideas often revolved around assumptions about servant character and employer responsibility that referred to wider and changing notions of gender and class difference.

On the 17th of December 1850 *The Times* reported a speech made by Mr Wortley, Recorder of the Central Criminal Court, at the commencement of the December sessions, in which he drew attention to the large number of charges of robberies by servants. He suggested that there was 'a very good remedy in the hands of employers themselves, and that a good deal of this class of crime was occasioned ... by not giving proper remuneration to the servants for their services'. Paying servants wages that were 'totally insufficient to enable them to support themselves', he argued, meant that 'the consequence almost necessarily was that they were compelled to resort to the expedient of plundering their employers in order to eke out a subsistence'.[3]

The next day the editorial in *The Times* ran a blistering attack on Mr Wortley. Choosing to entirely ignore Mr Wortley's suggestion that the economic exploitation of servants might drive them to steal, the writer of the editorial took the opportunity to express a specifically middle-class distaste for domestic servants. The writer claimed to 'protest, with all the force of the deepest conviction, against the truth of these assertions' and argued that Mr Wortley's words appeared 'calculated to do so much mischief that it cannot be passed over without remark'.[4] The following paragraph quotes from this editorial:

> We do not address ourselves now to the highest or to the humblest classes of society. The highborn lady ... is not in a condition to appreciate the miseries of which we are about to speak. So at the social antipodes the wife of a workman or the artisan who merely hires the occasional Betsy to look after the children while she is steaming the potatoes for her husband's dinner, or washing out with her own hands the family stock of linen, is ... equally removed from the annoyances inflicted by domestics on their employers. We speak of the average run of London households, in which two, three, or four servants are kept, and we appeal to every mistress of a family in London if it be not true that a very considerable portion of the waking hours of her life is spent day after day in the midst of

---

3 Recorder's Speech, *The Times*, 17 December 1850.
4 Editorial, *The Times*, 18 December 1850.

turmoil and vexation arising from the conduct of her servants. The kindlier and more gentle her nature the greater the annoyance she is doomed to endure ... She begins by submitting to trickery and negligence of every kind. Advantage is taken of her gentleness of temper until at last she is fairly exasperated into action, and driven ... to consider the "kitchen" as a hostile power, which must be dealt with by a strong hand. If otherwise, filth accumulates ... everything fragile in the house is shattered to atoms ... the dinner is late; and the cook drunk ... or wasteful, or a thief, or *en rapport* with a policeman.[5]

It is noteworthy that the author stressed that mistresses were pushed into using a 'strong hand' to ensure the respectability of their households. In the previous week, the shocking details of the case of Jane Wilbred, a pauper servant who was starved and physically abused almost to death at the hands of her middle-class employers, were brought to the attention of the public in the pages of both national and local newspapers. Earlier that year, newspaper editors had been preoccupied by a similar case, in which another young pauper servant, Mary Ann Parsons, who had worked in a farming household in Devon, had died after suffering systematic abuse from her master and mistress. These two unfortunate girls caught the sympathies of a press and public horrified by the girls' treatment and the leniency of the sentences received by their abusers. There was also much meditation in the newspapers on how such tragedies could be avoided in the future, with calls being made for legislation to protect 'that unfortunate and helpless class' – young servants.[6]

Nevertheless, in this article the mistress was constructed as maligned and abused, pushed into severity towards her servants by their dishonesty and laziness. Furthermore, it was later asserted by the editorial writer that the majority of servants were 'as well off as any class of the labouring community', a dismissive statement that implied that the situation of servants need not elicit any special concern, despite the concurrent case of abuse, and which established a clear difference between the 'labouring community' and the employing class.

The article sparked off a rash of letters to the *Times*. Almost all of these letters appeared in *The Times* after a letter was published by 'JW', a 'humble servant'. 'JW' openly acknowledged the power of the newspaper, pointing out that 'an article in *The Times*, well pointed and wittily expressed, is more forcible than a homily'.[7] He sought to use the newspaper to express the 'hope that the 200,000

[5] Editorial, *The Times*, 18 December 1850.
[6] Letter, *The Times*, 13 December 1850.
[7] Letter, *The Times*, 20 December 1850.

may not be branded with the crimes of the 20' and to articulate the point of view of servants.[8] 'JW' claimed his opinion was representative of that of other servants, writing that

> many of my class feel, like myself, aggrieved by an article in this day's *Times*, that seems to reflect on our whole body (which in this metropolis exceeds 200,000), and the gist whereof is not calculated to elevate our character in the social scale, much less to smooth the asperities that lie in the path of domestic servants.[9]

'JW''s letter gave an alternative perspective on the nature of servants' dependence. He did not make an argument for more formality within the employer-servant relationship, or even for more wages, but asked for more respect for servants. 'I feel and know that a good master makes a good servant – a bad master cannot have one', he wrote, 'good places ... retain their servants, and the domestics are rarely ungrateful or unattached to their superiors'.[10] Although this sounds like the kind of statement the more benevolent employers might have made, 'JW''s perspective on the nature of his role was rather different from that which his employers might have expected. Cynical and frustrated, 'JW' clearly was not blind to the limitations imposed on him by his role. He pointed out the exacting standards to which many servants had to conform in order to secure places: 'the first postulate is, that the applicants, in proof of steadiness, must have lived some years (at least) in his or her last place; that they are sober, honest, diligent, capable, cleanly, orderly, and civil. I will not here speak of being also healthy, young or even good-looking.'[11] He went on to ask

> in what other position these qualifications are indispensable? Yet after all these superhuman qualifications, to what end are they attained and preserved? – why, to obtain a bare subsistence, in many cases, 5L a year, but generally nothing, for futurity, whilst that futurity is wholly dependent upon the happy continuance of their qualities in the estimation of their employers.[12]

'JW' thus not only highlighted the unique requirements of service as compared with other forms of employment and the paucity of the financial reward, he also pointed towards the vulnerability entailed by a servant's dependence on his or her employer's goodwill. 'JW' went on to expand upon this theme, arguing that because a servant needed a good 'character' in order to get another place, and

---

[8]   Letter, *The Times*, 20 December 1850.
[9]   Letter, *The Times*, 20 December 1850.
[10] Letter, *The Times*, 20 December 1850.
[11] Letter, *The Times*, 20 December 1850.
[12] Letter, *The Times*, 20 December 1850.

the employer wrote that 'character' at his or her discretion, employers effectively controlled a servant's livelihood, and particularly controlled a servant's ability to express an independent opinion:

> Is it not notorious that a stray look, mayhap in a moment of excitement or irritation, gives offence to a master or mistress, or that even the best regulated domestic may be betrayed into a word of retort? If so, the servant's irritability is an immitigable fault, whilst the objurgation of an angry master or mistress is but a passing cloud of temper ... I feel confident that no one will assert that simply because a servant gives a reply in a case of aggravation, where he is right, and he simply asserts that right, he should be on that account ejected from his calling, and become an outcast in the world.[13]

'JW' was arguing that the relationship between servants and their employers should be a reciprocal, interdependent one. He was asserting what he saw as his right as a servant to some measure of independence of mind and to some leeway in the regulation of his behaviour. He was asking for servants to be treated with respect and promised that if a servant was so treated by his or her employer, the employer would be rewarded with greater attentiveness. 'JW' seemed to think that the servant-employer relationship should ideally be a properly reciprocal one, and implied that, in fact, in many houses the emphasis was on control rather than mutual regard. By writing to *The Times*, he was able to express the opinion he felt denied in his role as a servant.

The correspondence from employers of servants exhibited ambivalence towards servants in terms of their 'character'. Ambivalent attitudes were also evident in employers' letters in relation to the degree to which an employer was responsible for a servant. Some people responded in defence of servants, such as John Davis, Ordinary of Newgate Prison, who wrote that 'good female domestic servants are a class as highly meritorious and as undervalued as any class in the community'.[14] However, his praise was qualified; in his experience the 'larger number of female servants committed and convicted of dishonesty at the Central Criminal Court are poor Irish girls' who were 'lamentably short of clothing' and yet 'too often fond of fine and tawdry dress'.[15] This need for clothing, combined with the paucity of the wages they received, drove them to steal. Although the overall tone and argument of Mr Davis's letter were supportive of Mr Wortley's point of view – indeed, he explicitly sided himself

---

[13] Letter, *The Times*, 20 December 1850.
[14] Letter, *The Times*, 20 December 1850.
[15] Letter, *The Times*, 20 December 1850.

with the Recorder, claiming that Wortley had 'merely spoken for the public good', Davis reconstituted a common ethnic prejudice alongside a gendered assumption that as females, it was a love of dress that motivated these servant girls' stealing. It was Davis's opinion that these girls stole because they were poor Irish girls, rather than because they were servants. Ireland was still a British colony at this time, with the Irish still to some degree excluded from the category of 'whiteness'.[16] By locating dishonesty in the Irishness of these women, Davis implicitly claimed honesty as an English characteristic. By contrast, the editorial writer at *The Times* saw the problem as one specific to urban servants. In a second article the leader argued that

> thousands among them who would shrink from appropriating a stray half crown do, nevertheless, day after day abstract the property of their employers in other shapes. We do not speak of the wanton and criminal waste that cripples the means of so many families, but of the straightforward pilfering of property other than money, &c ... We repeat it most emphatically, there is a very low conventional standard of morality among the bulk of domestic servants throughout London.[17]

This attitude was supported in a letter from 'A Mistress of London Servants' who argued that the servant-keeping classes were extremely careful about who they hired and that it was 'preposterous' to suggest that servant employers risked their property by paying minimal wages. Having absolved the employing class of any blame, she went on to suggest that robberies by servants couldn't be due to those servants being Irish because '[s]o great indeed is the caution of the housekeeping community with regard to servants, that they will actually have nothing to say to the inhabitants of the sister isle but exclude them altogether from their service'.[18] The remaining implication of the letter was that servants stole because they were essentially dishonest; like magpies, it was in their nature to thieve.

On the same day, incidentally Christmas Eve, a letter written by 'One who has not been plagued with his servants' was published in *The Times*. This letter offered a slightly different perspective on the issue. The author reintroduced the idea articulated by Mr Wortley and Mr Davis, that 'the misconduct in domestic servitude' was largely 'attributable to the employers themselves'.[19]

[16] Laura Schwartz, *Feminism and the Servant Problem. Class and Domestic Labor in the Women's Suffrage Movement* (Cambridge: Cambridge University Press, 2019), 160.
[17] Editorial, *The Times*, 21 December 1850.
[18] Letter, *The Times*, 24 December 1850.
[19] Letter, *The Times*, 24 December 1850.

However, while he acknowledged that 'hiring upon an uncertain character' and 'unreasonableness of masters in their behaviour to and exactions from servants' were reasons for problems in the servant-employer relationship, for this author 'the root from which a great amount of evil arises' was 'the lamentable indifference of masters to the behaviour and conduct of their servants'.[20] This author raised the issue of employer responsibility beyond the need to provide sufficient remuneration for domestic work to ensure servants didn't pilfer from the household. 'Fathers are held responsible for the behaviour of children; do masters consider themselves responsible for the behaviour of their domestics, or that their own personal respectability may be compromised by the general character of their servants?'[21] In asking this rhetorical question, the writer invoked a comparison with the responsibilities of the parent-child relationship to remind readers of the paternalistic responsibilities the employer bore in relation to a servant's dependence. The relationship between servant and employer, in this formulation, went beyond the transaction of work for wages and was implicated in the construction of the identities and 'character' of employer and servant alike, specifically paternalistic master and servant. For this letter writer, the master's role included teaching servants their place, ensuring the establishment and maintenance of the display of differences associated with the intersection of class and gender. The failure of masters to do this resulted in difficulties:

> A female domestic is engaged, and, besides other requisites, she is expected to be neat and clean in her person; but it does not stop there only; she may dress as she thinks proper; ape the habits and style of her mistress, and, upon 10L or 12L per annum, flaunt in her silk, veil, parasol, &c, the fine lady to market, to church or to an evening visit. What is station in life to her? She has as good a figure, is as straight in the back, and dapper in the waist, and perhaps has as pretty a face as her mistress; why should she not adorn her person to the utmost? And, moreover, she may catch a sweetheart. What check, I would ask, is ever exercised in restraining that universal female foible of dressing beyond their means, and above their natural station in life?[22]

Several assumptions underpinned this statement: that servants were flighty, lusty and as women, they were victim to a dangerous love of clothes. Furthermore, in this formulation, servants neither understood nor appreciated the important meaning of the distinctions between women associated with class. To them

---

[20] Letter, *The Times*, 24 December 1850.
[21] Letter, *The Times*, 24 December 1850.
[22] Letter, *The Times*, 24 December 1850.

class was ephemeral, something that could be breached with silk, parasol and fancy airs and graces. Of course, class *is* ephemeral as the writer cleverly implied – its distinctions must be policed and maintained, which is exactly what he was claiming was part of the employer's responsibility. He went on to argue that this disrespect for class difference was sometimes encouraged by well-meaning mistresses, who continued the once common custom of giving servants hand-me-down clothing:

> It is a most common custom that the half-worn out dresses of the mistress are handed over to the domestic, – that dresses whose original cost was probably the wage of half a year's servitude should bedizen the person whose daily subsistence is dependent on daily toil, – or even worse than this, that encouragement should be held out by employers to their servants to dress as smart and fine as possible.[23]

The love of dress was a problem identified by several correspondents. While it was generalized as a female characteristic, in this debate it was suggested that servants were particularly prone to resort to dishonest and even criminal acts in order to satisfy their dress habit and that this habit was peculiar to servants as it was cultivated by employers who continued the custom of giving servants cast-off clothing. This had the doubly undesirable effect of giving servants ideas above their station, and inducing them to dishonesty so that they could fund an aspirational lifestyle. As 'One who has not been plagued by his servants' wrote, 'where the dress exceeds what the wages will provide they [servants] must rob in some way or other their employers, and those employers may thank themselves for having, perhaps unwittingly, been the cause thereof'.[24] In this assumption, an idea about gender – that women find fine clothing irresistible – intersected with a pejorative notion associated with class – that the poor will rob to get what they can't afford – and with an interpretation of the effects of the lifestyle of a servant – a young girl constantly surrounded by finery and beauty will succumb to the idea that she too can be fine and beautiful – to produce an explanation for domestic thefts that while agreeing that employers were responsible, entirely circumvented the question of wages. Perhaps it was uncomfortable for employers to think about wages in relation to domestic work because the domestic sphere was supposed to be free from the taint of the cash nexus. Perhaps, in emphasizing the employer's responsibility to teach servants their place, this writer was trying to find a solution to the problem that did not compromise the ideal of secluded

[23] Letter, *The Times*, 24 December 1850.
[24] Letter, *The Times*, 24 December 1850.

domesticity and did not threaten to upset the status quo of gender and class difference that was understood to underpin British 'civilisation'.

'One who has not been plagued by his servants' was not alone in his opinion that employers carried a responsibility to regulate their servants' conduct. Subsequent letters to *The Times* articulated variations on his theme. One writer claimed that as domestic servants 'are not selected, as a class, from the better educated, so it appears to me unreasonable [to expect them] to be free from the errors and vices common to the class from which they have emanated'.[25] He had a benevolently paternalistic solution to this problem of class-based depravity:

> In proportion, however, to this want of education, so ought greater attention to be paid, where practicable, to remedy such defects, and to endeavour to improve their moral and social position; and where the attempt to effect that object is really and fairly made by heads of families and an anxiety shown for the welfare of their servants, I do not think that the complaint will be at all general, that they are found difficult to manage or ungrateful for kindness afforded.[26]

Another letter writer emphasized the need for mistresses to keep tight control of servants. Claiming that servants were 'creatures liable to all the temptations which youth, poverty, imperfect education and undisciplined minds expose them to', she argued that 'the knowledge that the eye of a mistress, just and kind, but intolerant of falsehood, concealment, and all the "permitted degrees" of dishonesty, and resolute to know the works and ways of all beneath her roof and rule, was always upon them' would constitute 'remedies of the evils we complain of'.[27] This letter reprised the notion articulated by other letter writers that because of the combination of their class background, which predisposed them to dishonesty, and the nature of their role, which placed them in the way of temptation, servants were likely to succumb to that temptation and therefore needed to be carefully monitored by their employers. Furthermore, in this letter the writer argued that '[o]ther demoralizing influences arise out of the mischievous sensitiveness now in fashion … So much is done to confuse the notions of right and wrong, to efface the great landmarks of justice, and to enfeeble and pervert the moral judgement of the people'. Jane Wilbred's case was in the newspapers at the time and calls were being made for legislation

---

[25] Letter, *The Times*, 28 December 1850.
[26] Letter, *The Times*, 28 December 1850.
[27] Letter, *The Times*, 3 January 1851.

that would enable Poor Law officers to inspect households employing pauper girls in order to ensure they were free from physical cruelty. Is the 'mischievous sensitiveness' to which this writer refers, what the writer sees as a potential effect of the Wilbred case? Does the writer mean that servants will take advantage of sympathetic attitudes to their vulnerability, while the employers' ability to punish could be restricted?

As the letters progressed, the debate shifted from the question of whether servants were paid enough, to a focus on what were constructed as inherent characteristics that predisposed servants to steal. From these constructs, letter writers developed recommendations for action on the part of employers. The mistress or master in these formulations was represented as a guiding paternalistic force. The recommendations reconstituted the idea of the master/ mistress-servant relationship as a reciprocal one, structured along lines of dependence and obligation, rather than a transactional one between and employer and an employee. On first reading, the motivation behind these letter writers' arguments can be interpreted as pecuniary: they did not like being told they did not pay enough for servants and they did not want to have to pay more. But given the centrality of domestic service to the lives of so many people in the mid-nineteenth-century society, the arguments made in these letters were also about defending the form of a relationship that was fundamental to nineteenth-century class and gender identities and the differences that organized them. In his speech about employer-servant relations, quoted earlier, the Recorder of the Central Criminal Court explicitly highlighted the problematic cash nexus. In doing so, he pointed to a source of instability at the heart of middle-class servant employers' ambivalent attitude towards their servants. Through writing these letters, which all avoided the question of money, employers addressed their ambivalence by defining service as a relationship structured by 'character', dependence and reciprocity rather than wages paid for work done.

Intermittently through our period, letters would be written in to *The Times*, or editorials would appear that addressed one or another of the facets of the rather amorphous 'servant problem'. Sometimes there was no apparent external stimulus for these letters or editorials. In fact, the sense is often of an ongoing discussion that periodically bubbled up into the pages of the newspaper. Some letters by servants appear to have been spontaneously written, in order to highlight issues they believed to be important. For example, in January 1853 a 'Married Butler' wrote in to *The Times* with a complaint about 'the custom of separating married servants, partially or entirely, from their wives'. He claimed the custom was an evil the effects of which can be little known to the rich and great ... The more trustworthy the man is the more he feels the degradation and injustice of this custom. Hence they may desert the employment they are best qualified for to seek a precarious subsistence in some other way than domestic service preferring the meanest fare, with the privilege of sleeping at their own homes, to comparative luxury without it ... where it is possible, do not justice, religion and morality require it?[28]

In this letter the author asserted his masculinity and his right to independence, invoking justice; it was his right as a married man to sleep with the family of which he was head. He showed that he saw his role as a domestic servant as a job, and a job that he would leave if his employers did not respect his rights as a man. Perhaps most importantly, through writing this letter, the author sought to draw the attention of the 'rich and great' to what he saw as a degrading and unjust system for a manservant to live under. He was making a public argument for his rights as a man within the terms of his employment. Similarly, in May 1859 *The Times* published a letter from 'A Married Man' who also complained that he had been 'told that, being married I am of no use'.[29] He went on to point out that this meant that either he would be forced to leave service, or to lie and pretend he was unmarried. Like the 'Married Butler', 'Married Man' was using the correspondence column of *The Times* to articulate his grievance publicly: 'I think that ladies and gentlemen should consider how poor servants, married, are to live and live honest and truthful; and I hope this letter may open the eyes of the gentry and teach them to be charitable to those that strive to get an honest living'.[30]

Male servants wrote the letters considered above. As has been discussed elsewhere in this book, service was ideally work that working-class girls did before they got married. Located in the domestic sphere, service did not compromise a poor girl's gender identity, indeed it was often argued that service constituted excellent training for the domestic duties faced by a working-class wife. For a man, combining the indices of masculinity - which included maintaining a wife and children - with the residential dependence of domestic service was problematic, as these letters suggest. Perhaps simply taking the opportunity to articulate their grievance in this way would have boosted these menservants' sense of their right to a degree of mental and physical independence from their employers.

---

[28] Letter, *The Times*, 26 January 1853.
[29] Letter, *The Times*, 9 May 1859.
[30] Letter, *The Times*, 9 May 1859.

Occasionally, an editorial or a letter could provoke a correspondence debate. This happened early in 1864 when *The Times* carried an editorial comment on the giving of false characters to servants. A couple of days later, a letter from someone styling themselves as 'Truth' appeared in the correspondence column under the title 'Servants and their Characters'. The writer of the letter claimed to write 'in the interests of society at large, to call attention to a subject of deep interest to all classes'.[31] This writer had many complaints about servants. Most of these were elaborations on the themes underpinning the arguments of the earlier letter writers considered above. 'Servants nowadays', according to 'Truth', 'do not care either to obtain or to keep places where there are any restrictions as to dress, or as to hours for going out, or where regular attendance at church is required':

> The love of dress and finery among servants is quite a mania. They will by preference go to places where the work is hard and the wages low, but where they are allowed to be out late and to dress in an unsuitable and indeed, ridiculous manner. They care not how this mania is gratified. So long as the money can be had to be smart, it matters not how it is got. Often, of course, honesty suffers, and when this happens character is gone. When finery has been purchased, some opportunity for displaying it must be found, and I'm quite sure of this, that many a poor girl who now receives shelter in one of the refuges would never have had to seek such a home had it not been for love of dress and late hours.[32]

'Truth' made the familiar argument that the love of dress and going out, to which servants were supposedly particularly prone, could lead them into vice. However, the subtext was about her discomfort with servants evading control and expressing their individuality and independence. This became clearer as she developed her complaints. According to her, servant register offices were '[a]nother crying evil of the day' and existed to 'cause as many changes as possible in every household' because every time they found a servant a new situation they received a fee. This meant that servants who were 'comfortably settled and quite satisfied with their places' were tempted to change their places by the registry offices offering them new situations with 'higher wages and more liberty'. Servants exercising their right to change jobs unsettled 'Truth'; she did not like the idea of service working along market principles.

'Truth' was also annoyed by the fact, according to her, that there could 'be no doubt in the mind of any person of experience that servants are as a class

---

[31] Letter, *The Times*, 13 January 1864.
[32] Letter, *The Times*, 13 January 1864.

sadly devoid of principle and religion'. In relation to this, 'Truth' claimed that not only was there a widespread practice of giving false characters amongst servants, but also that London servant clubs had 'arranged a system of communication between servants which is perfectly marvellous' and that the 'name of any lady or gentleman who dares to speak the truth as to the faults of any servant is posted at these clubs, and to their houses no servant will on any account go'. She claimed to have known of a few incidences where employers had refused to give bad servants good characters and 'so great was the malice of servants with whom they had been obliged to part for misconduct which could not be concealed that they were forced to live in hotels or to go abroad for a time until the subject had been forgotten'! The dependence of the employer on the servant irritated 'Truth' – it was because she needed servants that their requirements and desires were problematic for her.

The idea that servants maliciously clubbed together against employers reflects the anxiety expressed by servant employers in India that Indian servants might be in league against Anglo-Indian employers.[33] Such anxiety was linked to the intimacy of the relation and the asymmetry of knowledge embedded in its structure, in an imperial context where white middle-class supremacy depended upon the exploitation of servant labour in both metropole and colony. Servants had intimate knowledge of their employers while employers often knew little of their servants' private lives. In India the anxiety this produced in employers was mapped onto the differences associated with race; in England it intersected with a gendered notion of class difference.

What of the mistresses of these difficult servants? 'Surely, the wives and mothers of England cannot be indifferent on such a subject as this. Wherever distress or sorrow comes, there they too are found, gentle, sympathizing, self-forgetting. Surely, then, they cannot see unmoved this serious evil within their doors' wrote 'Truth'. In referring to 'the wives and mothers of England' she meant the servant-employing class. Her words echoed those of *The Times* editorial of 1850, quoted earlier in this chapter, which conjured the tired and maligned mistress, driven to distraction by her evil servants. Nevertheless, like many of the earlier letter writers, 'Truth' saw the resolution to the problem as in the hands of those mistresses. 'Dress is one of the vices of the present day', she opined, 'and it is one of the favourite follies of women … I am sure there would

---

[33] Fae Dussart, "'To Glut a Menial's Grudge": Domestic Servants and the Ilbert bill Controversy of 1883', *Journal of Colonialism and Colonial History*, 14, 1 (2013) for an exploration of the potential political significance of the servant-employer relationship in British India.

be fewer refuges required if ladies would dress less extravagantly themselves, and at all events insist on plain servant-like dress among their servants'. Until ladies undertook such action 'there can be no improvement in those who ought to look up to us for an example'.[34]

Two days after the publication of the letter by 'Truth', a letter was published in the newspaper that articulated a servant's perspective. Written by X.Y.B, it is not entirely clear whether the author was a servant or not, but nevertheless she or he referred to the experience of an 'old servant friend of mine', and argued that 'ladies frequently refuse to give characters to servants when the servants do not suit them ... Being themselves dissatisfied with the capabilities of a servant, they think they had better say nothing about them, without reflecting that by such a course they are ruining their characters and prospects'.[35] 'X.Y.B' thus directly contradicted 'Truth's' argument that servants procured false characters, arguing that it was servants who were most frequently wronged by mistresses and pointing out the vulnerability of servants to the whim of their employers. 'X.Y.B' made curious use of the word 'character' in the above quotation. It is not clear whether she meant 'reputation' or 'reference'. Denial of character meant literally denial of testimonial, but 'X.Y.B' implied that the ramifications of such a denial involved loss of moral reputation or good qualities – the things that distinguish an individual. As a result of being denied a character a servant could lose out on a 'role' in another household. Her previous employer effectively owned her 'character'.

On the 28th of January another letter by 'Truth' was published, in which she illustrated her earlier remarks regarding servants' so-called 'love of dress' with an example. 'Truth' claimed that she had offered a place to a kitchenmaid at a wage of 18*l* per year with tea and sugar and then made her 'usual stipulations as to dress – viz:- That my servants did not wear flounces on their dresses or flowers or feathers outside their bonnets: that they wore white caps, and were required to attend church regularly'.[36] The girl to whom 'Truth' had offered the place apparently replied by letter, writing:

> I think everything is very clean, but I have one thing to name – that I have always been acustom to black caps; and I am sory to tell you that is one falt, that is all I have to name. If you alter this I should like to fill your place. I have been accustom to noblemans' kitchen, and understand my dutys. I think your serves

---

[34] Letter, *The Times*, 13 January 1864.
[35] Letter, *The Times*, 15 January 1864.
[36] Letter, *The Times*, 28 January 1864.

would sute me very well. I am sory to make any complaints but if it not your wish to alter this, I think I had better decline it.[37]

Assuming this letter was genuine, it seems the girl was stipulating her own terms within the contract of her employment. She was prepared to accept most of her potential employer's conditions but would only take the job if one particular requirement of her own – a right to wear her cap in the colour she preferred – was respected. In articulating her demand in this way she invited 'Truth' to negotiate with her. 'Truth' responded with annoyance. The 'effusion' she wrote, needed 'no comment from me'.[38] Nevertheless, her indignation got the better of her: 'The tone of the letter is more as if "A.B" were engaging me than the reverse. I have only to add that this is by no means an isolated case', she wrote.[39] The problem for 'Truth' was not so much to do with the servant's 'love of dress', as she claims, as it was to do with the fact the servant had her own 'stipulations as to dress' and did not think it unreasonable to state them. Such an attitude may be evidence of an increased willingness amongst metropolitan servants to make demands as employees in the later nineteenth century – a willingness, as we shall see, that was to result in servants' efforts to unionize less than a decade later.

On the same day as the second letter from 'Truth' was published, servants found an unlikely defender in the editorial writer of *The Times*. The writer acknowledged that the servant-employer relationship was a problematic one, writing that '[t]roublesome servants are one of those sources of annoyance in the little everyday matters of life which vex and irritate us', but that nevertheless 'we are very apt to exaggerate the extent of the mischief'.[40] This writer had little sympathy for ladies who 'represent themselves ... as almost helpless, obliged to put up with the annoyance of incessant change and anxiety in their households, and appear to consider servants little better than a necessary evil'.[41] In the view of the writer of this article, most of the faults claimed by correspondents such as 'Truth' to be specific to servants were 'either follies common to all classes, which are as troublesome, but as capable of control, in servants as in any others, or they are merely effects of the mischief complained of, and not its causes'.[42] Employers were responsible for their servants' conduct because

---

[37] Letter, *The Times*, 28 January 1864.
[38] Letter, *The Times*, 28 January 1864.
[39] Letter, *The Times*, 28 January 1864.
[40] Editorial, *The Times*, 28 January 1864.
[41] Editorial, *The Times*, 28 January 1864.
[42] Editorial, *The Times*, 28 January 1864.

the character of servants must largely depend upon the training they receive in the households where they are placed. Good masters and mistresses will, as a rule, make good servants, and keep them; and when a mistress is in a perpetual state of discomfort with her servants she is generally as much to blame herself as they are.[43]

This attitude stands in bald contrast to that expressed in *The Times* editorial fourteen years earlier, when it was written that 'Happy indeed the favoured few who have succeeded in securing good servants, or even one good servant, after many years of trial'.[44] In 1864, the editorial writer asserted servants' equal humanity, arguing that '[s]ervants are but human nature, and require as much care and consideration in their management as any other persons with whom we are brought into constant intercourse'.[45] He pointed out that employers' distrust bred dishonesty in servants, as by being mistrusted they lost self-respect 'like any other persons'.[46] He also highlighted the inequality of power in the relationship as a source of legitimate grievance for servants, writing that if 'servants could let us hear their side of the question, we are disposed to think they would have nearly as much ground of complaint on these scores against their masters as their masters have against them'.[47] In his view, the 'circumstances of the relation are naturally to the disadvantage of the servant' and employers often treated their servants as 'mere machines to do a certain amount of necessary service … without any consideration for a servant's natural prejudices and tastes'.[48] An example of this was when masters and mistresses restricted a servant's freedom to socialize with friends and sweethearts, not realizing that 'it is as hard for them as for any one else to give up a moderate amount of intercourse with their own class'.[49] According to the editorial writer, if masters and mistresses paid a little more attention to their servants' personal proclivities, then they would enjoy better service.

> Of course, domestic service must necessarily imply a considerable curtailment of personal liberty, but we believe that servants would be perfectly willing, as a rule, to obey even harsh regulations if they found their masters willing to consider their wishes wherever it was possible; whereas, on the other hand, if a servant

[43] Editorial, *The Times*, 28 January 1864.
[44] Editorial, *The Times*, 18 December 1850.
[45] Editorial, *The Times*, 28 January 1864.
[46] Editorial, *The Times*, 28 January 1864.
[47] Editorial, *The Times*, 28 January 1864.
[48] Editorial, *The Times*, 28 January 1864.
[49] Editorial, *The Times*, 28 January 1864.

finds her master regardless of her comfort and natural wants, it is but human nature if she becomes regardless of his. The fault, however, generally begins with the master, and at all events, as the better educated and more influential of the two parties, he ought to take the lead in the exercise of good feeling.[50]

The editorial writer was not suggesting that masters and servants were equal within the relationship. Rather, he was arguing that benevolent paternalism on the part of masters and mistresses would result in them receiving better service. That this attitude, which so contrasted with that expressed in editorials a decade earlier, should be articulated at this time is perhaps not surprising when we consider that women were beginning to organize in trade unions in other trades through this period.[51] It is likely some employers felt apprehensive about the implications of such shifts in thinking about women and work and wanted to mitigate the infiltration of such ideas into thinking about domestic service, hence the emphasis on reciprocity and benevolence rather than hours of work and wages in this apparent defence of servants' rights. Certainly, for this writer and as we shall see, other correspondents to *The Times,* a major source of tension was the issue of how money should work in the relationship between servants and their masters and mistresses. Indeed, in this editorial the writer argued that the 'worst feature of the relation upon which so much of the comfort of all rests' was the operation of the cash nexus within that relation. This, according to this writer, had become an evil in all employer/employee scenarios:

> It is the unfortunate tendency of the day to separate the interests of employer and employed. Masters in all trades and professions get to look upon their servants too much in the light of mere instruments for the production of a certain amount of work at a certain expense, and the employed inevitably come to regard their masters only in the light of a sort of mine from which by sufficient labour they can extract a certain amount of money.[52]

According to the editorial, this was bad enough when it infected relationships between employers such as builders and their workmen, but it was particularly 'painful that it should exist, as it nearly always does, between the inmates of the same household'.

This dislike of the cash nexus manifesting itself in relationships within the private world of home was not unusual during our period. The home was the place of family, ideally free from the taint of cash, the payment of which defined

---

[50] Editorial, *The Times,* 28 January 1864.
[51] The editor had not changed – the paper was under the control of John Delane from 1841 to 1877.
[52] Editorial, *The Times,* 28 January 1864.

'work'. In this writer's view, the notion that the amount and quality of domestic work done should relate to the amount paid for it was 'a disease that feeds upon itself, and it is harder to cure the longer it lasts'.[53] He saw it as undermining mutual confidence and amicability in the relationship between servants and their employers, resulting in mistrust and misery all round. Nevertheless, the remedy was in the employers', rather than the servants', hands:

> If master or mistress can acquire their confidence by treating them with trust, consideration, and kindness, he or she may call out all the good there is in them, and exercise almost any influence over them … servants are neither angels nor machines, but human beings, and they must expect to have to treat them with the same consideration and patience as they are forced to exercise towards any other inmates of their household. In this, as in every other office of life, it is generally a bad workman that complains of his tools.[54]

Even while the editorial writer asserted servants' humanity, the use of a metaphor of a tool to signify a servant effectively stripped servants of it. It is reminiscent of the use of the word 'hands' to describe factory workers and gives us the sense of the master working on a greater project, the construction of a definitively civilized way of life, the servants constituting the apparatus with which he achieves his aim.

C. Norton also wrote in defence of servants in a long letter that argued strongly that servants were often mistreated by ungrateful employers: 'As long as servants are treated as mere living machines, to execute for us tasks we cannot perform ourselves, our relations with them must be defective and unsatisfactory.'[55] Norton also focussed on the cash nexus as a problematic issue in the relationship between masters, mistresses and servants, claiming employers used it to avoid a 'kindly relation' with their servants, who gave much more than they were remunerated for either in cash or in kind:

> It is not an exaggeration of the alien and unnatural position servants occupy in some houses, as if they were a different race of beings from those who employ them. 'Well', the answer is, 'they *are* aliens and strangers, hired in and paid for their service'. True; but how much is given that you do not pay for? The pretty young girl goes to her opera or ball, and she is dressed by another pretty girl or respectable old servant. It is their duty, it is 'paid service'; but it is not paid service that makes them sincerely hope, when she returns, that it has been

---

[53] Editorial, *The Times*, 28 January 1864.
[54] Editorial, *The Times*, 28 January 1864.
[55] Letter, *The Times*, 2 February 1864. I was unable to establish if C. Norton was the social reformer Caroline Norton.

pleasant; that she has 'enjoyed herself' with the innocent gaiety of youth. It is not paid service that makes 'baby' almost as important in the eye of the numerous household, as in the eye of his doting mother ... All these things, and the pride in the successes and sorrow for the disaster of 'the family', have nothing to do with 'paid service' but with the quick, kindly, natural instincts of the human heart – instincts as easily awakened in our servants as in any other set or section of the community.[56]

The reference to servants as 'a different race of beings from those who employ them' points towards the development of a heightened awareness of racial difference and its possible meanings in British society in the 1860s. Scientists and social commentators were elaborating racial hierarchies and attributing 'inherent' characteristics to 'the Negro', 'the Indian' and of course, 'the Englishman'. It is possible that the sense of a common humanity shared by white, British servants and employers alike, so lacking in the earlier discussion of servant character in 1850, was stressed by both *The Times* editorial writer and C. Norton in 1864 as a by-product of new thinking about race. The commonality between British people, even of different classes, was highlighted by the difference between the British and people of other, supposedly inferior races. Thus, a point obliquely made in this quotation was that domestic servants, despite being strangers in the household, were of the same race as their employers, understanding and sharing the family's joys and sorrows. Therefore, it was not acceptable to treat them in the same way as one would treat a member of a different race. In this way racial hierarchy was implicitly endorsed. Such was the pervasiveness of racial thinking in ideas about British society in the second half of the nineteenth century.

Like the writer of the editorial featured in *The Times* a few days earlier, C. Norton believed that it was masters and mistresses who carried the responsibility for any problems within their relationships with their servants. Norton also argued that the 'love of dress' and other faults associated with domestic servants were foibles learned by servants from their employers. Speaking about crinolines, Norton asked

is the servant girl who persists (as *Punch* pictures her) in opening the door to the sweeps in that enormity, a whit more ridiculous, in fact, than the young lady stooping to enter her carriage with her real corporeal frame, slender and central as the tongue of a bell, set within the balloon circuit of her expanded petticoat,

---

[56] Letter, *The Times,* 2 February 1864.

or the portly and well-dressed mother of a family, who, lifting her little one to her lap, lays it fondly down on a sort of concealed gridiron, covered with silk and muslin?[57]

Similarly, Norton believed that servants could not be expected to live sober and honest lives if their employers did not do so. If masters and mistresses wanted good and faithful servants, then they had to treat them with kindness and set them a good moral example, else they would end up with servants who did nothing but 'ape the exterior luxury and apparent frivolity around them.'[58] Norton thus made an assumption about the malleability and suggestibility of servant character; in Norton's view servants did not have much personality of their own, but were constructed almost entirely by their employers. In Norton's letter even while servants were defended, they were somehow reduced.

Other letters to *The Times* demonstrated that servants not only had individual personalities, they also had their own ideas about the problems between masters, mistresses and servants and how they could be resolved. On the same day as C. Norton's letter was published, a letter from a servant, 'P', was also published in the correspondence column of *The Times*. This servant began her letter by claiming a right to speak about servants as a result of her long experience in service and then went on to discuss servants' dress. Like the editorial writer and C. Norton, 'P' saw the problems with servants' dress as largely the responsibility of the employer. However, in 'P's' eyes it was not because employers set a poor example, but because they preferred to hire servants 'that are smartly dressed than they do them that come plain and neat, and that is one of the reasons that servants are dressed so smart'.[59] 'P' also pointed out that some ladies 'go quite to the extreme the other way':

> I lived with a lady some years who would not let any of her servants (with the exception of her own maid) wear any crinoline in the house or out, and made them wear caps tied under their chin, like old women. Of course, young servants don't like that, and will not stay long in such a situation, because other servants laugh at them.[60]

'P' drew attention to servants' need for some recognition by their employers of their femininity and the fragility of their young egos, and indicated how the hierarchy of service within the household might be expressed through dress.

---

[57] Letter, *The Times*, 2 February 1864.
[58] Letter, *The Times*, 2 February 1864.
[59] Letter, *The Times*, 2 February 1864.
[60] Letter, *The Times*, 2 February 1864.

While they were servants, they were still young girls, and disliked ridicule as much as anyone. 'P' highlighted the fact that there was a person inside the servant's costume; the employers' needs did not necessarily entirely define the servants' existence. 'P' made this point explicitly later in her letter, claiming that 'masters and mistresses as a general rule don't speak kind to their servants' and advising employers that they should

> be kind to their servants, and not treat them as mere machines, only to get as much work out of them as they can for the money they pay them, and think, although they are beneath them, they are fellow creatures, and have the same feelings as they have. Then they will find they will soon get good servants.[61]

Like the editorial writer and C. Norton, here 'P' uses the metaphor of 'machines' to emphasize servants' personhood, and mentions money in a negative way. In 'P's' view, the degree to which servants were remunerated was not equivalent to the work expected of them. Because there was no standard wage for servants and no fixed hours of work, an employer could conceivably work a servant as many hours as he or she liked, for as much money as he or she cared to pay. The servant could of course reject or leave a place, but that was the extent of her bargaining power. Though for 'P' being treated with kindness would appear to have gone a long way towards mitigating her dissatisfaction, in the later decades of the nineteenth century servants in some parts of the country were making increasingly loud complaints about hours of work. With the advent of increased educational provision and the possibilities of other forms of employment for women emerging, servants had more choices available to them and this may have made them feel more confident about making demands of their masters and mistresses. Nevertheless, for servants in areas such as Wales, where there was little other work available for women, such complaints were rare.

'P' also pointed out that it was servants' lack of free time, rather than an inherent ungodliness, that made it difficult for them to attend church regularly, whether because they were working on Sundays, or because they were loath to spend the hour or two they had free on a Sunday sitting in church. Once again, 'P' drew attention to the fact that a servant was not necessarily satisfied with the household being her whole world, as some employers may have assumed:

> A young girl leaves home to go in service either as underservant in a large family or a small family ... When she gets to her situation she finds she has to work

---

[61] Letter, *The Times*, 2 February 1864.

from early in the morning until late at night, on Sundays hardly time to go to church once. There are scores of places in London where servants do not go a hundred yards from the house from month to month. You can hardly blame a servant when she gets another situation, and gets time to go to church, that she goes for a walk in the Park instead.[62]

On 6 February 1864 a letter from 'A Butler' appeared in *The Times*. 'A Butler' flatly contradicted 'Truth's' assertions that there was a scarcity of good servants. He acknowledged that he had 'no doubt many of your correspondents have suffered all the annoyance of which they complain'. However, in his view this was not because of some inherent immorality in servants, rather it was because employers were not prepared to accept that they had to pay for quality. According to 'A Butler', 'many employers keep establishments quite beyond what they can legitimately afford, and expect more than can in reason be expected'. Employers commonly parted 'with a good, respectable servant in whom they can, do, and may confide, for the sake of a paltry 1*l* or 2*l* a year'. This view of the relationship between cash and service differed from those articulated by the editorial writer, C. Norton and 'P', who all seemed to think that kindness would mitigate servants' dissatisfaction with pay. On the contrary 'A Butler' clearly thought that there was no substitute for a fair wage.

'A Butler' asserted servants' right to combine if they so wished, claiming that 'surely servants have an equal right with any other class to do so'. Also, like 'JW' fourteen years earlier, he highlighted a servant's vulnerability to the whim of his or her mistress, arguing that the root of evil was not so much servants supplying false characters as mistresses withholding true ones for petty reasons:

> Is there no such thing as a false character against as well as on behalf of a servant? Ask a wretched 'bookmaker' hanging about 'The Corner', or, still worse, many a fallen woman pacing the cheerless streets on a winter's night; and they will tell you one word or so omitted from the scented note of an angry mistress to an inquiring one has been their ruin.

The miserable state of the 'bookmaker' and the 'fallen woman' evocatively contrasted with the apparent innocuousness of the 'scented note' to highlight the vicious effects of a mistress's, perhaps momentary, malice. It was subversive in that it gave an alternative explanation for a servant's descent into vice from the usual one of a servant's 'love of dress' or lack of morality leading them down the path of ruin and regret. Furthermore, it was an explanation that placed

---

[62] Letter, *The Times*, 2 February 1864.

the blame for a servant's 'fall' squarely at the feet of unfeeling, unthinking mistresses. In this formulation, the servant was not so much fallen, as pushed. The medium of the newspaper made it possible for 'A Butler' to suggest such a possibility directly to members of the servant-employing class, implicitly chiding their selfishness in only considering how the problem of 'character' affected them.

In 'A Butler's' view, it was the lack of independence resulting from the need for a character that led servants to seek other kinds of employment, as well as the increased availability of other occupations in the late nineteenth century:

> In such circumstances is it to be wondered at that servants are anxious to find some other employment as soon as possible where, if there is more labour and fewer comforts, they are not so dependent on the caprice of an individual? There are now so many ways open to a man of activity, industry and honesty by which a living may be obtained that the subject is worth the consideration of employers.[63]

The fundamental element of manliness for the Victorians was independence.[64] 'A Butler' did not seem as concerned about the potential loss of his character as he was by his dependence on 'the caprice of an individual'. By referring to a servant as a 'man of activity, industry and honesty', he invoked other important features of ideal Victorian masculinity, making it clear that he was a man before he was a servant, and that these 'manly' qualities could suit him to other forms of employment apart from service.

It was not simply the link between domesticity and femininity that precipitated the decline in numbers of menservants through the second half of the nineteenth century. Male domestic servants were not necessarily feminized by the kind of work they did. After all, a gender division of labour operated within domestic service, with outdoor work being seen as men's work. In our period, this division intensified precisely because menservants refused to risk being feminized by doing women's work. The increasing availability to working-class men of a range of occupations in which a man could be independently engaged was also crucial. In the nineteenth-century imperial metropole, a dependent male could never fully achieve adult masculinity.

As Davidoff and Hall have shown, manliness and domesticity were not mutually exclusive, while John Tosh has argued that the 'Victorian ideal of

---

[63] Letter, *The Times*, 6 February 1864.
[64] See Leonore Davidoff and Catherine Hall, *Family Fortunes: Men and Women of the English Middle Class 1780–1850*, 2nd edn (London: Routledge, 2002),

domesticity was in all respects the creation of men as much as women'.[65]
Dominant discourses rooted in evangelicalism defined a 'manly' man as one
who involved himself with domestic life. However, in order to be 'manly' this
domestic life had to take place in a man's own home, with his own family. A
male domestic servant was always subject to, and a dependant of, the head of the
household for which he worked. The male servant's obligation to the employer's
family complicated his ability to enjoy a family life of his own, which frustrated
his claims to adult masculinity. It is no coincidence that alongside sons living at
home, soldiers living in barracks, lunatics, paupers and women, male domestic
servants were excluded from the franchise extensions of 1867 and 1884. All
these groups shared the characteristic of dependence on another individual or
institution. It is easy to see how male servants might have regarded their line
of work as compromising their masculinity, as state and society refused to
acknowledge their status as citizens, full adult men, while awarding that right to
other working-class males.

On 30 March 1864 the final intervention in the epistolary debate begun by
'Truth' was published. It was from a servant calling himself 'West End'. His letter
was generally in agreement with that written by 'A Butler' in terms of the issue
of characters, arguing that servants were 'often refused characters from the
whim or caprice, or – why mince the matter, Sir? – the unfeeling hearts of their
employers'.[66] 'West End' supported this argument with an anecdote from his own
experience, in which he described how one of his employers had refused him a
character simply because he wanted to leave her service and she wanted him to
stay. 'West End' claimed that it 'never entered her head that I was a free agent
and could have an opinion of my own about going or staying'.[67] 'West End' thus
highlighted the tension between the self and the role of servant that all these
servants' letters point towards.

'West End' went on to write generally about the vulnerability of servants
to their employers' whims and suggested employers follow the example of a
'venerable judge' who, on receiving a character for a servant he planned to engage,
decided to enquire into the character of the servant's last employer, in order
to determine whether the servant's character was likely to be honestly written.
Asserting servants' human equality with their employers, 'West End' sought

---

[65] See Leonore Davidoff and Catherine Hall, *Family Fortunes;* John Tosh, *A Man's Place, Masculinity
and the Middle-Class Home in Victorian England* (New Haven and London: Yale University Press,
1999), 50.
[66] Letter, *The Times*, 30 March 1864.
[67] Letter, *The Times*, 30 March 1864.

to appeal to employers' consciences, writing that 'it would be well for many a poor, houseless, homeless fellow-being were ladies and gentlemen to take a hint from the good old judge before they shut their doors on a poor creature whose only fault may have been a trifle easily explained away'.[68] He closed his letter by suggesting that the matter was one of serious social concern, commenting sharply on the selective philanthropy of mistresses and implying (like 'A Butler') that it was the uncharitable nature of many mistresses that drove girls onto the streets. In this way 'West End' linked into contemporary misogynist discourses on the hypocrisy of 'dutiful' ladies, arguing that 'gentlemen' who had 'done so much at the "midnight meetings"' could 'strike at the root, or at least a great root of the evil' by organizing

> a crusade against the hard-hearted mistresses who have driven many and many poor girls to be what they never would have been had they been treated with a more Christian spirit. I would advise gentlemen to begin with 'the sense of duty' ladies. They are always doing hard things from a duty, they say, they owe to society; always straining at the gnat, but quite as often swallowing the camel.[69]

Domestic servants' unions

From 1850 the number of men in service was in decline, partly as a result of the increased availability of alternative occupations for men in the second half of the nineteenth century. Though the number of women in service was not in decline as such, there was a slowdown in the rate of expansion of female service from the 1870s and female servants seem to have been increasingly willing to complain publicly (if anonymously) about their conditions of work. This may have been a by-product of developments in ideas about women's and workers' rights from the 1840s onward. In the 1870s women were organizing in increasing numbers to campaign on a range of issues such as the Contagious Diseases Acts and the right of married women to retain property, as well as suffrage. These early feminists were by no means a united movement, but they were growing in number and vociferousness. Though often divided by class, some of them were concerned with women's rights as workers.

---

[68] Letter, *The Times*, 30 March 1864.
[69] Letter, *The Times*, 30 March 1864. The 'Midnight Meeting' movement held meetings in areas known for 'vice' to provide an alternative space for women at risk of prostitution, where they would be provided with tea and food, and 'benevolently' lectured by middle-class men about the sinfulness of sex work.

There was a general price rise in the 1870s, with trade recession setting in by the mid-1870s.[70] The early 1870s also saw an expansion of trade union activity, as groups of previously unorganized workers, such as builders, railwaymen, gasworkers, labourers and agricultural workers (whose situation, in terms of the paternalism and dependence structuring their working lives, was not dissimilar to that of servants) began to make efforts to establish unions.[71] All over Britain women workers in various trades began to involve themselves with unions in increasing numbers in this period, some with more success than others.

Domestic servants were not very successful at establishing unions, but this was not for want of trying, nor does it mean that their efforts are not worth consideration.[72] Living and working in the houses of their employers with very little free-time, opportunities to meet and discuss unionization were limited for domestic servants. Also, the patriarchal nature of the relationship between master or mistress and servant was a hindrance to effective union organization. For example, in April 1872 domestic servants in Dundee met with a view to establishing a union. Despite 'numerous attendance' letters 'expressive of the regret of the writers because of the inability to be present were read – almost all assigning as the cause of their non-appearance that their mistresses had stated that they would lose their characters if they did so'.[73] According to a report in the *Dundee Advertiser* this vulnerability was a motivating factor in the Dundee domestic servants' intention to establish a union. 'Some humorous remarks were made' according to the article in the *Advertiser*, 'as to the stringency with which mistresses inquired into the character of their servants' and it 'was pointed out that they were perfectly omnipotent in their control of their servants' career, and it was urged that it was high time that the domestic servants should form themselves into an organization.[74]

Other points of grievance raised at this preliminary meeting included servants' lack of free time and the unreasonable hours they were expected to work. Using the language of rights, the servants contended that they

> were entitled to have a half-holiday weekly and a free Sabbath every fortnight … it was strongly argued that no labour should be performed on Sunday except

[70] Sheila Lewenhak, *Women and Trade Unions. An Outline History of Women in the British Trade Union Movement* (London: Benn, 1977), p 85.

[71] Sheila Lewenhak, *Women and Trade Unions*, p83.

[72] There was a precedent in a union set up by Edinburgh maidservants in 1825. For details of the Edinburgh Maidservants Society see Sheila Lewenhak, *Women and Trade Unions*, 32–3.

[73] *Dundee Advertiser*, 20 April 1872.

[74] *Dundee Advertiser*, 20 April 1872.

what was absolutely necessary … on Sabbath there was usually special cooking, and that hence a great amount of labour was entailed on the servants which they did not experience on other days of the week; and that Sabbath, therefore, entailed an amount of drudgery which was unbearable.[75]

By implying it was inappropriate to perform domestic labour on a Sunday the servants used the language of Sabbatarianism (the movement against working on Sundays, which was particularly powerful amongst Presbyterians in Scotland) not only to underscore their point about hours of work generally, but also to subversively construct domestic work as 'proper' work.

The other major source of complaint centred on the issue of dress and mistresses' efforts to determine what servants wore, despite the fact that they paid for their own clothing. In this, as in the complaints over the issue of characters, the servants were protesting against the totality of the control mistresses attempted to exert over them: 'The stipulations as to what should be worn in the way of dress and jewellery were also considered, and it was thought the mistress had no right to interfere with their apparel in any way so long as it was paid for.'[76] Again, the servants believed they were entitled, as women who had earned the money to pay for their clothes, to make an independent decision as to what those clothes would be like. It is hard to imagine this happening in the mid-nineteenth century. Though, as we have seen, servants' tendencies towards customizing their clothing had long been a source of grievance for employers, a group of servants combining and openly complaining about their employers restricting their ability to dress as they pleased was novel in 1872. These servants seemed prepared to go further than simply writing letters to the newspaper in order to get their employers' attention.

The objections outlined above were elaborated upon in a subsequent meeting on 26 April 1872, which was reported, apparently verbatim, in *The Dundee Advertiser*. At this meeting the servants resolved to form the Dundee and District Domestic Servants Protection Association and appointed a President, a Treasurer and a Secretary. In discussing their demands, the servants repeatedly stressed that their strength lay in combination. As one speaker said there was 'no use for one doing it and not the rest'.[77] Their major grievance concerned the hours they were expected to work. One speaker declared that 'I really wonder why mistresses can think their servants are able to do what they expect of them.

---

[75] *Dundee Advertiser,* 20 April 1872.
[76] *Dundee Advertiser,* 20 April 1872.
[77] *Dundee Advertiser,* 27 April 1872.

I do believe they actually think we are not made of the same material!' and her comment was met with roars of laughter and assent.[78] The chairwoman, in her summing-up speech, drew a direct comparison between service and slavery, implicitly highlighting the commonplace nature of labour exploitation across the Empire Britain was a part of. She claimed that the hardships suffered by servants drove them to steal. She did not appear to see the union as an antagonistic organization, but one that, by campaigning on behalf of servants, would improve the lot of mistresses too:

> It is a mistake, I say, for anyone to argue that slavery only exists abroad ... We have been "slavered" too long – at any rate, enough; and I am astonished that servants have stood the treatment they have received for a long time back. (Applause) How servants have been able to do the work which has been taken out of them on the food they have received I cannot understand, but the treatment they have got has led them, I believe, often to take what was not their own and what they really had no use for (Applause) ... I am sure that there would be happier homes for both mistresses and servants if the latter were more generously dealt by and treated with more confidence (Applause).[79]

The editorial writer of the *Dundee Advertiser* first highlighted the potential implications of the organization of servants. According to this writer even the threat of a servants' strike was 'enough to strike terror into households where the work could not be carried on without them' and he painted a vivid and sarcastic picture of domestic disaster if 'a general stoppage of work by the cooks, housemaids, nurserymaids, laundrymaids, and tablemaids' was to occur, relating the issue directly to wider ideas about workers and women's rights:

> No fires lighted, no breakfast ready, the lobby not swept, the doorsteps not washed, the children screaming for nurse who won't come, the dirty clothes on the floor of the washhouse untouched, the meat and vegetables likely to remain in the larder uncooked, the cook presiding at a mass meeting of other servants in the kitchen, the tablemaid declaring the time has come to turn the tables on the stiff necked generation upstairs, and the housemaid waving a sweeping brush and insisting on 'No Surrender!' ... The mistresses had better beware. They have long had the upper hand; but can they refuse to admit Women's Rights? The great question between Capital and Labour now has to be settled between the Parlour and the Pantry, the Drawing Room and the Kitchen, Madame and Mary.

---

[78] *Dundee Advertiser,* 27 April 1872.
[79] *Dundee Advertiser,* 27 April 1872.

Clarissa and the cook must come to an amicable arrangement, or 'all the fat will
be in the fire'.[80]

Within a few days of the servants' first meeting, the story had been picked up
by many local and even national newspapers. The tone of many of the articles was
surprisingly sympathetic to the servants. For example, *The Newcastle Chronicle*
applauded the Dundee maidservants' efforts, claiming that the 'great movement
among all classes of workers for better terms with their employers has shown
itself in a new field ... We heartily wish this plucky movement success and it
will be interesting to mark its progress'. However, the *Chronicle* also wondered if
the 'labouring "lords of creation", who already have their Unions and restricted
hours' would 'come to the rescue of this fair combination of the kitchen against
bad temper and unreasonableness in the parlour'.[81] The language used here
evoked chivalry. The implication was that the Dundee maidservants need the
manly support of unionized working men in order to achieve their aims.

The *Bradford Observer* argued that girls in 'large towns like Bradford'
compared the restrictive dependence that characterized the average servant's lot
with the relative freedom of the factory worker, resulting in 'a great dearth of
servants. Poor girls born in the district naturally prefer a life of independence and
good earnings to the servility of domestic service'.[82] Furthermore, the attractions
of factory work tempted girls who had been hired from the country away from
jobs in service: 'it often happens that as soon as the girl from the country has
been able to look about her and observe the elevated position of the factory
girl, she gives her mistress notice and at once flies to the mills'.[83] According to
the *Bradford Observer*, the advent of unionization amongst servants could be
advantageous to both the 'hirer and the hired' as it would 'raise the condition of
the domestic servant', making the profession more attractive for young girls and
thus solving the problem of servant shortages.[84] The newspaper even suggested
that the temerity of the domestic servants might be inspiring to the 'timid clerk'
who might 'take courage after this display of bravery on the part of some of
the humblest of the weaker sex'.[85] This association of the clerk with unmanly
weakness relative to the 'weaker sex' points towards the future definition of

[80] *Dundee Advertiser*, April 23 1872.
[81] *The Newcastle Chronicle*, 24 April 1872.
[82] *The Bradford Observer*, 24 April 1872.
[83] *The Bradford Observer*, 24 April 1872.
[84] *The Bradford Observer*, 24 April 1872.
[85] *The Bradford Observer*, 24 April 1872.

secretarial work as women's work, and is reminiscent of the effeminacy projected onto middle-class Bengali men by Britons in India.[86]

The *Leeds Mercury* was less supportive of servants' unionizing. According to the *Mercury*, poor relations between mistress and maid were almost universal, arguing that 'the household which knows of no difficulty in the matter of servants ... is the rare exception to the rule'.[87] The writer of this article claimed that servant numbers were generally declining because 'the middle classes are to some extent reaping the consequences of their own want of gratitude and forethought' as girls chose 'better wages and shorter hours ... [and] ... an infinitely greater amount of personal liberty' as 'machine hands' rather than as domestic servants.[88] However, in this writer's opinion, the quality of servant had also deteriorated: 'Not only are the young girls who are to be seen in the houses of the poorer members of the middle classes far more independent than their predecessors ever ventured to be; but they are fonder of dress and less ready and able to work than servants of former days'.[89] The solution to the problem lay in women learning how to cook and clean so that they would not be so dependent on servants: 'With all our anxiety for the "higher education" of women, we have a sneaking kindness for that which will enable them in an emergency to make a home comfortable by their own exertions'.[90] This notion echoed the idea, expressed in an article in *The Times* just over a decade earlier, that increased education for women made the middle-class girls poor mistresses, and the working-class girls poor servants:

> Intellectual have taken the place of domestic pursuits, and the upper and middle classes no longer exercise that constant supervision over their household affairs which they used to do. It is regarded as beneath their dignity, and they are incompetent for it; for the highest ambition of a young woman is that which she least of all qualifies herself for – namely, to become a wife. Many influences have operated to change the character of domestic servants. There is the asserted growing insubordination and love of independence on the part of the rising generation; the larger demand for women in other employments as well as in this; the love of change and locomotion generated by the increased facility of communication; and the multiplied temptations to gaiety which prove so

[86] See Mrinalini Sinha, *Colonial Masculinity. The 'Manly Englishman' and the 'Effeminate Bengali' in the Late Nineteenth Century* (Manchester: Manchester University Press, 1995).
[87] *The Leeds Mercury*, 24 April 1872.
[88] *The Leeds Mercury*, 24 April 1872.
[89] *The Leeds Mercury*, 24 April 1872.
[90] *The Leeds Mercury*, 24 April 1872.

attractive to the young. But the school itself, it is said, by a too ambitious course of instruction, often tends to raise girls above domestic service while imperfectly fitting them for it.[91]

In this article education for women was made responsible for 'the servant problem' and the servant problem was given as indicative of wider social ills. The writer implied that education and increased opportunities for other kinds of work were eroding not only the institution of service, but also the institution of marriage. Young women were increasingly unqualified for what should be their 'highest ambition'. Their lack of qualification showed in their inability, or unwillingness, to focus on managing their households, or working in the households of others. It was implied in this letter that women should not be educated, not because they were intellectually incapable, but because the effect of their being educated pressurized the order of servant-employer and even marital relations, thus destabilizing society.

The antagonistic attitude expressed by this writer towards these shifts in womanhood was not uncommon in the late nineteenth century and in relation to domestic servants could become tangled with hostility towards the increasingly assertive working class. For example, a letter written to the *Surrey Comet* when servants in Surbiton threatened to strike suggested the servants' demands for better pay were illegitimate because they didn't do skilled work, and associated the servants' and wider working-class agitation with the ill effects of too much education disrupting the proper order of society:

> Since education has been introduced amongst the poorer classes, their heads are full of nothing else but striking for higher wages, and now this monstrous thing has even spread to the domestic servants of our households. Why, the servants of this present time are not to be compared with those of twenty years ago, and may I ask what do they want? Do they want paying by the hour, the same as skilled mechanics? It is my opinion, and the opinion of others, that the working classes of the present day are ruining the country.[92]

Other newspapers highlighted the potential mass power of domestic servants. For example, an article in the *Daily News* suggested that domestic servants, by virtue of their sheer numbers and their importance in Victorian households, could force truly radical change if they wished:

[91] *The Times*, 20 September 1861.
[92] Letter, *Surrey Comet*, 20 July 1872.

Domestic servants are a powerful body. In number they are far superior to the householders who send members to Parliament and get our laws constructed for us. If they were suddenly to rise, and demand and obtain direct political representation, it would be hard to say what surprising results, such as no advocate of women's suffrage has ever dreamed of, might be reached.[93]

Servants' potential power was figured as threatening in the *Saturday Review*, which described the organization of servants as a 'domestic cyclone' which would sweep the country.[94] The advantage for 'London housekeepers' was that they had had 'fair notice' of it moving towards them, and they had time before it arrived to 'consider how they should meet it, and to lay their plans accordingly'.[95] Certainly, the efforts of the Dundee maidservants were supported by servants in other parts of the country. At a meeting of menservants in Leamington, 'Cheers were given for maids of Dundee'.[96] Having seen a report in *The Times* on the Union, some servants calling themselves 'Southern Sisters' wrote to the *Dundee Advertiser* to 'urge them [the Dundee maidservants] on in this work'. Making a claim to equality with their employers, they too used a comparison with slavery to highlight the exploitative conditions under which they worked, asking, 'why should we be treated as slaves? Are we not all of one flesh and blood?'[97] Other commentators were rather more sceptical about the likelihood of the Union succeeding in achieving its aims, let alone spreading throughout the country. *The Spectator* painted a dismal, though probably accurate picture, claiming that 'the girls will be beaten of course, but even if they succeed they will be worse off than London Lodging house servants, who at all events sell their health for good round profits'.[98]

Though the Dundee maidservants union was shortlived, it appeared in the news fairly frequently throughout its existence, with reports and commentary on its progress appearing in publications ranging from *Punch* to the *Pall Mall Gazette*. By June, though, enthusiasm for the union appeared to be fizzling out. An article appeared in *The Times* which claimed that 'the terrors which this movement have inspired may now be shaken off, and the maids of Dundee, like many other personages who have created unnecessary commotion, are likely to suffer a total eclipse'.[99]

---

93 *Daily News*, 25 April 1872.
94 *Saturday Review*, 27 April 1872.
95 *Saturday Review*, 27 April 1872.
96 *Dundee Advertiser*, 30 April 1872.
97 Letter, *Dundee Advertiser*, 7 May 1872.
98 *The Spectator*, 27 April 1872.
99 *The Times*, 11 June 1872.

Lack of support may have been significant in the failure of the Dundee union. The precarious terms of a servant's employment, their isolation within households, their lack of freedom and the conventions of loyalty and obligation that structured their relationships with their employers meant that combination was difficult for them. As Lewenhak has written: 'Like the small women's societies fostered by the Women's Trade Union League, the various unions of agricultural workers, of dockers, gasworkers, and others received middle-class help' and though it is true that '[n]o amount of middle-class encouragement ... ever created a union', the aid of other unions or of middle-class supporters could have gone some way towards mitigating the disadvantages faced by domestic servants attempting to unionize.[100] The Dundee maidservants do not appear to have received any such support, as a rather irritated letter to the *Dundee Advertiser* from the Secretaries of the union indicated:

> It has been mockingly suggested that we might do worse than try to get the engineers amalgamated with us matrimonially. Now, had they come forward to assist us there might have been some fear of us being captivated with their manliness; but as it is, there is no fear of any such thing. But, we have done pretty well, so far, without their help; and if they mean to hold back like cowards and see the weaker sex fight it out for themselves, let us hope we will still be successful.[101]

This letter used language that would not have been out of place at a suffrage meeting. The servants asserted their strength by sarcastically caricaturing their feminine weakness. In caricaturing female feebleness, the letter writers also scornfully caricatured manliness. This made the servants' subsequent use of the notion of traditional gender roles, in order to berate the male unionists for failing to help the maidservants, even more effective. The engineers' unwillingness to support the nascent servants' union was given as an indication of the engineers' lack of masculine bravery. The women, however, intended to 'fight it out for themselves'.

Unfortunately, despite their apparent determination, on this occasion their efforts were to be unsuccessful. By June 1872, few servants had signed up as members of the union, though more had been enquiring about it.[102] The

---

[100] Sheila Lewenhak, *Women and Trade Unions. An Outline History of Women in the British Trade Union Movement* (London: Benn, 1977), 84.
[101] *Dundee Advertiser,* 8 May 1872.
[102] *The Times,* 11 June 1872.

Secretary and Treasurer were unwilling to accept office unless they could receive a guarantee that their salaries would be paid, presumably because they would have to give up their jobs in order to administer the union, but of course few members meant little funds.[103] The Dundee Trades Council taking the domestic servants 'under their sheltering wing' marked the demise of the union.[104] According to *The Times* this had happened because the Dundee Trades Council 'were of the opinion ... that the servants were unfit to manage their business'.[105] Removal of authority over the union from servants themselves could have done little to inspire confidence in would-be members that their interests would be properly acknowledged and represented. It is not surprising that at a meeting held by the Council 'only six or eight maids attended', in stark contrast to the 'numerous attendance' described at earlier meetings.[106]

Despite the failure of the Dundee union, servants in other parts of the country began to consider organization. In Leamington a meeting of menservants was held on the 29th of April 1872. Mainly coachmen, gardeners and stablemen, the Leamington servants complained about their long hours of work, poor pay and the separation of married couples. They 'unanimously adopted' a resolution to form 'a union of butlers, gardeners, grooms, footmen and porters'.[107] The following day, a meeting of menservants was held in Kensington. In June 1872, washerwomen in Norbiton went on strike to protest at their low wages and long working hours, given the relative affluence of their employers. They combined with the washerwomen of Surbiton and held two open-air protest meetings, which were reported in the *Surrey Comet*. Following this, domestic servants in Surbiton and Kingston wrote letters to the *Surrey Comet* throughout the summer of 1872 in which they complained about their working conditions and threatened to unionize.[108] 'If a strike is thought necessary, all those who wish bravely set to work with hearty goodwill as the tub thumpers did', wrote one correspondent, given confidence by the washerwomen's protest, while another suggested following the Dundee servants' example:

[103] *The Times*, 11 June 1872.
[104] *The Times*, 11 June 1872.
[105] *The Times*, 11 June 1872.
[106] *The Times*, 11 June 1872; *Dundee Advertiser*, 20 April 1872.
[107] *Dundee Advertiser*, 30 April 1872.
[108] *Dundee Advertiser*, 30 April 1872; *Surrey Comet*, June, July, August 1872; See also John Pink, *Country Girls Preferred* (Surbiton: JRP, 1998), 61 for analysis of the *Surrey Comet* material.

If a strike be contemplated among the domestics of Surbiton they should set about it in a proper way, as our sisters did in Dundee. Call a meeting, but not at a public house – like our friends the washerwomen – there draw up their resolutions with regard to a half a day every week, extra hour on Sunday evenings, followers allowed, their dress etc. and let them be laid before the mistresses of Surbiton.[109]

The complaints of the servants of Surbiton and Kingston were similar to those made by the Dundee maids and the servants who wrote into *The Times* in 1864. In all cases they revolved around issues of freedom of choice, independence and wages for work. Perhaps this is why a recurrent motif in all these cases was comparison of a servant's situation with that of someone enslaved whose existence was defined by the denial of freedom, independence and remuneration for work.

Wages were an issue for the Surrey servants. In one letter a servant complained about low wages and the fact that of a servant's annual wage of 'between £7 and £12 ... half that amount is needed for print dresses and indispensable cap'.[110] 'Another of your Readers' argued that servants would happily do plenty of work provided the remuneration was fair: 'Servants do not mind hard work if they are paid well for it.' He or she added that 'no good servant would leave a good place foolishly', making it clear that employers carried some responsibility when good servants gave notice.[111]

A major source of grievance for the servants writing to the *Surrey Comet* was the amount of free time allowed them. 'A Footman' objected to cooking on Sundays, asking 'is it right that there should be so much Sunday cooking, shall the domestic servant never have her Sunday rest?'[112] 'A Domestic Servant' claimed that servants should 'feel that they have something to look forward to more than continual drudgery'.[113] 'A Cook of Surbiton Hill' described that drudgery, contrasting it with the myopic pleasantness of life 'upstairs':

I dare say you ... have felt how oppressive the heat has been during the past week or two out of doors; but just fancy being indoors, over a blazing fire all day, and sometimes till late in the evening, how awful it must be! I can assure you it is, and none but those with strong constitutions can stand it. This goes on day after day, week after week, the same old thing. It is very nice to hear our young mistresses playing the pianoforte and singing upstairs while the mistress of the dripping pan – herself almost dripping – is preparing their dinner. There is a certain

[109] Letter, *Surrey Comet,* 6 July 1872.
[110] Letter, *Surrey Comet,* 29 June 1872.
[111] Letter, *Surrey Comet,* 29 June 1872.
[112] Letter, *Surrey Comet,* 6 July 1872.
[113] Letter, *Surrey Comet,* 29 June 1872.

amount of consolation in the music, but there would be more if I could only think that those above considered those below a little more. For this slavery – for it is nothing else – I am rewarded by being let out one evening in each week from 7 til 9 – a whole two hours – and on Sundays the same.[114]

Freedom of choice over what they did in their free time was also a common theme of servants' letters. Servants disliked their out-of-work activities being dictated by their employers. For example, for 'A Domestic Servant', the fact that on a Sunday 'we are sent out with strict orders to go straight to church and back' was an unfair infringement on her right to decide how she spent her free time. The rule enforced by many employers, that servants should not spend time with 'followers', was similarly resented. Speaking of footmen, 'E.M.A', a nurse, asked, 'When are they to see their young ladies? ... if ladies were not so strict about 'no followers allowed' they would have less cause to find fault with their servants, let all, even the poor Surbiton footmen join saying "Britons never will be Slaves"'.[115]

The other common theme of the Surrey servants' letters was the argument that, in the words of 'A Footman', 'if we were treated with more kindness, masters and mistresses would be treated with more respect'.[116] 'Another of your Readers' asserted servants' human equality with their employers, claiming that

> if some ladies shewed a little more consideration for their servants, and treated them as though they were of the same flesh and blood as themselves, and not as though they were some kind of animal created expressly for their convenience, there would be less dissatisfaction amongst not only servants in Surbiton, but in general.[117]

Another servant believed that by being kinder to servants employers could neutralize the threat of combination: 'I think the best way to put down strikes is to deal kindly with searvants [*sic*] for no servant that have a good mistress will wish to strike and by doing so searvants strike would be cleared out of the distrack [*sic*] of surbiton.'[118] The notion that being shown kindness by their employers could mitigate servants' discontent, and the resonance of this idea with the themes of the letters considered earlier in this chapter, demonstrates the degree to which ideas about reciprocity and benevolence were embedded in servants' relationships with their employers, undermining claims to workers'

---

[114] Letter, *Surrey Comet*, July 1872.
[115] Letter, *Surrey Comet*, 6 July 1872.
[116] Letter, *Surrey Comet*, 6 July 1872.
[117] Letter, *Surrey Comet*, 29 June 1872.
[118] Letter, *Surrey Comet*, June 1872.

rights. The intimacy of the relationship meant that a kind word could go a long way, even while servants complained about wages and threatened to strike. The protest of the Surbiton and Kingston servants seemed to have died out by the end of August. Perhaps their employers heeded the servants' complaints.

Some historians have suggested that 'domestic service was almost untouched by the growth of trade unionism' because 'the conditions of effective association were all lacking for the domestic servant' and 'in an occupation so rigidly authoritarian and hierarchical there was little sense of common purpose or common injustice'.[119] It is certainly true that almost all efforts on the part of servants to unionize before the First World War failed. However, domestic servants were touched by the developments in thinking about workers' and women's rights, whether through community grapevines, reading the newspapers or contact with family and friends, or else they would not have made any effort to organize. It is easy to forget that although servants lived and worked in the households of their employers, many, if not most, of them maintained contact with the other worlds of family and community. Through these networks, servants would have been aware of shifts in thinking about employer-employee relations.

Although there was no effort to establish a servants union between 1872 and 1891, from 1891 to 1914 there were at least three separate attempts by domestic servants to combine.[120] In June 1891 the London and Provincial Domestic Servants' Union came into being, with the slogan: 'By our Industry we Live. Unity is Strength' and a number of its twelve member committee were butlers, cooks and ladies' maids, including its secretary, who had been a butler.[121] It held its first meeting a year later, in June 1892 and registered its rules the following November.[122] As well as demanding higher wages and fewer working hours, the union proposed to set up registry offices and to tackle the problem of characters.[123] Nevertheless, in the preface to the rule book, the union leaders made clear they did not see themselves as radical labour leaders:

> It is the desire of this Union to work in an educational way to raise the standard
> of domestic servants, and to endeavour to bring back the good feeling which
> formerly existed between servant and employers, and further wish it to be

---

[119] John Burnett, *Useful Toil, Autobiographies of Working People from the 1820s–the 1920s* (London: Allen Lane, 1974), 169.

[120] Pamela Horn, *The Rise and Fall of the Victorian Servant* (Stroud: Sutton, 1990), 180.

[121] Details of the London and Provincial Domestic Servants' Union are taken from Pamela Horn, *The Rise and Fall of the Victorian Servant*, 178–9.

[122] Pamela Horn, *The Rise and Fall of the Victorian Servant*, 179.

[123] Pamela Horn, *The Rise and Fall of the Victorian Servant*, 179.

thoroughly understood that the Committee do most strongly object to the strike policy of ordinary trade unions.[124]

It may have been the case that without such a disclaimer, the servants union would have garnered no middle-class support. Nevertheless, despite its non-militant approach, servants did not flock to join it. The isolated and hierarchical nature of domestic service did not lend itself to labour organization. Moreover, servants were afraid of losing their characters and their places, which may have dissuaded them from combination.[125] The union's membership remained small throughout the six years of its existence, reaching a peak of only 562 in 1895. In 1898 the London and Provincial Domestic Servants' Union was dissolved.[126] In 1910 however, another Domestic Workers Union was set up in London, while in Glasgow Jessie Stephen organized a union demanding higher wages, two hours' free time per day and regular days off each month. Because of good publicity, many employers in Glasgow honoured the claims for free time and pay rises.[127] However, membership of the Scottish union remained small. Stephen eventually found herself blacklisted by Glaswegian employers and registry offices and ended up travelling to London to join the Union there, working for a family who had 'no objection to engaging a trade unionist'.[128] However, despite the best efforts of Jessie Stephen and her fellow unionists, the London union also failed to recruit many members and was wound up in 1918, before the end of the war.

Conclusion

The record of domestic servants' trade unionism may seem to read as a record of failure. However, the efforts to unionize served as a 'barometer of discontent' and helped to alter the nature of the 'servant problem' as perceived by the employing class.[129] By the 1890s, articles were being published in journals that were concerned less with the paucity of good servants, than with the means by

---

[124] quoted in Pamela Horn, *The Rise and Fall of the Victorian Servant*, 179.
[125] Pamela Horn, *The Rise and Fall of the Victorian Servant*, 179.
[126] *Membership of Trade Unions, 1892–99, PP,* 1900, LXXXIII.
[127] Sheila Lewenhak, *Women and Trade Unions* 181–2; Pamela Horn, *The Rise and Fall of the Victorian Servant*, 179. See Laura Schwartz, *Feminism and the Servant Problem*, chapter 5, for a discussion of the Domestic Workers Union of Great Britain and Ireland, which was established in the twentieth century, and of Jessie Stephen's career.
[128] Jessie Stephen quoted in Pamela Horn, *The Rise and Fall of the Victorian Servant*, 180.
[129] Pamela Horn, *The Rise and Fall of the Victorian Servant*, 180.

which girls could be persuaded to become and remain servants and how best to resolve the tendency towards mutual antagonism in the mistress-servant relationship. Many of these articles argued that domestic service should be put on a more formalized footing: girls, and even mistresses, should receive proper training, should work fixed hours and should even live out, coming to the houses in which they worked on a daily basis.[130] Even while the servants' unions failed to recruit members, the alterations in working conditions that servants increasingly demanded were being reconstituted by middle-class commentators as ways both of decreasing the likelihood of successful servant unionization and of improving the tenor of servant-employer relations without disrupting the social order. Of course, many servants continued to work in dismal conditions for little pay and less consideration, and many others left service when they got the chance, preferring regulated work in munitions factories to servility in a middle-class home. For some servants though, the articulation of their feelings about their work and themselves in the public sphere of the courtroom, the newspaper and the union meeting provided not only an opportunity to challenge the ascription of servant identities by employers, but also an opportunity to mark what servants themselves saw as the limits of acceptability in the servant-employer relationship. Metropolitan servants had an agency denied their indigenous colonial counterparts. The fact that Indian servants were not able to do the same reflects their relative oppression. This difference of agency within the imperial category of labour 'servant' was a part of the process through which inequalities of race and ethnicity were inscribed into the labour relations of the imperial, and later post-British imperial global service economy.

---

[130] See for example 'A Domestic College', *Englishwoman's Review* (hereafter EWR) (July 15 1890): 293–9; 'A Few Thoughts about the Technical College at Newnham-on Severn' *EWR* (July 15 1890): 293–9; Ellen W. Darwin, 'Domestic Service', *Nineteenth Century*, 28, 39 (August 1890): 286–96; John Robinson, 'A Butler's View of Men-service', *Nineteenth Century*, 184, 31 (June 1892): 925–33; Mrs E. Lewis, 'A Reformation of Domestic Service', *Nineteenth Century*, 191, 33 (January 1893): 127–38.

Conclusion

The relationship between master/mistress and servant was critical in the making of the nineteenth-century British imperial world. It interacted with discourses of gender, race and class to simultaneously underwrite and complicate the categorical distinctions through which 'Englishness' and 'Indianness' were mutually constituted by Britons in the period. The relationship was key within the development of an ideology of 'domesticity' which was expressed in a range of nineteenth-century texts. This imperial discourse defined a civilized society as one divided into the classed, gendered and raced constructions that were the 'private' and 'public' spheres. The private sphere, superintended by women, was the place where characters were made and broken, the foundation of empire, the heart of British civilization. The public sphere, managed by men, was the place where the important 'work' of business and politics went on. This domesticity was key in establishing the coloniality of households across imperial space, and in making the distinctiveness of metropole and colony within the broad coherence of the Empire as a whole.

Conformity to idealized domestic arrangements signified the respectability of households across imperial space. Respectability was a catch-all term for a set of values and associated behaviours: broadly, temperance, cleanliness, neatness, propriety. It was expressed through the performance of specific forms of domesticity, which were acculturated to the particularities of place, and which intersected with differences of gender, race and class. The association of degrees of morality with these particular forms of domesticity – the extent to which they might be respectable or not – allowed domesticity to be used to constitute degrees of 'civilization', so that domesticity became a prism through which difference between human groups was refracted, giving meaning to the unstable categories of gender, race and class through which power and privilege were organized in the nineteenth century. 'Civilization' in the nineteenth century was a concept whose inheritance was in eighteenth-century evangelicalism and Enlightenment notions of stadial development, which had emerged in the context of European imperial expansion. Civilized domesticity was a product of empire in both a material and an abstract sense: empire created the conditions for the emergence and implementation of domestic ideology and its plant across imperial space, defining the places and power relations that made the British Empire what it was.

Domestic servants across the British Empire were instrumental in the maintenance of the distinction between the public and private worlds, and all the other trappings of domesticity. They were like magicians; as they scrubbed, polished, scoured, washed, bowed and scraped, they helped to maintain the illusion that the home could be a place free of the taint of the public world and helped bring into being a hierarchy of status, in which each household had a place. They also were the border police of both metropolitan and colonial households. They occupied a liminal zone created through the material practices of their labour, marking not only the physical boundaries of the house and family, but also the categorical boundaries of class, gender and racial difference. However, in keeping the borders, servants could not help but cross, challenge and even undermine them.

Edward Higgs has drawn attention to the fact that servants were 'employed in the homes of … members of all social classes to perform productive work; caring for animals, making cheese, tending the shop, cooking, cleaning, making fires, fetching and carrying water, helping out during times of domestic crisis and so on.'[1] Higgs is talking about metropolitan households, but the same was true for India. Across metropole and colony, the productive capacity of servants was not limited to material goods. The master/mistress-servant relationship was productive of the gradations and intersections of class, gender and racial difference that shaped household, nation, metropole and colony.[2] Within the British Empire people learned their place through their relation to domestic service.

Because of the weight of available material, this study has been primarily concerned with middle-class households and has argued that such households would rarely do without servants. At the same time, it suggests that the idea that the difference between middle-class and working-class status was defined by servant-keeping is overly simplistic.[3] In terms of class difference, the difference that was produced through the master/mistress-servant relationship

---

[1] Edward Higgs 'Domestic Service and Household Production' p136.
[2] Edward Higgs 'Domestic Service and Household Production' p136.
[3] See Edward Higgs 'Domestic Service and Household Production' for a discussion of this argument.

did not necessarily correspond to broad designations such as working-, middle- or upper-class, but rather to power differentials that were linked to subtle degrees of status within those groupings. Similarly, though servants did mark the difference between colonizer and colonized, the specificities of servant-employer relationships in India also marked differences within those categories. The variability of the master/mistress-servant relationship across metropole and colony helped produce different kinds of Britishness, different kinds of whiteness, as the way people conducted their domestic lives shaped their position on a spectrum of imperial belonging. For example, on return to England, rumours of Anglo-Indians' allegedly harsh treatment of their servants in Bedford marked them as different from their metropolitan neighbours. According to the *Bedfordshire Times* in 1891 there were

> tales about of "kitchen hunger" in some houses in Bedford, where the servants have not enough to eat … this is what happens with some of the rulers of our "great dependency", their ideas of what is necessary to keep up the strength and physique of an English servant being derived from their experience with natives who live on rice and wear scanty raiment.[4]

Artisans and labourers could hire servants cheaply, or employ kin to do materially productive work, but could also insist on those servants' observance of deference rituals that signified hierarchical difference within and between households. The deference of servants was central to the identity of 'colonizer' in India. Colonizers closely linked control of domestic servants to control of 'the native' more generally. In Britain contemporary commentators suggested that the effects of the ideas of the labour movement on servants, in their potential for undermining employers' authority, could potentially engender a catastrophe of wide social significance. Thus, the relationship between servants and their employers produced stabilizing status difference through the materially productive work that sustained imperial 'domesticity', and also through the acting out of difference.

Household manuals recommended routines and rituals designed to ensure a mistress's control of her household and the proper subjection of her servants to the family's needs and whims. Running a household took considerable organization and relatively few mistresses, certainly in the metropole, could be completely free from household tasks. Nonetheless, domestic servants' labour allowed the release of female family members in households in both metropole

---

[4] *Bedfordshire Times*, 24 Jan 1891 quoted in Elizabeth Buettner, *Empire Families*, p236.

and colony from drudgery that would compromise their positions in a classed spectrum of white femininity, without forfeiting household cleanliness and comfort. Mistresses figured their superintendence of their households as work of national and imperial importance. In teaching servants their places, constantly marking the difference between them and their employers, mistresses saw themselves doing the work of civilization. In households across India and England servants took on the dirtiest and most unpleasant chores and with them, a mantle of social inferiority in which shifting ideas about gender, race and class were interwoven. However, even while class, gender and racial difference were produced and invested with power through the workings of the master/mistress-servant relationship, the security of those categorical distinctions was being challenged by none other than those individuals whose work constituted an effort to close social boundaries – domestic servants.

Domestic servants crossed and contested the boundaries they upheld both physically and psychically. By their very presence within the home they breached the sanctity of the private sphere as exclusively the place of the family. They crossed between inside and outside, mediating much of the traffic between the public and private worlds. Crucially, domestic servants were paid for their labour. The introduction of the cash nexus into the master/mistress-servant relationship belied the naturalness of the structures of gender, class and race that the relationship underpinned and that organized it. Domestic servants' paid-for labour brought the cash nexus into the very sphere that was supposed to be, at least in part, defined by its absence.

Male servants complicated any straightforward association of household work with women. In India, the majority of servants were male and the problem of their masculinity was only partly solved by infantilizing them. The fear of servants expressed during moments of crisis, such as the 1857 uprising or the Ilbert Bill controversy of 1883, was articulated both in terms of their potential for violence and in terms of their possible politicization by nationalists, and was linked to their maleness. Male servants' exclusion from franchise extensions in Britain indicates state-sanctioned ambivalence towards any claim they might have made to full adult masculinity. Defined as dependents rather than as employees, to allow them to vote would undermine the indices of masculinity on which citizenship was predicated. By denying male servants this right, law-makers neutralized the challenge such servants' masculinity posed to notions of the private sphere as the woman's place and household work as women's work. It is no coincidence that in our period the numbers of men in service declined. As servants, English men were if not exactly feminized, then neutered.

Though the balance of power was weighted in the employer's favour – the master and mistress after all, had the power to hire, fire and give characters – domestic servants were by no means powerless. Many households were dependent on servants' labour to maintain the family's livelihood and lifestyle; a servant's refusal to fulfil certain tasks was potentially very disruptive to the smooth running of a household, hence the necessity for employers to maintain their authority through insisting on deference rituals. However, employers' need to control their servants in this way was also about power in a different sense. Employers in India and England needed to subject servants in order to maintain their sense of identity. In India controlling native servants was seen as instrumental in the maintenance of British prestige and to Anglo-Indians' sense of themselves as British citizens, working in the service of the British Empire. In both England and India, the power of the master or mistress over the servant was linked to maintaining the imagined hierarchy of status underpinning race, class and gender difference. The imagining of this hierarchy produced ambivalent attitudes in employers towards their servants as it involved repressing the knowledge that the difference between servant and employer was not natural, but man-made. In England, this was particularly difficult when servants moved towards making collective demands for employment rights towards the end of the nineteenth century, while in India servant employers feared the effect on servants of the claims of Indian nationalists to the right to self-rule and equality with Englishmen.

Servants possessed intimate knowledge of the families they worked for, often more intimate knowledge than family members had of each other. Privy to secrets shared intentionally and accidentally, the possibility of servants communicating their knowledge of the family's private affairs to others beyond the household was a cause of significant anxiety in many masters and mistresses. Many of the court cases considered in this book speak of instances when tension spilled into violence, when some of the negative by-products of intimacy, such as jealousy and fear of duplicity, resulted in hostility and injustice. Anglo-Indian employers often wrote about their Indian servants as if they were interlopers 'poised … at thresholds of European homes, intruders into the very domestic spaces where they worked, where women were confined, and where white children were reared'.[5]

For servants in both India and England the tensions of intimacy were heightened by asymmetries of knowledge. Masters and mistresses did not have

5   Ann Laura Stoler, 'Tense and Tender Ties: The Politics of Comparison in North American History and (Post) Colonial Studies', *The Journal of American History*, 88, 3, (2001): 843.

the same access to knowledge of their servants' lives as the servants had of their employers'. In Anglo-Indian households this was particularly consciously felt, as the difference between English and Indian servants was linked into the difference of Indian from English men and women. Indian servants, apart from their different skin colour, language, eating and religious habits, were mostly adult males, often with wives and children and lives beyond the household of which the servants' employers had no comprehension. In English households, servants' connection to their own family and friends was problematic for many employers. In households in metropole and colony, fearing betrayal, masters and mistresses encouraged silence; like children, servants were to be seen and not heard. But employers could only insist on silence within the household. Tongues could and did wag in the kitchen, in the marketplace, in the park, at the tradesman's entrance, in the courtroom. Furthermore, silencing servants meant not hearing anything of their lives, perpetuating the asymmetry of knowledge that produced such tension on the part of many masters and mistresses.

There was a double axis of power operating in the master/mistress-servant relationship. Employers exercised formidable power over their servants in their circumscription of their servant's lives. Meanwhile, consciously or unconsciously, servants possessed another kind of power over their employers, in which they had the ability to betray their employer's trust and shatter the illusion of their superiority. The disregard of servants' point of view has been a problem for this book, but perhaps indicates servants' agency – claiming privacy from those who would exploit them. Accessing the servant voice has been difficult and for India has proved more or less impossible. Masters and mistresses chatter at us from the archives while servants work silently in the background, occasionally coming forward at times of particular pleasure, irritation or exploitation, visible, but often inaudible.

This study has sought to demonstrate the importance of the master/mistress-servant relationship in British households in Britain and in India for our understanding of nineteenth-century social identities. Rather than compare two different sites, I have attempted to juxtapose them, exploring aspects of a relationship that existed within an imperial continuum that included both Britain and India. The specificity of each site lent the master/mistress-servant relationship its particular idiosyncrasies, but the broader dynamics of the relationship developed within the field of imperial domesticity. What it meant to be a master or a servant was constructed across imperial space; it was key in distinguishing metropolitan and colonial places in a relationship of exploitation that privileged the economic and political development of Britain and the white people who identified as belonging to it.

In both Britain and British India the relationship between master, mistress and servant involved quotidian negotiations and struggles over power linked to gendered hierarchies of class and race. The relationship in both sites resonated with similar feelings of tension, fear, frustration and pleasure even while the differences between households in India and in Britain were plain. There are many possibilities for future research in this field. Comparing and connecting the master/mistress-servant relationship, and its mobilities, across a range of sites of empire and in different contexts within those sites could deepen our understanding of the way in which the intimate relation of servant and employer worked to construct tensely classed, gendered and raced identities across the globe, embedding inequalities of power in the everyday on a scale from the local to the global, right up to the present day.[6] Exploring the master/mistress-servant relationship in particular places, but with attention to the wider imperial context they share, could enable us to break down the categories that limit us to thinking in terms of national *or* colonial histories. Such work would bring us to a better understanding of the ways in which imperial identities were configured through the intimacies shared by master and servant, ruler and ruled, and the ways in which the shifting and variegated contents of the category 'imperial' were constructed across time and space. Domestic service was critical in the making of the inequalities that have underpinned the development of the 'modern' world: it's time we attended to its history.

---

[6] Work in this direction has begun. See Julia Martinez, Claire Lowrie, Frances Steel and Victoria Haskins, *Colonialism and Male Domestic Service across the Asia Pacific* (London: Bloomsbury, 2018) and Olivia Robinson, 'Travelling Ayahs of the Nineteenth and Twentieth Centuries: Global Networks and Mobilization of Agency', *History Workshop Journal*, 86, 1, (2018): 44–66.

Bibliography

Primary sources

Unpublished material

Anson, George, Letter 1857, MSS/Eur/A162
Beveridge, Annette, Journal of Annette Beveridge MSS/Eur/C176/104
Clwyd County Record Office
Cullwick, Hannah, Diaries and Letters 1854–1864, Munby Collection, Box 98
Diaries of Louisa Yorke, Erddig MSS D/E/2816
Galton, Emma, 1829–98 Diary, Galton papers, item 37
India Office Records in Asia Pacific and Africa Collections at the British Library
King, Lucas White, Letters and t/s memoir, MSS/Eur/C852
Letters from Lucy Hitchman, Erddig MSS D/E/2831
Letters from servants, Erddig MSS D/E/595
Lloyd, Gertrude, *Biography of Gerald Braithwaite Lloyd* (unpublished manuscript) Mrs Judy Lloyd.
Lyall, Alfred, Letters 1863–67, Lyall Collection, MSS/Eur/F132
Lytton Collection, MSS/Eur/E218
Poynder, Rev E. Journal, MSS/Eur/Photo/Eur/385
Privately owned manuscripts
Shore, Frederick John, Frederick John Shore Collection, MSS/Eur/E307/5
Stokes, May Florence, *Impressions of a Memsahib*, t/s memoir, 1896, MSS/Eur/Photo/ Eur 326
Thornhill Collection, MSS/Eur/B298
Torrington, Elinor, Memoir, MSS/Eur/D1197
University College London Library
Ward, Mary Augusta, 1885–87, 1892–98 Diary, UCL Library, MS ADD 202, Item 2
Walter, Emma, Journal of Emma Walter, MSS/Eur/B265/1
Westmacott Papers, MSS/Eur/C376
Wonnacott Collection, MSS/Eur/C376
Wood, Minnie, Letters of Maria Lydia Wood, MSS/Eur/B210
Wren Library, Trinity College, Cambridge University

Oral archives

Edith Dixon MSS/Eur/T26
Essex University Oral Archive

India Office Records
Katherine Mabel Pearse MSS/Eur/R202
Lady Sylvia Corfield MSS/Eur/T17
Mary Carroll MSS/Eur/T12
Thompson, Paul and Thea, 'Family Life and Work Experience before 1918'
Vere Lady Birdwood MSS/Eur/T7

Official sources

1881: *PP*, 1883, LXXX
1891: *PP*, 1893–94, CVI
1901: *PP*, 1904, CVIII
1911: *PP*, 1913, LXXVIII
APAC = Asia Pacific and Africa Collections at the British Library
Proclamation by the Queen in Council to the Princes, Chiefs and the People of India,
    Governor General, Allahabad
'Bill for the Better Protection of Young Persons under the Care and Control of Others as
    Apprentices or Servants', *PP*, 1851 (32) I.97.
Census of 1851: Ages and Occupations, 1852–3, *PP*, LXXXVII, parts I and II
Census Returns for 1851, 1861, 1871 and 1881, PRO
General Reports of the Censuses of Population: 1871: *PP*, 1873, LXXI
Hansard's Parliamentary Debates
IOR L/P+J/5/410, APAC
Local Government Board, *Third Annual Report: Report by Mrs Nassau Senior on the
    Education of Girls in Pauper Schools,*
Lord Lytton. Letters Despatched. 1876 MSS Eur/E218/18, APAC
Membership of Trade Unions, 1892–99, PP, 1900, LXXXIII
Miss C.E. Collett, *Report on the Money Wages of Indoor Domestic Servants, PP,* 1899,
    XCII
Miss C.E. Collett, *Report on the Statistics of Employment of Women and Girls, PP,* 1894,
    LXXI, pt II
PP, XXV (1874)
PP = Parliamentary Papers
PRO = Public Record Office
The Queen vs Gerald Meares. Authenticated Print of the Proceedings, 1874
Report on the Census of British India Taken on the 17 February 1881, vols I, II, III,
    London
Ripon Papers: *Abstract of Proceedings of the Governor General of India in Council*, XXII,
    British Library
Ripon Papers: *The Marquis of Ripon. Correspondence with Persons in England*, 1883, BP
    7/5, British Library
Ripon Papers: *The Marquis of Ripon. Correspondence with Persons in India.* 1883. BP
    7/6, British Library

Statistics of the British-Born Subjects Recorded at the Census of India, 17 February 1881.
  Superintendent of Government Printing
*The Viceregal Papers of the Marquess of Dufferin and Ava. Correspondence in India, July–
  September 1885*, MSS Eur IOR Neg 4337, APAC

Newspapers and journals

The Bengal Times
Bedfordshire Magazine
Blackwoods Edinburgh Magazine
The Bradford Observer
The Calcutta Review
Carmarthen Journal
Carmarthen Weekly Reporter
The Civil and Military Gazette
Daily News
The Daily Telegraph
Dundee Advertiser
English Woman's Journal
The Englishman
Englishwoman's Domestic Magazine
Englishwoman's Review
Fortnightly Review
The Indian Daily News
The Leeds Mercury
Legislative Acts of the Governor General in Council Vol I, 1834-1851, IOR/V/8/117,
  APAC
Legislative Acts of the Governor General in Council Vol III, 1859-1861, IOR/V/8/119,
  APAC
Madras Mail
The Morning Chronicle
National Review
The Newcastle Chronicle
Nineteenth Century
The Pioneer
Punch
Saturday Review
The Servants Magazine
The Spectator
The Surrey Comet
The Times

The Western Times
Westminster Review

Published books and articles

Aberdeen, Isobel, 'Household Clubs: An Experiment', *Nineteenth Century*, 181, 31 (March 1892)

Adams, Samuel and Sarah, *The Complete Servant* (London: Knight and Lacey, 1825)

Adams, Samuel and Sarah, *The Complete Servant* (London: Knight and Lacey, 1925)

Aitken, E.H., *Behind the Bungalow*, 14th edn (London, Calcutta and Simla: Thacker and Co, 1929)

Allen, Rose, *Autobiography of Rose Allen* (London: Longman, 1847)

An Anglo-Indian, *Indian Outfits and Establishments: A Practical Guide for Persons about to Reside in India* (London: L. Upcott Gill, 1882)

'An Old Servant', *Domestic Service* (London: Constable and Co, 1917)

Bain, James. S., *A Bookseller Looks Back. The Story of the Bains* (London: Macmillan, 1940)

Baker, Lady, *Our Responsibilities and Difficulties as Mistresses of Young Servants* (London: Hatchards, 1887)

Bell, Mrs J.N., *The ABC of Housekeeping or Mistress and Maid* (London: H. J. Drane, 1902)

Benedict, A. *Mistresses and Servants, or Servants and Mistresses; Which Shall Be First?* (London: John Hatfield, 1859)

Benson, A.C. *The Life of Edward White Benson, Sometime Archbishop of Canterbury*, 2 vols (London: Macmillan and Co, 1899)

Benson, E.F., *Mother* (London: Hodder and Stoughton, 1925)

Benson, M.E. 'In Defence of Domestic Service: A Reply', *The Nineteenth Century*, 164, 28 (October 1890)

Black, Clementina, 'The Dislike to Domestic Service', *The Nineteenth Century*, 193, 33 (March 1893)

Booth, Charles and Argyle, Jesse, *Life and Labour of the People in London*, Vol. VIII, part II (London: Macmillan,1896)

Braddon, Edward, *Life in India* (London: Longmans, Green and Co, 1872)

Buckton, Catherine, *Comfort and Cleanliness. The Servant and Mistress Question* (London: Longmans, Green and Co, 1898)

Bulley, A. Amy, 'Domestic Service. A Social Study', *Westminster Review*, 135, 2 (February 1891)

Burnett, John (ed.), *Useful Toil: Autobiographies of Working People from the 1820s–the 1920s* (London: Allen Lane, 1974)

Burnett, John (ed.), *Destiny Obscure: Autobiographies of Childhood, Education and Family from the 1820s to the 1920s* (London: Allen Lane, 1982)

Callcott, Maria Hutchins, *A Few Household Hints and Lessons of Conduct for Female Servants in the Form of Narrative Letters* (London: SPCK, 1856)

Carlyle, Alexander, *New Letters and Memorials of Jane Welsh Carlyle* (London: John Lane, 1903)

Cassell's Book of the Household: A Work of Reference on Domestic Economy, Vol. 1 (London: Cassell's Book of the Household, 1890)

Caswell, J.D., *The Law of Domestic Service* (London: Grant Richards Ltd, 1913)

Christian Knowledge Society, *A Mistress's Counsel* (London: Christian Knowledge Society, 1871)

Collins, Wilkie, *The Moonstone* (London: Collins, 1953)

Cooper, J. Fenimore, *England* (London: Richard Bentley, 1837)

Cosnett, Thomas, *The Footman's Directory and Butler's Remembrancer* (London: T. Cosnett, 1825)

Cumming, Constance Frederica Gordon, *In the Himalayas and on the Indian Plains, 1884* (London: Chatto and Windus, 1901)

Darwin, Ellen.W., 'Domestic Service', *The Nineteenth Century*, 28, LLXII (August 1890)

Deputation to the Secretary of State for India, 26 July 1883

Dickens, Charles, 'Nurse's Stories' in *An Uncommercial Traveller* (New York: George Munro, 1958) 104–12

Dickens, Charles, *David Copperfield* (Oxford: Oxford University Press, 1981)

'A Domestic College', *The Englishwoman's Review* (15 July 1890)

Duncan, Mabel (ed.), *A Lady's Maid in Downing Street* (London: T. Fisher Unwin, 1922)

Ellis, Sarah, *The Women of England* (London: Fisher and Son, 1839)

Engels, F., *The Condition of the Working Class in England*, 2nd edn (Oxford: Blackwell, 1971)

Fay, Mrs Eliza, *Original Letters from India (1779–1815)* (London: Hogarth, 1925)

'A Few Thoughts about the Technical College at Newnham-on-Severn', *The Englishwoman's Review* (15 July 1890)

Fraser, Patrick, *Treatise on Master and Servant* (Edinburgh: T and T Clark, 1875)

Froude, J.A. (ed.), *Letters and Memorials of Jane Welsh Carlyle*, 3 vols (London: Longmans, 1883)

Glimpses of Anglo-Indian Life Here and at Home (Madras: SPCK, 1901)

Grant, Colesworthy, *Anglo-Indian Domestic Life* (Calcutta: Thacker, Spink and Co, 1862)

Greaves, Charles Sprengel, *Lord Campbell's Acts* (London: n.p., 1851)

Greg, W.R. 'Why Are Women Redundant?', *National Review*, 15 (1862)

Garrett, Elizabeth, *Morning Hours in India* (London: Trubner and Co, 1887)

Godden, Rumer, *Breakfast with the Nikolides* (London: Peter Davies, 1942)

'A Friend', *A Word to Maidservants* (London 1864)

Hamilton, Margaret, 'Household Clubs: How Will They Affect Small Household', *Nineteenth Century*, 183, 31 (May 1892)

Hobhouse, Mary, *Letters from India 1872–1877* (Edinburgh: Printed for Private Circulation, 1906)

Anon, *Home Difficulties or Whose Fault Is It? A Few Words on the Servant Question* (London: Griffith and Farron, 1866)

Household Work; or the Duties of Female Servants, no III, The Finchley Manuals of Industry (London: Finchley Manuals, 1849)

Howell, Constance, *Married in India. A Story of Anglo-Indian Life in the Sixties* (London: John Ourseley, 1910)

Huxley, Leonard (ed.), *Jane Welsh Carlyle: Letters to Her Family, 1839–1863* (London: John Murray, 1924)

The Ilbert Bill. A Collection of Letters, Speeches, Memorials, Articles, &c, Stating Objections to the Bill (London: W.H. Allen and Co, 1883)

'Internuncio' *Mistresses and Servants* (London: John F. Shaw, 1865)

James, Mrs Eliot, *Indian Household Management* (London: Ward, Lock and Co, 1879)

James, T.S. (ed.), *The Works of John Angell James*, 17 vols (Birmingham, 1860–64)

Kaye, John, *Peregrine Pulteney; or Life in India* (London: J. Mortimer, 1844)

Kilvert, Adelaide Sophia, *Home Discipline or Thoughts on the Origin and Exercise of Domestic Authority* (London: Joseph Masters, 1847)

Kipling, Rudyard, *Kim* (Leipzig: Bernhard Tauchnitz, 1901)

'A Lady' *Instructions in Household Matters or the Young Girl's Guide to Domestic Service*, 5th edn (London: John W. Parker and Son, 1852)

'A Lady Resident' *The Englishwoman in India* (London: Smith, Elder, 1864)

Lanceley, William, *From Hall-Boy to House-Steward* (London: Arnold, 1925)

Lethbridge, Katherine (ed.), *Letters from East and West* (Devon: Merlin, 1990)

[Maitland, Julia], 'A Lady', *Letters from Madras during the Years 1836–1839* (London: John Murray, 1846)

My Secret Life (New York: Grove Press, 1966)

Lewis, Mrs, *Domestic Service in the Present Day* (London: Hatchards, 1889)

Lewis, Mrs, 'A Reformation of Domestic Service', *The Nineteenth Century*, 191, 33 (January 1893)

The Local Opinions on the Criminal Procedure Code Amendment Bill (Calcutta, 1883)

Lockwood, Mrs Josiah, *An Ordinary Life 1861–1924* (London, 1932)

Malabari, Behramji Mehrbanji, *The Indian Eye on English Life* (London: Constable and Co, 1893)

Marryat, Florence, 'Gup' *Sketches of Anglo-Indian Life and Character* (London: Reprinted from Temple Bar, 1868)

Mayhew, Henry, *London Labour and the London Poor*, IV (London: Charles Griffin and Co., 1864)

McCullock and Others, *India: Geographical, Statistical, and Historical*, Compiled from the London *Times* Correspondence (Toronto: Bostwick, 1858)

McQueen Simpson, Alan and Mary (eds.), *I Too Am Here. Selections from the Letters of Jane Welsh Carlyle* (Cambridge: Cambridge University Press, 1977)

'A Medical Practitioner', *Domestic Guide to Mothers in India* (Bombay: American Mission Press, 1848)

Mill, James, *History of British India* (London: Baldwin, Cradock and Joy, 1820)

Miller, Herbert P, *The Scarcity of Domestic Servants: The Cause and the Remedy* (London, 1876)

'A Mistress and a Mother', *at Home* (London: Macintosh and Co., 1874)

A Mistress's Counsel (London: Christian Knowledge Society, 1871)

Mitchell, Mrs Murray, *In India: Sketches of Indian Life and Travel from Letters and Journals* (London: T. Nelson and Sons, 1876)

Morris, Sir Malcolm, *The Annals of an Anglo-Indian Family* (Ludgate Hill: Printed for Private Circulation, 1920)

Motherly, Mrs, *The Servants Behaviour Book* (London: Bell and Daldy, 1859)

Munby, A.J., *Ann Morgan's Love: A Pedestrian Poem* (London: Reeves and Turner, 1896)

Munby, A.J., *Benois; Poems* (London: John Oliver, 1852)

'The National Housewifery Association', *The Englishwomen's Review* (15 January 1890)

Oram. G, *Masters and Servants: Their Relative Duties* (London: Hatchard 1858)

Panton, Mrs J.E., *From Kitchen to Garrett* (London: Ward and Downery, 1893)

Pelly, Lewis (ed.), *The Views and Opinions of Brigadier-General John Jacob, C.B.* (London: Smith, Elder, 1858)

Petition of the Residents of Dibrugarh and Neighbourhood – To the Chief Commissioner of Assam, April 16 1883 (published in *The Englishman*, 6 July 1883)

Petition of Englishwomen in India 1883

Postans, T., *Hints to Cadets, with a Few Observations on the Military Service of the Honourable East India Company* (London: William Allen and Co, 1842)

Powell, Margaret, *Below Stairs* (London: Pan, 1968)

'A Practical Mistress of a Household', *Servants as They Are and as They Ought to Be* (London: W. Tweedie, 1859)

Quennell, Peter (ed.), *Mayhew's Characters* (London: Spring Books, 1951)

Report of a Public Meeting Held at Silchar on Saturday the 29 September 1883 to Further Protest against the Passing of the Ilbert Bill (Calcutta: The Englishman Press, 1883)

Riddell, Dr R., *Indian Domestic Economy and Receipt Book* (London: Thacker and Spink, 1871)

Roche, George and Terrell, Richard (ed.), *Childhood in India: Tales from Sholapur* (London and New York: Radcliffe Press, 1994)

Roberts, Emma, *Scenes and Characteristics of Hindoostan, with Sketches of Anglo-Indian Society*, Vol. I (London: W. H. Allen, 1837)

Robertson, William, *A Historical Disquisition Concerning the Knowledge Which the Ancients Had of India* (Basil: J. J. Tourneisen, 1792)

Robinson, John, 'A Butler's View of Men-service' *Nineteenth Century*, 184, 31 (June 1892)

Rowntree, Seebohm B., *Poverty: A Study of Town Life*, 2nd edn (London: Macmillan, 1903)

Ruskin, John, *Sesame and Lilies*, 1864 pocket edn (London: Georgen Allen, 1906)

Russell, Bertrand and Patricia (ed.), *The Amberley Papers*, 2 vols (London: L and V Woolf, 1937)

Salmon, Edward, 'Domestic Service and Democracy', *Fortnightly Review* (March 1888)

Salmon, Lucy Maynard, *Domestic Service* (New York: Macmillan, 1911)

Sanyal, Ram Gopal (ed.), *Record of Criminal Cases as between Europeans and Natives for the Last 60 Years* (Calcutta: J.N. Dutt, 1893)

Scudder, Townsend (ed.), *Letters of Jane Welsh Carlyle to Joseph Neuberg 1848–1862* (London: Oxford University Press, 1931)

Shore, Frederick John, *Notes on Indian Affairs*, 2 vols (London: John W. Parker, 1837)

Spike, Edward, *The Law of Master and Servant* (London: Shaw and Sons, 1839)

Stanley, Liz (ed.), *The Diaries of Hannah Cullwick, Victorian Maidservant* (New Jersey: Virago, 1984)

Steel, F.A. and Gardiner, G., *The Complete Indian Housekeeper and Cook* (London: W. Heinemann 1898)

Stocqueler, J.H. *The Hand-book of India, a Guide to the Stranger and the Traveller, and a Companion to the Resident* (London: W.H. Allen, 1844)

Taylor, Mrs, *Practical Hints to Young Females on the Duties of a Wife, a Mother and a Mistress of a Family* (London: Taylor and Hessey, 1815)

Taylor, S. *Relation of Master and Servant as Exhibited in the New Testament* (Richmond: T.W. White, 1836)

Thackeray, W.M., *Vanity Fair* (London: Penguin, 1968)

Thackeray, W.M., 'On a Chalk-Mark on the Door', *Roundabout Papers* (London: Smith, Elder and Co, 1876)

Thompson, Edward, *An Indian Day* (London: A. A. Knopf, 1927)

Thompson, E.P. and Yeo, Eileen (eds.), *The Unknown Mayhew. Selections from the Morning Chronicle 1849–1850* (London: Merlin, 1971)

Vansittart, Jane (ed.), *From Minnie with Love* (London: Peter Davies, 1974)

Veritas, Amara, *The Servant Problem* (London: Simpkin, Marshall and Co, 1899)

Waring, Edward J., *The Tropical Resident at Home: Letters Addresses to Europeans Returning from India and the Colonies on Subjects Connected with Their Health and General Welfare* (London: J. Churchill, 1866)

Williamson, Thomas, *The East India Vade-Mecum; or Complete Guide to Gentlemen Intended for the Civil, Military or Naval Service of the Honourable East India Company* (2 vols, London: Black, Parry and Kingsbury, 1810)

Wilson, Lady and Anne C. Macleod, *Letters from India* (Edinburgh: William Blackwood, 1911)

Wise, Dorothy (ed.), *Diary of William Tayler, Footman, 1837* (London: St Marylebone Society Publications Group, 1962)

Young, G.M. (ed.), *Early Victorian England* (London: Oxford University Press, 1934)

Secondary sources

Books

Adams, K. and Sara Dickey (eds.), *Home and Hegemony; Domestic Service and Identity Politics in South and South East Asia* (Ann Arbor: University of Michigan Press, 2000)

Allen, Charles, *Plain Tales from the Raj: Images of British India in the twentieth century* (London: Abacus, 1994)

Alexander, Sally, *Women's Work in Nineteenth Century London* (London: The Journeyman Press, 1983)

Ally, Shireen, *From Servants to Workers: South African Domestic Workers and the Democratic State* (Ithaca: ILR, 2009)

Anderson, Benedict, *Imagined Communities. Reflections on the Origin and Spread of Nationalism* (New York: Verso, 1991)

Anderson, Bridget, *Doing the Dirty Work? The Global Politics of Domestic Labour* (London: Zed Books, 2000)

Armstrong, A., *Stability and Change in an English County Town* (Cambridge: Cambridge University Press, 1974)

Attar, Dena, *A Bibliography of Household Books Published in Britain 1800–1914* (London: Prospect, 1987)

Ballantyne, Tony, *Webs of Empire: Locating New Zealand's Colonial Past* (Wellington: Bridget William Books, 2012)

Ballhatchet, Kenneth, *Race, Sex and Class under the Raj: Imperial Attitudes and Policies and Their Critics, 1793–1905* (London: Weidenfeld and Nicolson, 1980)

Banerjee, Swapna M. *Men, Women, and Domestics: Articulating Middle-class Identity in Colonial Bengal.* (New Delhi: Oxford University Press, 2004)

Banks, J.A., *Prosperity and Parenthood* (London: Routledge and Kegan Paul, 1954)

Banton, Michael, *Racial Theories*, 2nd edn (Cambridge: Cambridge University Press, 1998)

Bayly, C.A., *Indian Society and the Making of the British Empire* (New Delhi: Orient Longman, 1990)

Bayly, C.A., *The Raj. India and the British 1600–1947* (London: National Portrait Gallery Publications, 1990)

Bhaba, Homi.K., *The Location of Culture* (London: Routledge, 1994)

Bolt, Christine, *Victorian Attitudes to Race* (London: Routledge and Kegan Paul, 1971)

Boyce, George, Curran, James and Wingate, Pauline (eds.), *Newspaper History from the Seventeenth Century to the Present Day* (London: Constable for the Press Group of the Acton Society, 1978)

Branca, Patricia, *Silent Sisterhood. Middle-Class Women in the Victorian Home* (London: Routledge, 1975)

Breckenridge, C.A. and Van Der Veer, P. (eds.), *Orientalism and the Postcolonial Predicament: Perspectives on South Asia* (Philadelphia: University of Pennsylvania Press, 1993)

Briggs, Asa, *Victorian People. A Reassessment of Persons and Themes 1851–67* (Chicago: University of Chicago Press, 1972)

Buettner, Elizabeth, *Empire Families. Britons and Late Imperial India* (Oxford: Oxford University Press, 2004)

Burton, Antoinette, *At the Heart of Empire: Indians and the Colonial Encounter in Late Victorian Britain* (Berkeley: University of California Press, 1998)

Burton, Antoinette, *Burdens of History. British Feminists, Indian Women, and Imperial Culture, 1865–1915* (Chapel Hill: University of North Carolina Press, 1994)

Butler, Judith and Scott, Joan Wallach (eds.), *Feminists Theorize the Political* (New York: Routledge, 1992)

Cannadine, David, *Ornamentalism. How the British Saw Their Empire* (London: Penguin, 2001)

Chaney, Elsa. M. and Castro, Mary Garcia (eds.), *Muchachas No More. Household Workers in Latin America and the Caribbean* (Philadelphia: Temple University Press, 1989)

Chang, Grace, *Disposable Domestics: Immigrant Women Workers in the Global Economy* (Cambridge: South End Press, 2000)

Chatterjee, Indrani (ed.), *Unfamiliar Relations: Family and History in South Asia* (New Delhi: Permanent Black, 2004)

Chatterjee, Partha, *The Nation and Its Fragments: Colonial and Post-Colonial Histories* (Princeton: Princeton University Press, 1993)

Chaudhuri, Nupur and Stroebel, Margaret (eds.), *Western Women and Imperial Power: Complicity and Resistance* (Bloomington: Indiana University Press, 1992)

Clancy Smith, Julia and Gouda, Frances (eds.), *Domesticating the Empire, Race, Gender and Family Life in French and Dutch Colonialism* (Charlottesville: University Press of Virginia, 1998)

Cleall, Esme, *Missionary Discourses of Difference. Negotiating Otherness in the British Empire, 1840–1900* (London: Palgrave, 2012)

Colley, Linda, *Britons. Forging the Nation 1707–1837* (London, Pimlico: Vintage, 1996)

Collingham, E.M., *Imperial Bodies. The Physical Experience of the Raj c.1800–1947* (Cambridge: Polity, 2001)

Collini, Stefan, Whatmore, Richard and Young, Brian (eds.), *History, Religion and Culture: Essays in British Intellectual History, 1750–1850* (Cambridge: Cambridge University Press, 2000)

Cooper, Frederick and Stoler, Ann Laura, *Tensions of Empire: Colonial Cultures in a Bourgeois World* (Berkeley: University of California Press, 1997)

Cox, Rosie, *The Servant Problem: Domestic Employment in a Global Economy* (London: I.B. Tauris, 2006)

Conley, C., *The Unwritten Law: Criminal Justice in Victorian Kent* (Oxford: Oxford University Press, 1991)

Crosbie, Barry, *Irish Imperial Networks. Migration, Social Communication and Exchange in Nineteenth Century India* (Cambridge: Cambridge University Press, 2011)

Cunningham, Hugh, *Children and Childhood in Western Society since 1500* (London: Routledge, 1995)

Davidoff, Leonore, *The Best Circles. Society Etiquette and the Season* (London: The Cresset Library, 1986)

Davidoff, Leonore, *Worlds Between. Historical Perspectives on Gender and Class* (Cambridge: Polity, 1995)

Davidoff, Leonore, Doolittle, Megan, Fink, Janet and Holden, Katherine, *The Family Story. Blood, Contract and Intimacy 1830–1960* (London: Pearson, 1999)

Davidoff, Leonore and Hall, Catherine, *Family Fortunes: Men and Women of the English Middle Class 1780–1850*, 2nd edn (London: Routledge, 2002)

Davidoff, Leonore and Hawthorn, Ruth, *A Day in the Life of a Victorian Domestic Servant* (London: Allen and Unwin, 1972)

Davis, Mary (ed.), *Class and Gender in British Labour History: Renewing the Debate (or Starting It?* (Pontypool: Merlin, 2011)

Dawes, Frank, *Not in Front of the Servants. Domestic Service in England 1850–1939* (London: Hutchinson, 1973)

D'Cruze, Shani, *Crimes of Outrage. Sex, Violence, and Victorian Working Women* (London, Routledge, 1998)

Delap, Lucy, *Knowing Their Place. Domestic Service in Twentieth Century Britain* (Oxford: Oxford University Press, 2011)

Don Vann, J., Don, J. and VanArsdel, Rosemary.T. (eds.), *Victorian Periodicals: A Guide to Research*, Vols. 2 and 5 (New York: Modern Language Association of America, 1989)

Douglas, Mary, *Purity and Danger: An Analysis of Concepts of Pollution and Taboo* (London: Routledge and Kegan Paul, 1970)

Ebery and Preston, *Domestic Service in Late Victorian and Edwardian England, 1871–1914* (Reading: University of Reading, 1976)

Fauve-Chamoux, Antoinette (ed.), *Domestic Service and the Formation of European Identity: Understanding the Globalization of Domestic Work, 16th–21st Centuries* (Bern: Peter Land, 2004)

Finn, Margot and Kate Smith, *The East India Company at Home 1757–1857* (London: UCL Press, 2018)

Fischer-Tiné, Harald, *Low and Licentious Europeans: Race, Class, and 'White Subalternity' in Colonial India* (New Delhi: Orient BlackSwan., 2009)

Fairchilds, Cissie, *Domestic Enemies: Servants and the Masters in Old Regime France* (Baltimore: Johns Hopkins University Press, 1981)

Foucault, Michel, *The Archaeology of Knowledge* (London: Routledge, 1972)

Gatrell, V.A.C., Lenman Bruce and Parker, Geoffrey (eds.), *Crime and the Law. The Social History of Crime in Western Europe since 1500* (London: Europa, 1980)

Gerard, Jessica, *Country House Life: Family and Servants 1815–1914* (Oxford: Blackwell, 1994)

Ghose, Indira (ed.), *Memsahibs Abroad. Writings by Women Travellers in Nineteenth Century India* (New Delhi: Oxford University Press, 1998)

Ghosh, Durba, *Sex and the Family in Colonial India: The Making of Empire* (New York: Cambridge University Press, 2006)

Goldberg, David Theo (ed.), *Anatomy of Racism* (Minneapolis: University of Minnesota Press, 1990).

Gopal, S., *The Viceroyalty of Lord Ripon 1880–1884* (Oxford: Oxford University Press, 1953)

Gillis, John.R., *A World of Their Own Making. Myth, Ritual, and the Quest for Family Values* (London: Harvard University Press, 1996)

Hall, Catherine, *White, Male and Middle Class. Explorations in Feminism and History* (Cambridge: Polity, 1992)

Hall, Catherine (ed.), *Cultures of Empire. Colonizers in Britain and the Empire in the Nineteenth and Twentieth Centuries. A Reader* (Manchester: Manchester University Press, 2000)

Hall, Catherine, *Civilising Subjects. Metropole and Colony in the English Imagination 1830–1867* (Cambridge: Polity, 2002)

Hammerton, A. James, *Cruelty and Companionship. Conflict in Nineteenth-century Married Life* (London: Routledge 1992)

Hamlett, Jane, *Material Relations. Domestic Interiors and Middle-class Families in England 1850–1910* (Manchester: Manchester University Press, 2010)

Hamlett, Jane (ed.), *A Cultural History in the Age of Empire* (London: Bloomsbury, 2021)

Haskins, Victoria, *One Bright Spot* (London: Palgrave, 2005)

Heuman, Gad, *Between Black and White. Race Politics, and the Free Coloureds in Jamaica 1792–1865* (Oxford: Clio Press, 1981)

Higman, Barry, *Domestic Service in Australia* (Melbourne: Melbourne University Press, 2002)

Hill, Bridget, *Servants. English Domestics in the Eighteenth Century* (Oxford: Clarendon Press, 1996)

Hirschmann, Edwin, *White Mutiny: The Ilbert Bill Crisis in India and the Genesis of the Indian National Congress* (New Delhi: Heritage, 1980)

Hoerder, Dirk, Elise van Nederveen Meerkerk and Silke Neunsinger (eds.), *Towards a Global History of Domestic and Caregiving Workers* (Leiden: Brill, 2015)

Horn, Pamela, *The Rise and Fall of the Victorian Servant* (Stroud: Sutton, 1990)

Horn, Pamela, *Children's Work and Welfare 1780s–1880s* (Stroud: Sutton, 1994)

Horn, Pamela, *Flunkeys and Scullions: Life below Stairs in Georgian England* (Stroud: Sutton, 2004)

Hudson, Derek, *Munby, Man of Two Worlds: The Life and Diaries of Arthur J.Munby, 1828–1910* (London: Abacus, 1974)

Huggett, Frank. E., *Life below Stairs* (Stevenage: Robin Clark, 1977)

Hutchins, Francis.G., *The Illusion of Permanence* (Princeton: Princeton University Press, 1967)

John, Angela V., *Unequal Opportunities. Women's Employment in England 1800–1918* (Oxford: Blackwell, 1986)

Jones, Aled, *Powers of the Press. Newspapers, Power and the Public in Nineteenth-century England* (Aldershot: Scolar Press, 1996)

Joyce, Patrick (ed.), *The Historical Meanings of Work* (Cambridge: Cambridge University Press, 1987)

Joyce, Patrick, *Democratic Subjects* (Cambridge: Cambridge University Press, 1994)

Joyce, Patrick (ed.), *Class* (Oxford: Oxford University Press, 1995)

Kolsky, Elizabeth, *Colonial Justice in British India. White Violence and the Rule of Law* (Cambridge: Cambridge University Press, 2010),

LaCara, Dominic and Kaplan, Steven.L. (eds.), *Modern European Intellectual History: Re-appraisals and New Perspectives* (New York, 1982)

Leong Salobir, Cecilia, *Food Culture in Colonial Asia: A Taste of Empire* (London: Routledge, 2001)

Lester, Alan, *Imperial Networks: Creating Identities in Nineteenth-Century South Africa and Britain* (London: Routledge, 2001)

Levine (ed.), *Gender and Empire* (Oxford: Oxford University Press, 2004)

Lewenhak, Sheila, *Women and Trade Unions. An Outline History of Women in the British Trade Union Movement* (London: Benn, 1977)

Lewis, Jane (ed.), *Labour and Love: Women's Experience of Home and Family 1850–1940* (Oxford: Blackwell, 1989)

Light, Alison, *Mrs Woolf and the Servants* (London: Penguin, 2008)

Locher-Scholten, Elspeth, *Women and the Colonial State. Essays on Gender and Modernity in the Netherlands Indies 1900–1942* (Amsterdam: Amsterdam University Press, 2000)

Lorimer, Douglas, *Colour, Class and the Victorians: English Attitudes to the Negro in the Mid-Nineteenth Century* (Leicester: Leicester University Press, 1978)

Lowrie, Claire, *Masters and Servants. Cultures of Empire in the Tropics* (Manchester: Manchester University Press, 2016)

Lowrie, Victoria (eds.), *Colonization and Domestic Service. Historical and Contemporary Perspectives* (London: Routledge, 2015)

Mackenzie, John M. with Nigel R. Dalziel, *The Scots in South Africa. Ethnicity, Identity, Gender and Race, 1772–1914* (Manchester: Manchester University Press, 2012)

Macmillan, Margaret, *Women of the Raj* (London, 1988)

Majeed, Javeed, *Ungoverned Imaginings. James Mill's 'The History of British India' and Orientalism* (Oxford: Oxford University Press, 1992)

Manktelow, Emily, *Missionary Families. Race, Gender and Generation on the Spiritual Frontier* (Manchester: Manchester University Press, 2013)

Marshall, Dorothy, *The English Domestic Servant in History* (London: George Philip 1949)

Marshall, P.J. (ed.), *The Cambridge Illustrated History of the British Empire* (Cambridge: Cambridge University Press, 1996)

Martinez, Julia, Claire Lowrie, Frances Steel and Victoria Haskins, *Colonialism and Male Domestic Service across the Asia Pacific* (London: Bloomsbury, 2018)

Massey, Doreen, *For Space* (London: Sage Publications, 2005)

May, Andrew J., *Welsh Missionaries and British Imperialism. The Empire of Clouds in North-East India* (Manchester: Manchester University Press, 2012)

May, Trevor, *The Victorian Domestic Servant* (Princes Riseborough: Shire, 1998)

McBride, Theresa, *The Modernisation of Household Service in England and France 1820–1920* (London: Croom Helm, 1976)

McClintock, Anne, *Imperial Leather: Race, Gender and Sexuality in the Colonial Context* (New York: Routledge, 1995)

McKim Marriott (ed.), *India through Hindu Categories* (New Delhi: Oxford University Press, 1990)

Mehta, Aban, *The Domestic Servant Class* (Bombay: Popular Book Depot, 1960)

Mendus, Susan and Rendall, Jane (eds.), *Sexuality and Subordination* (London: Routledge, 1989)

Metcalf, Thomas. R., *The Aftermath of the Revolt: India, 1857–1870* (Princeton: Princeton University Press, 1964)

Metcalf, Thomas R., *Ideologies of the Raj* (Cambridge: Cambridge University Press, 1994)

Metcalf, Thomas R. and Metcalf, Barbara, *A Concise History of India* (Cambridge: Cambridge University Press, 2002)

Mizutani, Satoshi, *The Meaning of White: Race, Class, and the 'Domiciled Community' in British India 1858–1930* (Oxford: Oxford University Press, 2012)

Newton, Judith. L, Ryan, Mary P. and Walkowitz, Judith R. (eds.), *Sex and Class in Women's History* (London: Routledge, 1983)

Parker, Vanessa, *The English House in the Nineteenth Century* (London: Historical Association, 1970)

Pink, John, '*Country Girls preferred' Victorian Domestic Servants in the Suburbs* (Surbiton: JRP, 1998)

Poovey, Mary, *Uneven Developments. The Ideological Work of Gender in Mid-Victorian England* (London: Virago, 1989)

Porter, Andrew (ed.), *The Oxford History of the British Empire. The Nineteenth Century* (Oxford: Oxford University Press, 1999)

Procida, Mary, *Married to the Empire. Gender, Politics and Imperialism in India, 1883–1947* (Manchester: Manchester University Press, 2002)

Proudfoot, Lindsay and Hall, Dianne, *Imperial Spaces. Placing the Irish and Scots in Colonial Australia* (Manchester: Manchester University Press, 2011)

Rabinow, Paul, *The Foucault Reader* (London: Penguin, 1991)

Ray, Raka and Seemin Qayum, *Cultures of Servitude: Modernity, Domesticity and Class in India* (Stanford: Stanford University Press, 2009)

Rendall, Jane, *Women in an Industrialising Society, 1780–1880* (Oxford: Blackwell, 1990)

Renford, Raymond. K., *The Non-Official British in India to 1920* (Delhi: Oxford University Press, 1987)

Robbins, Bruce, *The Servant's Hand. English Fiction from Below* (London: Duke University Press, 1993)

Robinson, Shirleene, *Something like Slavery? Queensland's Aborginal Child Workers, 1842–1945*) (Melbourne: Australian Scholarly Publications, 2008)

Romero, Mary, *Maid in the USA* (London: Routledge, 1992)

Roper, Michael and Tosh, John, *Manful Assertions. Masculinities in Britain since 1800* (London: Routledge, 1991)

Rose, Sonya O., *Limited Livelihoods. Gender and Class in Nineteenth-Century England* (London: Taylor and Francis, 1992)

Rowbotham, Sheila, *Hidden from History. 300 Years of Women's Oppression and the Fight against It* (London: Pluto 1973)

Said, Edward, *Orientalism* (London: Penguin, 1995)

Scott, Joan Wallach, *Gender and the Politics of History* (New York: Columbia University Press, 1988)

Schwartz, Laura, *Feminism and the Servant Problem. Class and Domestic Labor in the Women's Suffrage Movement* (Cambridge: Cambridge University Press, 2019)

Searle, G.R., *Morality and the Market in Victorian Britain* (Oxford: Clarendon,1998)

Sen, Samita and Nilanjana Sengupta, *Domestic Days: Women, Work and Politics in Contemporary Kolkata* (New Delhi: Oxford University Press, 2016)

Sinha, Mrinalini, *Colonial Masculinity. The Manly Englishman and the Effeminate Bengali* (Manchester: Manchester University Press,1995)

Sinha, Nitin and Nitin Varma (eds.), *Servants' Pasts. Late-Eighteenth to Twentieth Century South Asia*, Vol. 2. (Hyderabad: Black Swan Pvt Ltd, 2019)

Stallybrass, Peter and White, Allan, *The Politics and Poetics of Transgression* (Ithaca: Cornell University Press, 1986)

Stedman Jones, Gareth, *Languages of Class* (Cambridge: Cambridge University Press, 1983)

Steedman, Carolyn, *Master and Servant: Love and Labour in the English Industrial* Age (Cambridge: Cambridge University Press, 2007)

Steedman, Carloyn, *Labours Lost. Domestic Service and the Making of Modern England* (Cambridge: Cambridge University Press, 2009)

Stepan, Nancy, *The Idea of Race in Science. Great Britain 1800–1960* (London: Palgrave Macmillan, 1982)

Stoler, Ann Laura, *Race and the Education of Desire* (Durham: Duke University Press, 1995)

Stoler, Ann Laura, *Carnal Knowledge and Imperial Power. Race and the Intimate in Colonial Rule* (Berkeley, Los Angeles, London: University of California Press, 2002)

Straub, Kristina, *Domestic Affairs: Intimacy, Eroticism and Violence between Servants and Masters in Eighteenth-Century Britain* (Baltimore: Johns Hopkins University Press, 2009)

Taylor, Barbara, *Eve and the New Jerusalem. Socialism and Feminism in the Nineteenth Century* (London: Virago, 1983)

Thompson, Dorothy, *Outsiders. Class, Gender and Nation* (London: Verso, 1993)

Tosh, John, *A Man's Place. Masculinity and the Middle-Class Home in Victorian England* (New Haven and London: Yale University Press, 1999)

Tosh, John, *The Pursuit of History* (Harlow: Longman, 2000)

Vicinus, Martha, (ed.), *Suffer and Be Still: Women in the Victorian Age* (Bloomington: Indiana University Press, 1973)

Visram, Rosina, *Ayahs, Lascars and Princes: Indians in Britain 1700–1947* (London: Pluto, 1986)

Waterfield, Giles, French, Anne and Craske, Matthew, *Below Stairs. 400 Years of Servants Portraits* (London: National Portrait Gallery Publications, 2003)

Waterson, Merlin, *The Servants' Hall. A Domestic History of Erddig* (London: National Trust, 1990)

Williams, James and Felicitas Hentschke (eds.), *To Be at Home: House, Work, and Self in the Modern World* (Berlin: De Gruyter, 2018)

Williams, Raymond, *The Long Revolution* (London: Chatto and Windus, 1961)

Wohl, Anthony S. (ed.), *The Victorian Family: Structures and Stresses* (London: Routledge, 1978)

Wurgaft, Lewis. D. *The Imperial Imagination. Magic and Myth in Kipling's India* (Connecticut: Wesleyan University Press, 1983)

Articles and book chapters

Anderson, Michael, 'Mis-specification of Servant Occupations in the 1851 Census: A Problem Re-visited', *Local Population Studies*, 60 (1998): 58–64

Arnold, David, 'European Orphans and Vagrants in India in the Nineteenth Century', *The Journal of Imperial and Commonwealth History*, 7, 2 (1979): 104–27

Barber, Jill, '"Stolen Goods": The Sexual Harassment of Female Servants in West Wales during the Nineteenth Century', *Rural History*, 4, 2 (1993): 123–36

Bayly, Susan, 'The Evolution of Colonial Cultures: Nineteenth Century Asia' in Porter, Andrew (ed.), *The Oxford History of the British Empire. The Nineteenth Century* (Oxford: Oxford University Press, 1999): 447–69

Bailkin, Jordanna, 'The Boot and the Spleen: When Was Murder Possible in British India?', *Comparative Studies in Society and History*, 48, 2 (2006): 462–93

Blunt, 'Imperial Geographies of Home: British Domesticity in India, 1886–1925', *Transactions of the Institute of British* Geographers, 24, 4 (1999): 421–40

Bressey, Caroline, 'Looking for Work: The Black Presence in Britain 1860–1920', *Immigrants and Minorities*, 28, 2–3 (2010): 164–82

Bressey, Caroline, 'Black Women and Work in England, 1880–1920' in Mary Davis (ed.), *Class and Gender in British Labour History: Renewing the Debate (or Starting It?* (Pontypool: Merlin, 2011)

Buettner, Elizabeth, 'Problematic Spaces, Problematic Races: Defining Europeans in Late Colonial India' *Women's History Review*, 9, 2 (2000): 277–98

Buettner, Elizabeth, 'From Somebodies to Nobodies: Britons Returning Home from India', in Daunton, Martin and Rieger, Bernhard (eds.), *Meanings of Modernity. Britain from the Late-Victorian Era to World War II* (Oxford: Berg, 2001): 221–40

Bush, Barbara, 'White "Ladies", Coloured "Favourites" and Black "Wenches"; Some Considerations on Sex, Race and Class Factors in Social Relations in White Creole Society in the British Caribbean', *Slavery and Abolition*, 2, 3 (1981): 245–62

Chartier, Roger, 'Intellectual History or Sociocultural History? The French Trajectories', in LaCapra, Dominic and Kaplan, Steven. L. (eds.), *Modern European Intellectual History: Re-appraisals and New Perspectives* (New York: Cornell University Press, 1982)

Chattopadhay, Swati, 'Goods, Chattels and Sundry Items', Constructing 19th Century Anglo-Indian Domestic Life', *Journal of Material Culture*, 7, 2 (2002): 243–71

Chaudhuri, Nupur, 'Memsahibs and Their Servants in Nineteenth-century India', *Women's History Review*, 3, 4 (1994): 549–62

Cooper, Di and Donald, Moira, 'Households and "Hidden" Kin in Early-Nineteenth-century England: Four Case Studies in Suburban Exeter, 1821–1861', *Continuity and Change*, 10, 2 (1995): 257–78

Dussart, Fae, '"To Glut a Menial's Grudge": Domestic Servants and the Ilbert Bill Controversy of 1883', *Journal of Colonialism and Colonial History*, 14, 1 (2013): n.p.

Elbourne, Elizabeth, 'The Sin of the Settler: The 1835–36 Select Committee on Aborigines and Debates over Virtue and Conquest in the Early Nineteenth-Century British White Settler Empire', *Journal of Colonialism and Colonial History*, 4 (2003): n.p.

Davidoff, Leonore, 'Domestic Service and the Working Class Lifestyle', *Society for the Study of Labour History*, Bulletin 26 (1973): n.p.

Davies, Russell, 'In a Broken Dream: Some Aspects of Sexual Behaviour and the Dilemmas of the Unmarried Mother in South-west Wales 1887–1914', *Llafur*, 3 (1983): 24–33

Dawkins, H., 'The Diaries and Photographs of Hannah Cullwick', *Art History*, 10 (1987): 154–87

de Groot, Joanna, '"Sex" and "Race": the Construction of Language and Image in the Nineteenth Century' in Susan Mendus and Rendall, Jane Rendall (eds.), *Sexuality and Subordination* (London: Routledge, 1989): 89–130.

Derrett, J.D.M, 'The Administration of Hindu Law by the British', *Comparative Studies in Society and History*, 4 (1961): 10–52

Dirks, Nicholas.B., 'The Original Caste: Power, History and Hierarchy in South Asia' in McKim Marriott (ed.), *India through Hindu Categories* (New Delhi: Sage, 1990)

Dirks, Nicholas.B., 'Castes of Mind', *Representations*, 37 (1992): 56–78

Dobbin, Christine, 'The Ilbert Bill: A Study of Anglo Indian Opinion in India, 1883', *Historical Studies Australia and New Zealand*, 13, 45 (October 1965): 87–102

George, Rosemary Marangoly, 'Homes in the Empire, Empires in the Home', *Cultural Critique*, 26 (1993): 95–127

Gerard, Jessica. A., 'Invisible Servants: The Country House and the Local Community', *Bulletin of the Institute of Historical Research*, 57, 36 (1984): 178–88

Gillis, John, 'Servants, Sexual Relations and the Risks of Illegitimacy in London, 1801–1900' in Newton, Judith. L, Ryan, Mary P. and Walkowitz, Judith R. (eds.), *Sex and Class in Women's History* (London: Routledge, 1983): 114–45

Gray, R., 'Factory Legislation and the Gendering of Jobs in Britain, 1830–1860', *Gender and History* 5 (1993): 56–80

Habermas, Jurgen, 'The Public Sphere', *New German Critique* 1, 3 (1974): 49–55

Hall, Catherine, 'Politics, Post-structuralism and Feminist History', *Gender and History*, 3, 2 (1991): 204–10

Hall, Catherine, 'Introduction: Thinking the Post-colonial. Thinking the Empire' in Hall, Catherine (ed.), *Cultures of Empire. Colonizers in Britain and the Empire in the Nineteenth and Twentieth Centuries. A Reader* (Manchester: Manchester University Press, 2000)

Hammerton, A. James, 'The Targets of "Rough Music": Respectability and Domestic Violence in Victorian England', *Gender and History*, 3 (1991): 23–44

Harper, Marjory 'British Migration and the Peopling of the Empire' in Andrew Porter (ed.), *The Oxford History of the British Empire. The Nineteenth Century* (Oxford: Oxford University Press, 1999): 75–87

Haskins, Victoria, 'Domesticating Colonizers: Domesticity, Indigenous Domestic Labor, and the Modern Settler Colonial Nation', *The American Historical Review*, 124, 4 (2019): 1290–301

Higginbotham, Evelyn, 'African-American Women's History and the Metalanguage of Race', *Signs*, 17 (1992): 251–374

Higgs, Edward, 'Domestic Servants and Households in Victorian England', *Social History*, 8, 2 (1983): 201–10

Higgs, Edward, 'Domestic Service and Household Production' in John, Angela V. (ed.) *Unequal Opportunities. Women's Employment in England 1800–1918* (Oxford: Blackwell, 1986): 125–52

Higgs, Edward, 'Women, Occupations and Work in the 19th Century' *History Workshop Journal*, 23 (1987): 17–38

Higman, B.W., 'Domestic Service in Jamaica since 1750' in Chaney, Elsa. M., Castro, Mary Garcia (eds.), *Muchachas No More. Household Workers in Latin America and the Caribbean* (Philadelphia: Temple University Press, 1989)

Higman, B.W., 'Long Term Trends in Domestic Service in Jamaica', conference paper, *Engendering History: Current Directions in the Study of Women and Gender in Caribbean History* (Mona, Jamaica, 1993)

Hinde, P.R.A., 'Household Structure, Marriage and the Institution of Service in 19th Century Rural England', *Local Population Studies*, 35 (1985): n.p.

Johnson, Michele '"Decent and Fair": Aspects of Domestic Service in Jamaica, 1920–1970', *Journal of Caribbean History*, 30, 1–2 (1996): 83–106

Kaul, Chandrika, 'England and India: The Ilbert Bill, 1883: A Case Study of the Metropolitan Press', *The Indian Economic and Social History Review*, 30, 4 (1993): 413–36

Kent, Christopher A., 'Victorian Periodicals and the Constructing of Victorian Reality' in Don Vann, J., Don, J. and VanArsdel, Rosemary.T. (eds.), *Victorian Periodicals: A Guide to Research*, Vols. 2 and 5 (New York: Modern Language Association of America, 1989)

Kent, D.A., 'Ubiquitous but Invisible: Female Domestic Servants in Mid-eighteenth Century London', *History Workshop Journal*, 28 (1989): 111–28

Kerber, Linda 'Separate Spheres, Female Worlds, Woman's Place: The Rhetoric of Women's History', *Journal of American History*, 75, 1 (1988): 9–39

Koditschek, Theodore, 'The Gendering of the British Working Class', *Gender and History*, 9 (1997): 333–63

Lewis, Judith, 'Separate Spheres: Threat or Promise?', *Journal of British Studies*, 30, 1 (1991): 105–15

Locher-Scholten, Elsbeth, 'So Close and Yet So Far: The Ambivalence of Dutch Rhetoric of Javanese Servants in Indonesia, 1900–1942' in Clancy Smith, Julia and Gouda, Frances (eds.), *Domesticating the Empire, Race, Gender and Family Life in French and Dutch Colonialism* (Charlottesville: University Press of Virginia, 1998): 85–120

Marshall, P.J., '1783–1870: An Expanding Empire' in Marshall, P.J. (ed.), *The Cambridge Illustrated History of the British Empire* (Cambridge: Cambridge University Press, 1996): 24–51

Marshall, P.J., '1870–1918: The Empire under Threat' in Marshall, P.J. (ed.), *The Cambridge Illustrated History of the British Empire* (Cambridge: Cambridge University Press, 1996): 52–80

Marshall, P.J. '1918–1960s: Keeping Afloat' in Marshall, P.J. (ed.), *The Cambridge Illustrated History of the British Empire* (Cambridge: Cambridge University Press, 1996): 80–107

Marshall, P.J. 'Imperial Britain' in Marshall, P.J. (ed.), *The Cambridge Illustrated History of the British Empire* (Cambridge: Cambridge University Press, 1996): 318–38

McBride, Theresa, 'The Modernization of "Woman's Work"', *Journal of Modern History*, 2, 49 (June, 1977): 231–45

Moore, Robin.J., 'Imperial India, 1858–1914' in Porter, Andrew (ed.), *The Oxford History of the British Empire. The Nineteenth Century* (Oxford: Oxford University Press, 1999): 422–46

Paton, Diana, 'Decency, Dependence and the Lash: Gender and the British Debate over Slave Emancipation, 1830–34', *Slavery and Abolition*, 17, 3 (1996): 163–84

Prochaska, F.K., 'Female Philanthropy and Domestic Service in Victorian England', *Bulletin of the Institute of Historical Research*, 54 (1981): 79–85

Quijano, Anibal, 'Coloniality and Modernity/Rationality', *Cultural Studies* 21, 2–3 (2007): 168–78

Rattansi, Ali, 'Postcolonialism and Its Discontents', *Economy and Society*, 24, 4 (1997): 480–500

Raychaudhuri, Tapan, 'British Rule in India: An Assessent' in P.J.Marshall (ed.), *The Cambridge Illustrated History of the British Empire* (Cambridge: Cambridge University Press, 1996): 357–69

Roberts, Michael, '"Waiting upon Chance": English Hiring Fairs and Their Meanings from the 14th to the 20th Centuries', *Journal of Historical Sociology*, 1, 2 (1988): 119–60

Rocher, Rosanne, 'British Orientalism in the Eighteenth Century: The Dialectics of Knowledge and Government' in Breckenridge, C.A. and van der Veer, P. (eds.), *Orientalism and the Postcolonial Predicament: Perspectives on South Asia* (Philadelphia: University of Pennsylvania, 1993): 215–49

Samuel, Raphael, 'Reading the Signs: II.Fact-grubbers and Mind-readers', *History Workshop Journal*, 33 (1992): 220–51

Sarti, 'Historians, Social Scientists, Servants, and Domestic Workers: Fifty Years of Research on Domestic and Care Work', *International Review of Social History*, 59, 2 (2014): 279–314

Schwarz, Leonard, 'English Servants and Their Employers during the Eighteenth and Nineteenth Centuries', *Economic History Review*, 52, 2 (1999): 236–56

Scott, Joan.W., 'Experience', in Judith Butler and Joan Wallach Scott (eds.), *Feminists Theorize the Political* (New York: Routledge, 1992)

Seccombe, Wally, 'Patriarchy Stabilised: The Construction of the Male Breadwinner Wage Norm in nineteenth-century Britain', *Social History*, 11 (1986): 53–76

Sen, Indrani, 'Colonial Domesticities, Contentious Interactions: Ayahs, Wet-nurses and Memsahibs in Colonial India', *Indian Journal of Gender Studies*, 16, 3 (2009): 299–28

Singha, Radhika, 'Nationalism, Colonialism and the Politics of Masculinity' *Studies in History* [India] 14, 1 (January–June 1998): 127–46

Smith, R.J., 'Early Victorian Household Structure: A Case Study of Nottinghamshire', *International Review of Social History*, xv (1970): 69–84

Stallybrass, Peter and White, Allan, 'Below Stairs: The Maid and the Family Romance' in Stallybrass, Peter and White, Allan (eds.), *The Politics and Poetics of Transgression* (Ithaca: Cornell University Press, 1986): 149–70

Steedman, Carolyn, 'Servants and Their Relationship to the Unconscious', *Journal of British Studies*, 42 (July 2003): 316–50

Stoler, Ann Laura, 'Tense and Tender Ties: The Politics of Comparison in North American History and (Post) Colonial Studies', *The Journal of American History*, 88, 3 (December 2001): 829–65

Tinsman, Heidi, 'The Indispensible Services of Sisters: Considering Domestic Service in United States and Latin American Studies', *Journal of Women's History*, 4 (1992): 37–59

Todd, Selina, 'Domestic Service and Class Relations in Britain 1900–1950', *Past and Present*, 203 (2009): 181–204

Trodd, Anthea, 'Household Spies: The Servants and the Plot in Victorian Fiction', *Literature and History*, 13, 2 (1987): 45–68

Varma, Nitin, 'Servant Testimonies and Anglo-Indian Homes in Nineteenth-Century India' in James Williams and Felicitas Hentschke (eds.), *To Be at Home: House, Work, and Self in the Modern World* (Berlin: De Gruyter, 2018): 219–4

Vickery, Amanda, 'Historiographical Review. Goldern Age to Separate Spheres? A Review of the Categories and Chronology of English Women's History', *Historical Journal*, 36 (1993): 383–414

Washbrook, D.A., 'India, 1818–1860: The Two Faces of Colonialism' in Porter, Andrew (ed.), *The Oxford History of the British Empire. The Nineteenth Century*. (Oxford: Oxford University Press, 1999): 395–421

Wiener, Martin.J., 'The Sad Story of George Hall: Adultery, Murder and the Politics of Mercy in Mid-Victorian England', *Social History*, 24, 2 (1999): 174–95

Wilcox, Penelope, 'Marriage, Mobility and Domestic Service in Victorian Cambridge', *Local Population Studies*, 29 (1982): 195–206

Wrigley, Julia, 'Feminists and Domestic Workers', *Feminist Studies*, 17, 2 (1991): 317–29

Young, Brian, '"The Lust of Empire and Religious Hate": Christianity, History and India, 1790–1820' in Collini, Stefan, Whatmore, Richard and Young, Brian (eds.), *History, Religion and Culture: Essays in British Intellectual History, 1750–1850* (Cambridge: Cambridge University Press, 2000): 91–111

Theses and dissertations

Dussart, Fae, *'Horrible Cruelty to a Servant Girl'*: *'Civilisation' and Domestic Service in mid 19th Century England'*, unpublished MA Dissertation (UCL, London University, 2000)

Travers, Judith, 'Cultural Meanings and Representations of Violence against Women, London 1790–1895', PhD thesis (State University of New York, 1997)

Index

Lightning Source UK Ltd.
Milton Keynes UK
UKHW020204120522
402847UK00003B/113